Also By Colin Mustful,

Fate of the Dakota: A Novel and Resource on the U.S. – Dakota War of 1862

Grace at Spirit Lake

A Welcome Tragedy: Factors That Led to the U.S. – Dakota Conflict of 1862

Unwarranted Expulsion: The Removal of the Winnebago Indians

The Generation of 1837: Attitudes, Policies and Actions Toward Indian Populations of Argentina

The Battle of Point Pleasant: A Critical Event at the Onset of a Revolution

The Tobacco Controversy of 1857: An Early Debate and Its Delayed Results

The American Tobacco Controversy: The Tobacco Controversy of 1857 Revisited

Unabashed Hypocrisy: A Dichotomy of Values

CEDING CONTEMPT

MINNESOTA'S MOST SIGNIFICANT HISTORICAL EVENT

COLIN MUSTFUL

EDITED BY JENNIFER QUINLAN

Copyright © 2016 Colin Mustful.

All rights reserved. No part of this book may be reproduced, stored, or transmitted by any means—whether auditory, graphic, mechanical, or electronic—without written permission of both publisher and author, except in the case of brief excerpts used in critical articles and reviews. Unauthorized reproduction of any part of this work is illegal and is punishable by law.

ISBN: 978-1-4834-4859-6 (sc)
ISBN: 978-1-4834-4860-2 (e)

Because of the dynamic nature of the Internet, any web addresses or links contained in this book may have changed since publication and may no longer be valid. The views expressed in this work are solely those of the author and do not necessarily reflect the views of the publisher, and the publisher hereby disclaims any responsibility for them.

Any people depicted in stock imagery provided by Thinkstock are models, and such images are being used for illustrative purposes only.
Certain stock imagery © Thinkstock.

Lulu Publishing Services rev. date: 03/29/2016

Contents

Dedication vii
Acknowledgements ix
Author's Note xi
Introduction xiii

Chapitre un 1
Chapitre deux 13
Chapitre trois 24
Chapitre quatre 36
Chapitre cinq 52
Chapitre six 67
Chapitre sept 82
Chapitre huit 94
Chapitre neuf 105
Chapitre dix 116
Chapitre onze 129
Chapitre douze 142
Chapitre treize 153
Chapitre quatorze 163
Chapitre quinze 172
Chapitre seize 182

Epilogue 187
Appendix A 193
Appendix B 195
Appendix C 197
Appendix D 199
Appendix E 209
Appendix F 212
Bibliography 215

Dedication

To my Mom and Dad. You did a good job.

Acknowledgements

Rachelle Kuehl

Sean Beggin

Jennifer Quinlan

Ryan Parsons

Sketches in this text were reproduced from the book, *With Pen and Pencil on the Frontier in 1851: The Diary and Sketches of Frank Blackwell Mayer* and are printed with the permission of the Newberry Library.

Author's Note

This is history. Parts are fictionalized and imagined, but for the most part it is written and described as discovered through historical documentation. Portions may seem bland or out of place from the story. They may not be a part of the narrative, but they are a part of the history. Some parts are weaved into the narrative while others are given to you directly. Don't be discouraged. What I have written is by no means a masterpiece of literature. It is more of a puzzle. The picture has always been there, I just had to put it together. But I do not believe that mitigates the value of what I have created. It is history, both fact and fiction, and I think you should know about this history. Though it happened before you, it plays an indissoluble role in who you are and the life you live. It is not as though the world would crumble if you were to go without this information, but it substantiates who you are as an individual and edifies us as a community. Or, at least this is what I have come to believe.

I am not without bias. I come to you with my own set of experiences and perspectives, something from which I cannot divorce myself. But I have, to the best of my knowledge and ability, written something that is informative and entertaining. It is a mixture of fiction and nonfiction, utilizing elements of both. I have relied on historical documents, both primary and secondary, to discover and convey these events while creating a fictional narrative that strings together the people, places, and things that happened. All of the characters are real, with one minor exception, and several of the speeches and dialogues are taken straight from the sources in which they were recorded. It is my own attempt to bring the history to life as it might have happened. In this case, I have relied on the journal of

Frank Blackwell Mayer, a young artist who traveled to Minnesota in 1851 and drew sketches of the things he saw. Utilizing his own experience, I have juxtaposed myself into his character. In other words, I have tried to explain and understand this part of history with Mr. Mayer as my eyes and ears. What you will read is a combination of my own thoughts and feelings placed alongside his own as expressed through his journal and other various sources. Again, I must remind you that the final result is not perfect. This is not the conclusive source on these historical events. Rather, it is a brief introduction conveyed as thoughtfully and objectively as I know how. I have every bit of respect for the people and groups involved, regardless if their actions are seen as good or bad, selfish or selfless. I merely wish to understand, just as you do, what happened and how we came to be who we are today.

    I'd like to thank Frank Blackwell Mayer who had the foresight to record these events as well as Bertha L. Heilbron who compiled and edited Mr. Mayer's journal. I would also like to thank William Watts Folwell who has, in the most thorough sense, done the real work of being a historian. Finally, I'd like to thank you, dear reader. I cannot express with enough gratitude how thankful I am that you have come here today to read this story. Welcome and enjoy.

Introduction

Thousands upon thousands, in and out of Minnesota are anxiously and impatiently waiting for this treaty and for the opening of the magnificent country, which is spread out west of us like a beautiful map—a country full of game and heavy timber, and delightful prairies and rich bottom lands—its resources of natural wealth not only not exhausted, but as yet scarcely seen. . . . The civilization of those bands . . . is utterly hopeless; and the welfare of the Indians requires their speedy removal from a neighborhood which makes them daily more dependent, and in which they learn the vices, but attain to none of the virtues of civilized life."
   -James Goodhue, Minnesota Pioneer Newspaper

How do I explain this? There were no epic battles. There was no damsel in distress. No "once upon a time" or "happily ever after." Yet, it was the most significant event in the history of Minnesota, the place you live. It was the beginning of everything you now know. It was the beginning of the world you live in, but you've never even heard of this event. You've never been told. For it happened long ago, too long ago for its effects to be seen as anything but ancillary. Commonplace. Routine.

Allow me to give you an example. Have you ever glanced upon the Territorial Seal of Minnesota? I suspect not. Upon that seal is an image. It is an image of a white man with a plow at the Falls of St. Anthony. In the distance is an Indian atop a horse who is riding toward the setting sun. Never mind that the sun is setting in the east. The motto, which is written in Latin, states, "I fain would see what lies beyond." In this rather brief rendition somehow lies the quintessential depiction of your history and how life came to be the way it is today. But you wouldn't know it if not for me and for others like me. Those who had the foresight to record your history as it happened. And those who had the curiosity to seek out, perpetuate, and preserve your history.[1]

I am speaking of the Treaty of the Traverse des Sioux in 1851. It was this event in which the United States Government negotiated the sale of some thirty-five million acres of land west of the Mississippi River from the Dakota Indians. Much of this land would become the state of Minnesota. But let me back up just briefly in order to give you a better perspective of the monumental event. At the time of the treaty, Minnesota was a very young territory, having been organized on April 9, 1849. It was a large territory consisting of all the land west of Wisconsin and north of Iowa reaching to the Missouri River in the west and the 49th parallel in the north. But the population was quite small, being less than 10,000, and those people in the territory being limited to the settlements of Stillwater, St. Paul, St. Anthony, and the Red River Valley.

It was in 1837 that the territory of Minnesota first began to take shape. At this time the United States government completed the first major land cession treaty with the Dakota and Ojibwe Indians living throughout the Minnesota region. According to these land cession treaties, the Dakota sold their lands east of the Mississippi River while the Ojibwe sold their lands between the Mississippi and St. Croix Rivers and south of the Crow Wing River. The land was purchased by the Americans in order to harness the rich timber resources in the triangle of land between the two rivers. But it also set into motion the destiny that lay ahead. The destiny that all the land would be open to settlement, to civilization, and to prosperity.

The agriculturally rich land west of the Mississippi was known by frontier newspapers as the Suland. The next major step toward acquiring the Suland and achieving the American destiny occurred on May 29,

---

[1] A drawing of the original seal can be found in William Watts Folwell's *A History of Minnesota*, Volume 1. I have relied on Folwell for multitudes of information and he will be cited throughout this text. William Watts Folwell, *A History of Minnesota*, Vol. 1, (St. Paul: Minnesota Historical Society, 1922), 459-462.

1848, when Wisconsin became the 30th state admitted to the Union. This was important because the western boundary of Wisconsin was fixed at the St. Croix River, thereby leaving those who lived west of the St. Croix in unorganized territory. This would not last long, as industrious and enterprising men such as Henry Hastings Sibley and Joseph R. Brown sought immediate action. These men, like nearly all men and women along the frontier, extolled popular sovereignty and they insisted upon controlling their own destiny.² This, of course, led to the establishment of the Minnesota Territory. This was no small task, by the way, but took much political maneuvering. That is a story for another time.

Upon the establishment of Minnesota as a territory came the duty of assigning its governor. This role was bestowed upon Alexander Ramsey, a Whig from Pennsylvania. The new governor arrived in Minnesota in May of 1849 where he took residence with Henry Sibley at Mendota. The two formed a friendship and a political bond which adverse political interests could not disturb.³ It also established an agreement of sorts: an agreement that the first and foremost political interest of the new territory was the opening of the Suland to white settlement. Congress itself called the region superior to any part of the American Continent because of its rich, fertile soil.⁴ People were clamoring for it, and after all, it was their destiny.

Before we go any further, allow me to introduce myself. My name is Frank Blackwell Mayer and I am a young artist from Baltimore, Maryland—or at least I was in 1851. I was born December 27, 1827, to a distinguished Baltimore family. My father, Charles F. Mayer, was a prominent lawyer while my mother, Eliza Blackwell, was the daughter of Captain Francis Blackwell, a commander in the merchant service.⁵

---

2   William E. Lass, *Minnesota: A History*, 2nd Ed., (New York: W.W. Norton and Company, 1998), 108.
3   Folwell, *A History*, 249.
4   Ibid., 254.
5   The story of Frank Blackwell Mayer and his travels to Minnesota were edited and published by Bertha L. Heilbron in a book titled, *With Pen and Pencil on the Frontier in 1851*. Much of what follows was taken directly from what Mayer has related through his journal entries. Bertha L. Heilbron, Ed., *With Pen and Pencil on the Frontier in 1851: The Diary and Sketches of Frank Blackwell Mayer*, (St. Paul: Minnesota Historical Society Press, 1986).

At this point you may be wondering what a young artist from Baltimore has to do with the history of Minnesota. Please bear with me as I try to explain.

As a child my parents encouraged my artistic talent. When I was still very young they hired for me a tutor named Alfred J. Miller, a local artist of some fame, who, in 1837, traveled all the way to the great Rocky Mountains in the far west. He divulged the tales of his travels and shared with me his experience with the strange and mysterious aborigines that populated the west. These stories inspired within me a sort of wanderlust: a thirst for travel. Just as Mr. Miller before me, I longed to utilize my skills and talents as an artist, to capture scenes of the now-shrinking frontier and to share those scenes with the rest of the world.

My ambition led me to Washington City, the nation's capital, in order to obtain an appointment as an official artist to one of the government expeditions being sent west. I had a number of interviews, including one with the Office of the Topographical Bureau, but such appointments were scarce and I met only with rejection. But, early in 1851 I had heard of an expedition going to Minnesota to purchase from the Indians a land called the Suland. This immediately sparked my interest as I recalled a great explorer named Joseph Nicollet who had established himself near St. Mary's College in Baltimore.[6] My readers, you no doubt recognize that name as it has been given to a large island above the Falls of St. Anthony, a principal street in Minneapolis, a town, and a county. During the 1830s Joseph Nicollet led several expeditions throughout the upper Mississippi River Basin which included the land that would become Minnesota Territory. After visiting the region, Nicollet himself called it the garden spot of the Mississippi Valley.[7] This, I knew, was the region that I must see. This was the region I must record.

It was with this inspiration that I once again traveled to Washington to apply not only as an artist, but for any position connected with the treaty negotiations in Minnesota Territory. Again I was disappointed, being told that all positions had been filled. But I remained undaunted. As luck would have it, while I was at Washington I was introduced to Captain Seth Eastman. Years before Captain Eastman had been stationed

---

[6] Folwell, *A History*, 126.
[7] Ibid., 287.

at Fort Snelling where he, as an illustrator, was instrumental in recording the life of the Dakota Indians who lived within close proximity of the fort. Throughout our meeting he gave me much information and advice about travel in the west and he furnished me with many useful letters. Following this fortunate meeting I determined once and for all to undertake the trip at my own expense. Just a year earlier I had earned four hundred fifty dollars illustrating a book for my uncle, which I had saved and could then use for travel expenses. It was my hope that my exchange with the Indians and others and the sketches I would make might amply repay me for any expenditures I would incur.

Hindsight proved me wrong. Yes, I made a living as an artist. But my journal and sketches from the 1851 treaty never became valuable. I thought perhaps I could create a volume from my journal with watercolor drawings worked out from my sketches to be offered to the Historical Society. My idea received some interest and in 1887 I was asked to send the journal and sketchbooks to St. Paul for inspection. However, the society decided against its publication and also against its purchase.

Sadly, this was not the only time I was rejected in trying to create a lasting piece of Minnesota history through my art and through my experience. I sought wholeheartedly to prepare a painting of the Treaty of the Traverse des Sioux. Not just any painting but an original American work of art: the crowning effort of my life. I first submitted my proposal to the Minnesota state legislature in 1871, but the legislature did not see fit to spend money on an oil painting. Immediately thereafter I retained the hope that I might secure funds through private subscription but once again I was disappointed.

For years nothing became of my project until interest was revived in 1885. Though the legislature again failed to pass a bill ordering the painting, the executive council at the Historical Society asked me to send a rough sketch that they might evaluate. Thusly I did so, but even with the sketch before them, members of the executive council decided they could not procure funds necessary for a larger painting. I was devastated.

I made one last attempt to obtain an order from the state to paint a larger picture. This was in 1893 when I had heard that Minnesota planned to build a new capitol building. I immediately wrote the governor of Minnesota and proposed that I be allowed to develop my sketch of the treaty signing to fill a panel on the walls of the new state House. But my proposal was too early. It was not for another ten years, after my own passing, that America's most talented artists were assigned to decorate the capitol. The project I so longed to do was given to Francis D. Millet. Following my own design and composition, Millet created a painting of the Treaty of the Traverse des Sioux which now decorates the governor's reception room at the Minnesota State Capitol.

I have now given you the information to understand who I am and the brief role I played in your history. What follows is my story and my experience as told through a thoughtful observer. As you might have guessed, I am no longer living, but my story is—or rather the story I witnessed. Believe what you will. Parts may be embellished or changed, dialogue imagined, thoughts projected. But among those things is an important and valuable history. A history that I sought to capture and preserve. This history has unthinkable relevance in your life today. I knew it then and I am sure of it now. Whether right or wrong, it happened, and you ought to know about it. That is why I wrote my story down. That is why I am sharing it once more.

Chapitre un

===◦(◉)◦===

"Instead of the solitary wilderness of tangled forest and swampy plain, we see, over all the land, cultivated farms, seamed everywhere with the avenues of commerce. Instead of a few remote clusters of smoking wigwams, we see a country thickly dotted with pretty homesteads and magnificent marts of trade."
  – Thomas Hughes, *The Treaty of the Traverse des Sioux*

"All aboard!" came the call of the boatswain.
"All aboard!" he shouted again, only to be drowned out by the ship's loud, elongated, and reverberating whistle.

The *Excelsior* was the name of the side-wheeler I now boarded. It was a large enough vessel with a double deck, white in color with red trim and a single dark chimney rising well above the rest of the ship. On the prow was the antlered head of a deer. This was not the first, nor the second, but now the third steamer I entered upon since departing Baltimore on May 7. I was anxious to reach my destination of St. Paul's Landing.[8] The date was June 8, 1851, which signifies that I had already spent over a month in travel. But despite the encumbrance and the knowledge that St. Louis, my point of departure, lay nearly eight hundred miles south of St. Paul, I knew

---

[8] For a detailed history of the city of St. Paul, read *A History of the City of St. Paul* by J. Fletcher Williams. J. Fletcher Williams, *A History of the City of St. Paul and the County of Ramsey, Minnesota*, (St. Paul: Minnesota Historical Society, 1876).

I had another month before the treaty negotiations were to commence. Thusly, I accepted the next leg of my journey with guarded perseverance.

The boat, much to my dislike, was crowded with freight, immigrants, and cabin passengers. It was alive with movement and noise. There existed all types of people from all walks of life, both rich and poor, both young and old, making the boat seem more of a circus than a mode of transport. On deck I first noticed a number of Prussian immigrants due to their strange and distinct beards, good figures, and foreign costumes. Also there were Irishmen of a noble class. One in particular, who was undoubtedly royal, amused and astonished us by his wit and extensive information. I cannot forget to mention the merchants from St. Louis, raftsmen from the headwaters of the Mississippi, farmers from Iowa and Wisconsin, and perhaps folks from every state in the Union, Canada and Europe.

I found myself in a state-room along with a Mr. Charles Sexton. As I learned, Mr. Sexton was the editor of the *St. Croix Enquirer* and he proved himself to be a rather amusing and useful companion. To be honest, my initial perception of Mr. Sexton was disconcerting. He was a gaunt fellow with a ghastly smile almost like a grinning skull that expressed melancholy joy. His complexion, in fact, was so death-like that I once was about to wake him to know if he was dead! An unavoidable bull I must confess. But despite his ghostlike appearance he was a man of energy, intelligence, and was good-hearted enough. Even more, he had ventured the Rocky Mountains, he had pierced the forests of Oregon, and he had gazed upon the ceaseless waters of the Pacific. I was most anxious to learn more about his travels.[9]

"How can I describe it?" Mr. Sexton said on our first evening as I prodded him for information.

"Well," I replied with a pause, "I reckon you could begin with the basics."

---

[9] Though it is true that Mr. Charles Sexton, editor of the *St. Croix Enquirer* at this time, had indeed traveled to the Rocky Mountains, I was unable to locate any written record. It is untrue then, that he traveled with Capt. John Charles Frémont as his story here follows. Therefore the details that follow are accurate as reported by Capt. John Charles Frémont in 1842, not Charles Sexton. John Charles Frémont, *The Exploring Expedition to the Rocky Mountains, Oregon and California* (New York and Auburn: Miller, Orton and Mulligan, 1856).

"The basics, you say?"

"Yes," I answered quickly. "What was the nature of the expedition? Who did you travel with, and so forth?"

"Well, my good lad," he said in his jubilant manner. "It was 1842 and I suppose I was about your present age. I traveled as a reporter with a government sponsored expedition led by Captain John Charles Frémont."

"Like the many expeditions I tried so ardently to acquire?" I asked assumingly.

"Perhaps," he nodded. "We started out from St. Louis where there was no shortage of men eager for work and experienced in the business of quests of this nature."

"They were voyageurs no doubt," I interjected with confidence.

"Indeed," Mr. Sexton replied with his almost ironic grin. "Twenty-one if I remember correctly, all of them Creole and Canadian voyageurs. They were a hearty band of men and willing to endure any hardship. We departed St. Louis by steamer traveling west along the Missouri River until we neared the mouth of the Kansas River. We disembarked at Choteau's Landing and proceeded twelve miles to Cyprian Choteau's trading house where we completed the final arrangements for our expedition."

Mr. Sexton spoke with alacrity like the journalist he was, eager to report his story. Being a captive audience in our chamber, I listened with great ease.

"Finally we set out. For what, precisely, I was unawares; being along just as an observer, I was not privy to all information. Together we formed quite a train of men and provisions. We were all armed and mounted with the exception of eight men who ushered as many carts. In addition there were a few loose horses and four oxen which had been added to our stock of provisions."

"You were well armed," I stated. "Was there much apprehension about a possible Indian attack?"

"Not necessarily apprehension," answered Mr. Sexton. "Just preparedness. We were by no means the first whites to travel though Indian country and an attack, however unlikely, was always a possibility."

I nodded.

"Our travels were somewhat tedious and monotonous, sometimes covering many miles, sometimes covering few. We were at the will and whim of Captain Frémont throughout the journey. He spent much time recording details and taking scientific measures of latitude, longitude, barometric pressure and temperature. In effect it was rather dull—rather routine, I must say."

I looked upon Mr. Sexton quizzically as I did not expect to hear him describe such a journey as dull.

"Our first major setback occurred while attempting to ford the swollen Kansas River. All but one last cart of supplies had crossed without peril when this final cart overturned midstream, sending our provisions floating down the river. Without consideration toward their own well-being or even concern over whether or not they could swim, several of the men jumped in after the provisions. Luckily the men were able to secure nearly all that had been lost and no one was drowned. However, we did lose a large bag of coffee which made up the bulk of our supply. It was a loss which none but a traveler in a strange and inhospitable country can appreciate. Often afterward, when excessive toil and long marching had overcome us with fatigue and weariness, we remembered and mourned over our loss in the river."

"Over coffee!" I exclaimed.

"Quite," returned Mr. Sexton with a laugh. "I might have rather lost my own appendages before suffering the loss of our precious coffee."

"Certainly, but there must have been something more interesting to report than just the loss of your coffee."

"I am getting there," continued Mr. Sexton with his skeleton-like finger held forward. "No, it wasn't all so dull. Our first encounter of note was with a massive band of Arapaho Indians. We could see them at a distance and they were coming at us with speed. Some two or three hundred in number all nearly naked save for their breech cloth. We endeavored to find a defensive position within a grove of trees on the opposite side of the river. But before we could even reach the bank the Indians were upon us."

I listened with anticipation, wanting to know if a struggle had ensued.

"Though it was useless in the presence of such an immense force, we acted out of instinct and removed the covers from our guns and put our fingers on the triggers. But just before they could attack, one of our men recognized the lead Indian and shouted to him in his native language. Surprised by the sound of his native tongue, the lead Indian flew passed us like an arrow. He soon recognized the man in our group as a trader who had previously lived among this band of Indians. The mood suddenly lightened and the next thing we knew we were in the midst of this massive horde of Indians. Immediately they began subjecting us to all sorts of questions."

"What a frightful experience," I said truthfully.

"It was," answered Mr. Sexton, "but we soon learned that the Indians, even in this western country, were hospitable and kind and most eager to build relationships with the whites. The chief invited us to his village and we accepted most heartily. Upon reaching the village we could see that it was a picturesque Indian town with close to one hundred and twenty lodges all placed neatly alongside the southern bank of the Kansas River. The lodges were tent-like structures made from tanned buffalo hide and stretched across long poles that met at a central location about the floor. Each lodge or tepee had a single flap that acted as a door. The structures appeared easy to take down and to put up, which was suitable for the Indians' nomadic lifestyle. As I gazed upon this new and curious city, I observed something I had never expected."

"And what might that have been?" I asked curiously.

"A buffalo hunt!" exclaimed the excited story-teller. "The Arapaho chief pointed out a herd on the north bank of the river and he invited us to witness the adept custom of these plains Indians. The chief asked us to remain on the south side so as not to raise the herd. We obliged, unsaddled our horses and sat down on the bank to view the scene. The Arapaho crossed the river about one hundred yards downstream. Behind them followed scores of wild-looking dogs, perhaps more wolf than dog. The hunters separated into two parties. One went directly across the prairie toward the hills and the other followed the shore upriver. Before long the herd caught wind of their soon-to-be attackers and the chase was on."

"How exciting!" I exclaimed while perched forward on the edge of my seat. Nothing like this happened in Baltimore.

"The buffalo scampered in the direction of the hills but they were immediately cut off by the second group of hunters. Soon clouds of dust covered the whole scene and it took on a very singular appearance. But every so often we could see two or three buffalo dashing along with an Indian close behind, his spear or other weapon held upright, but they would soon disappear again. The rapidity of the dim figures and the silence from where we sat gave the scene a dreamy effect, making it seem like more of a picture than something out of real life. After an hour we decided to continue back toward the village. As we did, Indian after Indian came dropping along laden with meat. As we reached the village the backward road was covered with horseman. It was a most successful hunt."

"I cannot imagine such an experience," I said with wonder.

"It was so unique and different, as if I were daydreaming of things I had previously only read about," returned Mr. Sexton. "Soon you too will have such an experience."

"I suppose I will," I replied, realizing just how far I had come and now how close I was to the Minnesota frontier. "I have never seen a real Indian."

There was a silence as Mr. Sexton merely raised his eyebrows and subtly nodded his head.

"Did you share in their spoils?" I asked.

"Certainly," said Mr. Sexton, as he decided to light his pipe. "We were, many of us, invited to the lodge of the chief and headmen. That evening we enjoyed quite a pleasant affair. The Indians were most hospitable, giving us a robe to sit upon and offering us a large wooden dish of buffalo meat. We enjoyed as much as we could eat while smoking the pipe which was passed around the lodge. Gradually, however, the setting changed. The chiefs were very interested in the nature of our journey and began asking many questions. Captain Frémont concealed nothing and told them about the intentions of establishing forts on the way toward the Rocky Mountains. And although this information was of the highest interest to them, and by no means calculated to please them, it excited no expression of surprise, and in no way altered the grave courtesy of their demeanor. By the time we had finished they had given us a bundle of dry meat and we set off at dusk to find our companions and camp a few miles upriver. The entire encounter was most interesting, most pleasing."

"I am happy to hear that they provided you such comfort. It calms some of my own apprehensions about meeting with the Dakota of Minnesota."

"Yes," replied Mr. Sexton. "The Indians were all very helpful to us along our journey. Even warning us of potential dangers."

"What of the mountains?" I questioned. "I have not heard a single word of the great and majestic Rocky Mountains."

"Well, I have not got there yet," smiled Mr. Sexton, smoking his pipe pleasurably. "It just so happens that the day after we departed the Arapahos was the first day we could catch sight of the distant peaks. We could just barely discern Long's Peak, whose snowy summit appeared like a cloud just above the horizon. We continued west through ever-changing scenery which seemed to grow more beautiful with each passing mile. We were approaching the Wind River Mountains and though they remained constantly in view, it felt as if it took forever to finally reach them."

Never having seen such peaks myself, I listened with interest to Mr. Sexton's description.

"The natural beauty of the place is beyond compare. Once we passed over the foothills and into the valley, there opened a marvelous world where the air was crisp, the water clear, and the land almost one with the sky. Even the clouds could not escape the towering hills and the rocky cliffs that surrounded us on nearly every side. It seemed as if, when compared to the vast expanse of uninteresting prairie we had passed over, nature had collected all her beauties together in one chosen place."

"Remarkable," I said in honest awe of his description.

"Indeed it was," commented Mr. Sexton. "It was like nothing I could have imagined. And the higher we climbed the more elaborate became our view. Though the terrain was rough, it was equally beautiful. Rocky peaks that cut vividly against the bluest sky, lakes like mirrors to the exquisite beauty around them, endless forests, flowing and flowery meadows that swayed and rustled ever so gently with the breeze, dells and ravines that appeared by surprise all encompassed with the same wonder and mysterious beauty. Finally there was the peak itself which our rugged leader was determined to summit."

"And did you reach it?"

"Yes. After much toil we conquered the highest elevation where it seemed the whole world was revealed to us. On the one side were innumerable lakes and streams where among them was the source of the Colorado River. On the other side was the Wind River Valley where we could see the heads of the Yellowstone. And to the far north we could even see the snowy heads of the Trois Tetons. The whole scene had one main striking feature, which was that of terrible convulsion. But even that was not the most notable characteristic of this surreal country. Rather, it was the impression of seclusion it left upon my very being."

"Seclusion?" I asked with hesitation.

"Loneliness. Isolation. A stillness the most profound and a terrible solitude forced themselves constantly on the mind as the great features of the place. Here, on the summit, where the stillness was absolute, unbroken by any sound and solitude complete, we thought ourselves beyond the region of animated life. This I remember most."

"What an adventure," I declared with sheer amazement. "You have further inspired my yearning to discover the frontier for myself."

"And you shall," answered Mr. Sexton with a strange confidence. "You are young and you are ambitious. I may have captured the frontier through words, but there is much need for the skill you possess. There exists—I believe will *always* exist—a need to capture the frontier, to record its endless beauty and to encapsulate its fleeting existence through imagery. Through art."

"Perhaps it shall be my life's ambition," I said with a smile.

"Perhaps."

The following day I was gleaming with enthusiasm over my interim roommate's description of his western expedition. It filled me with wonder to hear about such an astonishing adventure. Unfortunately my enthusiasm was squelched as a terrible illness visited our boat and reminded me of the potential hazards of travel. Thankfully the illness did not afflict me, but it wrought itself upon several others and it was not without its unforgiving affect. Ere two days had passed aboard this vessel when we buried five deck passengers. These passengers no doubt died of cholera which was aggravated or induced by filthiness, exposure, fatigue, and improper diet. It made for a sad occasion that evening with the tolling of the bell and the mooring of the boat near a high bluff. Here a grave was speedily dug and therein laid an infant just as the orange glow of the sunset reflected off the gently flowing waters of the Mississippi. It was a harsh reality and it created a somber tone.

Ceding Contempt

Burial of the Cholera Dead

Notwithstanding these sad events I was able to pass my time aboard the *Excelsior* with some enjoyment. This I owe to my fellow passengers who proved most admirable. At Keokuk, for instance, we received a Mr. C. Butler of New York who was accompanied by Miss Anna C. Lynch, the authoress. Miss Lynch was a most fine acquaintance with whom I led off a Virginia reel in the cabin to a good old-fashioned fiddle. I cannot remember a time I had more fun. Still there were others with whom I became acquainted and I should not fail to mention. I recall with pleasure a Mr. George Richmond of Boston who was then residing in St. Louis and who was a happy combination of Eastern and Western man. There was a refinement about him as if he had been tutored at a renowned eastern university, while at the same time having an adventurous spirit and a wholesome appearance as if he'd seen his fair share of outdoor labor. There was also Tom Jackson, an open-hearted, good-natured soul. And the clerk of the boat, an intelligent German named Mr. Schultz. But I could go on forever about the many kind and jubilant people I met along this brief excursion.

There was a strange but unmistakable change in the scenery after passing Davenport and Rock Island. The physical difference was obvious as bluffs began to rise on either side ushering in new and various landscapes. On one side the land was clothed in lush green forests where trees grew in every possible opening except where the bluffs were too steep and their rocky crags too uninviting. On the other side were grassy knolls and undulating prairies for as far as the eye could see. The gentle flowing nature of the prairies seemed almost destined for the farmer's plow. Here and there the river would twist and turn as if guided by the numerous hills and knolls behind which the river would disappear only to reappear in some unexpected direction.

But the further we traveled there was expressed another change. This one not in the climate or the physical features, but in the state of being. There was a certain emptiness precipitated by the absence of man—by the absence of civilization. Here nature took up the characteristic of quiet solitude. It was its own living, breathing organism where the noise and movement of man was absent and instead ruled the gentle but constant flow of life. The translucence of the water, the coolness of the air, the clearness of the sky, and the subtle and swaying movement of the leaves and the grass, all working in concert as if never disturbed by even the notion of man's hand.

Before long the scenery changed once more. As we neared Lake Pepin we entered a new region. One not of solitude, but of a fledging new world. There existed here growth and progress, but also tradition and perpetuity. It was a dichotomy that was remarkably visible. On the one side of the river was civilization where the New England log frame house had been constructed and the land had been cleared and the soil tilled. On the other side was the Native Indian where council smoke still rose and the sun dance was still celebrated. Somewhere in between the two became mixed along with other varieties of people and cultures that were so unique to the American frontier. One needn't look far to see a Christian church, alongside a trading post, surrounded by Indians, half-breeds, French voyageurs, and Americans while birch bark canoes and peltries[10] lie by the side of the Yankee steamboat.

---

[10] Peltries are animal furs.

View of the Minnesota River Valley from Traverse des Sioux

"I have never met with an Indian," I admitted to my roommate Mr. Sexton.

"Yes, you told me," replied Mr. Sexton rather plainly.

"Oh, that's right," I said with embarrassment. "Being from the east coast I have lived in the modern world my entire life," I explained. "The days of the Delaware and Powhatans have long since passed."

"And they shall pass here too," responded Mr. Sexton with a puff of his pipe. "The savage Indian has no place in this world, his usefulness being antecedent at best."[11]

---

[11] This was a common notion expressed at this time in history. According to Minnesota Historian William E. Lass, the settlers of Minnesota "never saw themselves as expansionists in a derogatory sense. In pushing aside the Indians, breaking land, and building cities, they were only fulfilling their destiny." Furthermore the prejudiced attitude of the Native as a savage was also commonplace. Upon analyzing the results of the 1851 *Treaty of the Traverse des Sioux*, Thomas Hughes wrote, "Instead of eight thousand half starved, half naked savages, eking out a miserable existence in ignorance and filth, we see a million happy people, beaming with intelligence and blessed with abundance." William E. Lass, *Minnesota: A History* 2nd ed. (New York: W.W. Norton and Company, 1998), 97. Thomas Hughes *The Treaty of Traverse des Sioux in 1851, Under Governor Alexander Ramsey, With Notes of the Former Treaty there in 1841, Under Governor James D. Doty of Wisconsin,* in Collections of the

"Do you really believe that?" I asked. "That we will overrun all of the Indians? That they have no place in this world?"

"Indeed I do," said Mr. Sexton confidently. "The Indian's time has come and gone and his light is fading fast. The very reason you have traveled all this way is to witness the sale of the Indian lands. And as simple as the savage Indian may be, he recognizes the inevitability of American progress. If he does not sell it now and gain what he can, it will be taken later and he will gain nothing. It is the white man's destiny to harness this land, to save it from stagnation, and to make it productive."

"And the Indian," I said curiously. "What will happen to the Indian?"

"He must take up the plow and shed his savage nature or he shall disappear like all cumbersome obstructions."

He must I repeated in my own mind. *It* was a regrettable fact and one I hadn't considered with quite the same tone as the frontiersmen. I knew the world was changing, but it hadn't occurred to me just how intentional a change it was. Of course, I was aware that many people consider the Indians savage and useless, but I had never heard it spoken in such a direct and relevant nature. Was this true, I thought. Was the Indian somehow undeserving of the land upon which he lived? I would soon find out more. I would soon meet these children of the wilderness, these so called savages.

Minnesota Historical Society, Vol. 10, Part 1, (St. Paul: Minnesota Historical Society, 1905), 116.

Chapitre deux

"My! how this town is growing. I counted the smoke of eighteen chimneys this morning."
                         J.R. Clewitt, 1848, speaking of St. Paul

As the sun was setting on the eve of the 14th, I could make out two indistinct forms gliding across the water. Slowly the forms became more perceptible as our massive boat gained on the two travelers. All of the sudden I could see and it struck me; it was two canoes, one paddled by a Frenchmen, the other by an Indian. This was by no means unusual, but rather quintessential of the time and place I would soon arrive. Simple though it was, it seemed magnificent to me to witness this idealistic representation of the Minnesota frontier right within my realm. From that point forward, the canoes, the Indian women and their babies, and Dakota chiefs would be frequent sights.

We arrived at St. Paul's Landing on June 15. I bid my bunkmate Mr. Sexton a fond farewell and immediately set upon obtaining lodging. St. Paul was a burgeoning and picturesque little town. It was beautifully situated upon a bluff at a turn in the river. Standing about fifty feet above the surface of the water it commanded a fine view of the surrounding country and it invited gentle breezes that sweep down the river and over the adjacent hills.

Just two years earlier, St. Paul was little more than an Indian trading post that could not even be located on a map. But all of that changed when Minnesota officially became a territory and St. Paul was named its capital.

That is why it appears like a bustling New England village that well attests the presence of an energetic and free soil population. Still, this is all so hard for me to imagine, so hard to understand. I came from Baltimore where I spent whole life. Baltimore was a modern, industrial city that was established well over one hundred years before. Its population was over 150,000. But not here. This was something much different. Something on the edge. Something on the verge between past and future.

Until 1838, the city of St. Paul did not exist. One year prior the United States government signed a treaty with the Dakota Indians of Minnesota in which the Dakota agreed to relinquish their land east of the Mississippi River. This opened the territory to many eager settlers, most of them traders. These traders sought to do business with both the soldiers residing at Fort Snelling and the Indians who still lived in the surrounding country. After the opening of the region to settlement, among the first to lay claim was a French Canadian named Pierre Parrant. There is no gentle way to describe *Monsieur* Parrant, for he bore not the most enviable character. His personal appearance was not much different. He was a coarse, ill-looking, low-browed fellow, with only one eye, and that a sinister-looking one. He spoke execrable English and his habits were intemperate and licentious.[12] But when considering the history of St. Paul, Pierre Parrant cannot be ignored. He made his claim just beyond the boundary of the military reserve where he could sell whisky to the soldiers and the Indians. For such a spot he selected the mouth of the creek which flows from Fountain Cave. Here was a secluded and lonely gorge in the river bank which would provide convenience for his customers and his business. Before long others began to settle in the region around Parrant's claim. Many of them were refugees of the Red River settlement which had been flooded around that time. And so were the makings of a small community based, sadly enough, on the liquor traffic.

Things would eventually change, but before they did, this small and secluded frontier community was given the name "Pig's Eye" after its unseemly founder Pierre Parrant. This rather suitable and expressive

---

[12] As described by J. Fletcher Williams. Williams, *City of Saint Paul*, 1876; 65.

sobriquet was bestowed upon Parrant by the sutler's clerk at Fort Snelling, Roswell P. Russell. Indeed Parrant had a piggish expression and so after a little while he was generally known by that appropriate nickname. As for the locality, it became attached to the nickname oddly enough because of a letter. A young Canadian named Edmund Brissett was doing carpentry work for the settlers of the area and he wished to send a letter to the trading post at Grey Cloud Island. But he was not sure where he should date the letter. After some thought, he set upon to date it at "Pig's Eye" since Parrant was so well known and it was sure to be recognized. A letter was returned safely and it was addressed "Pig's Eye." The name stuck and from its beginnings then, St. Paul was known as Pig's Eye—or so the story goes. But being such an important place the name did not last for long.

In 1840 a French Reverend named Lucian Galtier was sent north from Dubuque to establish a mission at the newly settled place. Upon arriving at his destination, Rev. Galtier recognized the privation and hard trials he would endure in such a wild and uncivilized territory, but he immediately dedicated himself to the region despite that precarious and somewhat difficult condition. After a year of establishing relations with the community, Rev. Galtier set about selecting a site for a new church. In this Rev. Galtier was forward-thinking. He ardently wished to select a spot that would facilitate communication and navigation. In doing so he selected a spot along the river nearest Fountain Cave where Pierre Parrant no longer held claim. In October of 1841, Rev. Galtier built his church which he believed was destined to be the nucleus of a great city. On November 1, 1841, he blessed the new basilica and dedicated it to "Saint Paul," the apostle of nations. Before long a store and grocery was put up alongside the church and then steamboats began landing there. It became known as St. Paul's Landing and eventually as St. Paul.

The period prior to 1849 may be called the arcadian days of Minnesota. The population grew slightly each year, but things remained simple, quiet, and primitive. The people of the region were content with the even tenor of their ways and remained unconcerned with the exciting events that stirred other communities. They were isolated and seemed to prefer it that way. But things changed drastically in 1849 when Minnesota became a territory and St. Paul its capital. As if in an instant, immigrants began pouring in. Boat after boat landed, bringing with them crowds of people, so much so that it became a serious question of where they would lodge and on what they would subsist. Building began at a feverish pace. Immigrants were instructed to bring with them tents because there were not enough builders to keep up with demand. Everywhere were piles of lumber and building materials left in admirable confusion. It was said that in just three weeks over seventy buildings had been erected.[13] Anyone who was absent, upon returning might think he had taken a Rip Van Winkle like slumber. But among this confusion and unprecedented growth, the territory was organized and the future was set. While seated upon beds or trunks in a little room at the St. Paul House, the Territorial Officers drew up the "First of June Proclamation" and Minnesota was officially organized.

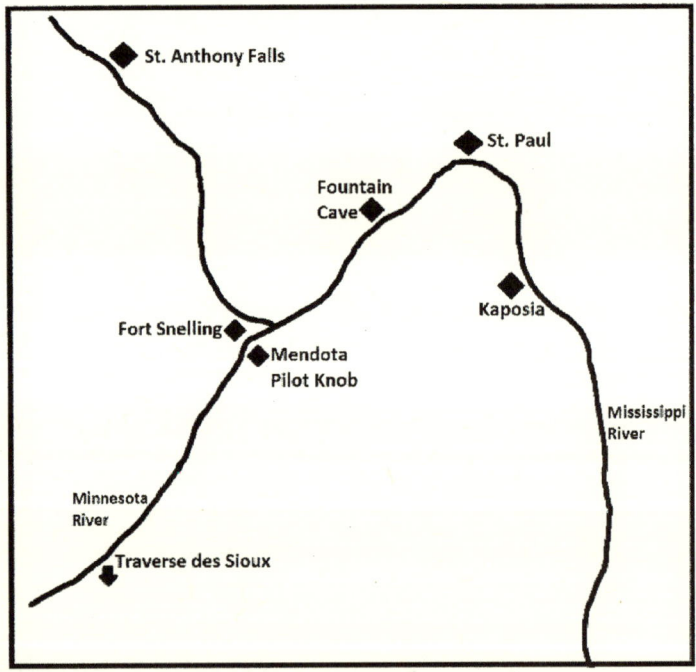

St. Paul and Surrounding Area, 1851

"Welcome to Minnesota!" exclaimed a stately looking man as I arrived at the St. Paul House. "I am Mr. Charles Smith, Secretary of the Territory."

I reached to grasp his already outstretched hand. "Pleased to make your acquaintance. I am—"

---

[13] *Minnesota Pioneer,* May 26, 1849.

"I know very well who you are, Mr. Mayer," Secretary Smith said, interrupting me. "The Governor has been expecting you."

"Very good," I replied with some shyness. The Secretary was hospitable to say the least and it may have thrown me off.

"Can I offer you anything?" asked the Secretary. "Coffee? Tea?"

Like nearly everyone in the city, Secretary Smith had not long been in the territory. He was a lawyer from Ohio appointed by President Taylor to his current position. He had about him a rather unique disposition marked by an intensified character and a strong individuality. What he was, he was decidedly.

"No, thank you," I responded. "I am quite comfortable."

"Well then," returned Secretary Smith in his direct but polite manner, "let us not lag. I have an honor upon which to bestow you."

"Upon me?" I said curiously.

"Yes, upon you," Secretary Smith immediately replied. "Governor Ramsey sends his apologies that he could not deliver it to you himself, but he is presently indisposed, as you will soon see, and he wanted that you have this honor right away."

My curiosity was piqued. I could not perceive what they may have for me and I also wished to know in what the Governor was presently engaged.

"Behold," stated the Secretary as he held in front of me a diploma of sorts. "Have a look."

The diploma, much to my surprise, instated me as a member of the Minnesota Historical Society.

"Congratulations!" exclaimed Secretary Smith. "As one of the founding members of the Historical Society I am glad to welcome a new member."

"But I am not deserving of such an honor," I said humbly but honestly.

"Nonsense. The Governor told me about your work with the Maryland Historical Society and we could not be more thrilled that you traveled all this way, upon your own volition, to record the historic events of our new territory."[14]

"I am speechless," I said trying to express my honest surprise and profound gratitude. I knew it was quite an honor to be welcomed to such

---

[14] In 1848, Mayer had accepted a position as librarian of the Maryland Historical Society in Baltimore, an organization that his father and his uncle, Brantz Mayer, had helped to found in 1844. Heilbron, *With Pen and Pencil*, 7.

a prestigious group in a place that was not my home. It also seemed to validate all the trouble I took in traveling so far.

"Never mind all of that," said Secretary Smith with a pat on my back. "Let me escort you to the Governor's temporary office where he is meeting with a deputation of Dakota Indians from Six's village. It will give you a chance to witness some of the Indian politics in which you will soon become immersed."

I was excited by this announcement. I had no idea I would so soon become witness to the Indian peoples. To me they were a vestige, something I read about in books. But not here. Here they were intertwined with the people, land, and culture.

As I was ushered down the hall to the Governor's office, I first observed dignified volumes of smoke billowing from the room. It was the Indians, who now came into view, who smoked from the pipe while seated around the Governor and his interpreter. As the Indians spoke with Governor Ramsey, I had the fine opportunity to observe their manners and mode of speech. It seemed they were discussing with the Governor their current starving condition and their need for supplies.

An old man stood and handed his pipe to his neighbor. He was dressed in a calico shirt and buckskin vest which was fringed around the edges. He wore leggings and a breech cloth along with moccasins and a beaded sash. His hair was long and dark, pulled straight back, plaited, and held together by several goose feathers. He looked every bit the part of an Indian as I had imagined them to be.

"Father," he said referring to Governor Ramsey. "We come on behalf of our brothers and kin," he said in his native Dakota. "We are starving and sick. There are no more buffalo to feed us and no more robes to keep us warm."

The man spoke with many expressive gestures and movements. He paused after each statement to shake hands with the Governor and to allow the interpreter to translate. It was clear that he was passionate about that of which he spoke.

"When we gave you our land, the Great Father promised to take care of us. He promised food for our children and money so that we would not have to beg. He promised land of our own where we could hunt and live like our ancestors had, without need or want."

In between each statement all of the other Indians exclaimed "Ho!" as if to say, *Yes, it is so.*

"But this is not what happened," continued the old man with his arms waving above his head. "The *wasicu* continue to come and encroach on the land promised us. They hunt our animals and leave the carcasses to rot. Yet the Great Father does nothing. He promised us money, but we do not receive it. He promised us implements, but you give us tools that we do not know how to use. You teach us to grow crops, but the crops fail. Now we are like starving wolves howling at the moon."

The man finished his speech abruptly and sat down. Before Governor Ramsey could respond, another man arose with his war-spear in hand.

"I agree with my elder," the man said. He was younger than the man who spoke before him and he appeared to be more of the warrior class. "We go out like sparrows for food and our young are like birds in the nest, crying for food. But we return with nothing."

"Ho!" they called in unison.

"Your traders fool us by making us stupid with fire-water. They indebt us until all of our money is gone. It passes through our hands like water from the stream."

"Ho!" they called again.

"The Great Father does not see our condition. He cannot hear our children crying. That is all I will say."

Another unified "Ho" followed but then there was silence. Governor Ramsey looked toward each member of the Indian band waiting for the next speaker to come forward. None came. Governor Ramsey stood and made ready to address the Indians.

"My friends," he began. "I call you this because we are neighbors who share in each other's good fortune and bad. I am pleased to meet you here today and I welcome you to our city at any time you see fit."

Governor Ramsey was exceedingly cordial, having the ability to make even a stranger feel like a close personal friend. I learned this about him earlier that spring when I met him in Washington City. He was exceptionally kind to me.

"You are right to allege that the treaty stipulations have not been upheld," continued the Governor in an honest and firm voice. "The traders sell whiskey without a license. The frontiersmen settle on your land without claim. Your monies have in part been withheld or misappropriated. I have heard your grievances and I understand why you have come here today."

The Indians sat still and quiet as they watched the Governor and listened to his interpreter. Alexander Ramsey was his full name. Of Scotch and German descent, he was born in Pennsylvania in 1815. He studied law at Lafayette College and was elected to Congress in 1843. Ramsey quickly became well-known among his colleagues as evincing those qualities of sagacity and firmness. He contributed largely to the election of Zachary Taylor as president and was therefore rewarded as being named Minnesota's first territorial Governor. Ramsey had a marked character, a stalwart form, and frank manners. He was a favorite with his associates and with all observers.[15]

"But I can assure you," continued the Governor in a frank tone, "that your wants and needs have not gone unheeded. The power of your Great Father extends from the rising to the setting sun and he will assert his authority on all those who do wrong. Those who steal from you will be punished and those who deceive you will be apprehended. Also, your monies are forthcoming and we wish to share with you the abundance of this land. None should remain hungry nor sick. Not in this land of plenty."

The Indians grunted as if in some form of reluctant agreement.

"I have for you supplies in a wagon just outside. They are yours to take. I have also for you tickets for bread. They can be redeemed here in town. I do not wish for you to go away dissatisfied."

The Indians stood and one by one grasped the hand of Governor Ramsey. There were no smiles or niceties exchanged, just a solemn accord. The Indians exited quietly and peacefully, walking directly passed where I stood. I held my breath, filled with nervous excitement. My first encounter with the Native Indian. He was just as I had imagined; strong and lean, dignified yet uncouth.

"Ah, young Mr. Mayer!" announced Governor Ramsey as he turned his attention toward me. "I must apologize, for there was business to attend to. Welcome to this new territory. Welcome to Minnesota."

"Thank you," I replied with a smile and a nod.

---

[15] As described by J. Fletcher Williams. *A History of the City of St. Paul*, 219.

"You must feel as if you are in a foreign country," said Governor Ramsey as he stepped close to shake my hand. "The people, the language, the environment. It must seem peculiar to a gentlemen of the east coast."

"Certainly," I agreed. "It will take some getting used to."

"Yes," the Governor laughed. "Well, there will be time for that. I understand you have received an invitation from Dr. Williamson to visit the Indian village at Kaposia."

"I have."

"Very good," replied Governor Ramsey. "Today you can relax. Explore the city, a work in progress though it may be, and on the morrow you can visit a real Indian village. You can see the frontier as it really exists."

"Splendid," I said in return. I did not wish to take any more of the Governor's time as I was certain he was busy establishing the young territory.

"Oh, and Mr. Mayer," said Governor Ramsey before I could exit. "We could not possibly be more grateful to have you here to record these historic events."

"Thank you, Governor. It is my pleasure to do so."

The Governor lowered his head and began scraping through the papers on his desk. With the direction of Secretary Smith, I exited the Governor's office ready for my adventure.

I spent the remainder of the day walking throughout the new and unique city of St. Paul. It was elegant in the way it was situated, but also in its multitude of new buildings and fresh, unworn streets. The glistening new paint and fresh-cut timber seemed to represent a hopeful and eager society. A society where everyone had a different beginning, but where each was given a new and equal start. Nearly the entire population was starting over. It created an uncommon mixture of peoples and customs, of languages and cultures. One such culture I could not fail to recognize were the French voyageurs. They were among the first to settle here and they still retained their national distinctions. The French language I heard spoken at least as much as English and it was often mixed with Dakota and English. These ancestors of Old France had a manner and appearance quite different from the typical American. They had a strange vivacity, merry-jest laugh, and were generally of smaller size than an American. The costume of the voyageur was a mixture of Indian and European which often included a scarf sash, moccasins, and a blanket coat reaching to about the knees and leggings. Their heads were often covered with a fur or felt hat adorned with feathers. Many of them, it appeared, had Indian wives which gave rise to another branch in the population of Minnesota. These were the mixed-breeds.[16]

Mixed-breeds, being neither Indian nor white, seemed to create an identity all their own. While they were welcome in all society, they had their own interests separate from those of the Dakota or the settler. During this time of cultural transition they sought to grow and protect their own communities. I could see that some people looked down upon the mixed-breeds for having both white and Indian blood. But I could also see that they carried a unique and useful influence. The mixed-breeds acted as a bridge between two very different and distinct cultures. Often they spoke both Indian and European based languages. They understood both white and Indian cultures and therefore could be rather shrewd in business and trade. It was obvious that those of mixed-race were an essential part of the frontier.

I found it curious to witness so many Native Indians in the streets of St. Paul. Like the Frenchmen they were clearly distinct but intermingled with the people of the city in the same capacity and manner of any other group. Throughout the course of the day I witnessed the very same Indians who had previously visited Governor Ramsey and so I observed them once more. Some of these were very fine specimens of Indians with a peculiar ease and grace of walk. They moved with lightness and nonchalance; they were very graceful in their movements. Yet they appeared powerful and fit with broad shoulders and muscular legs. They held over themselves large blankets with numerous pouches and trinkets which added to their picturesque appearance. Their hair was worn long, sometimes plaited, and vermillion was rubbed into the seam where parted, with feathers and beadwork known as wampum also adorning their heads. As I observed I came to presume that the use of moccasins contributed very much to the elegant walk of the Indian by giving the feet a natural elasticity. All in all I'd say that compared with the figures of the Anglo-Saxon, the Indian

---

[16] For more on the French Voyageurs, read *The Voyageur* by Grace Lee Nute. Grace Lee Nute, *The Voyageur*, (St. Paul: Minnesota Historical Society, 1987).

was lighter, graceful, and more erect, formed rather for feats of agility than strength.

By the close of the day I admit that sleep escaped me. I was excited. I had entered into a new world, one that I had previously only imagined. I came to wonder what it must be like to live in this new world. For some, like the settlers, it represented endless possibilities. For others, like the Indians, it represented adjustment and uncertainty, even fear.

Chapitre trois

―――◆―――

"I have seldom met with the same number of persons taken promiscuously from the ranks of civilized life who possessed so much genuine politeness, gentlemanly feeling and kindliness of manner as the Kaposia Indians."

― Frank Blackwell Mayer

"Ma-er? Ma-er?" said the Indian guide as he tried to speak my name.

"Yes," I replied. "Frank Mayer."

"Uh," he grunted as he pulled his dugout canoe on shore. "Ma-er," he uttered again evidently directing me to enter the canoe.

The boat was a fine piece of craftsmanship that appeared to be hollowed-out cottonwood. The front end was pointed while the rear was blunt and flat. It was light and smooth and probably maneuvered with ease along the water. Years of woodland dwelling had made the Dakota adept at constructing such an important and useful vessel.

Inside the canoe were two Dakota women, the wives of my guide. This was my first encounter with an Indian woman of any kind. They sat quietly on each end of the canoe with paddles in hand.

My guide spoke instructions to his wives as he gently eased the boat back into the water and then leaped in a sprightly manner into the canoe. He grunted out further instructions which I could not understand.

We moved along at a comfortable pace as the orange light of twilight danced across the waters of the Mississippi. My guide sat behind me as the two women did most of the work, the gentleman only helping when it pleased him to do so. My guide made conversation with his wife opposite him, while the woman opposite myself sat with a rather pensive expression, only joining the conversation at short intervals.

Both Indian women appeared pleasing to me. They were young with childlike expressions. Their pleasing appearance was greatly due to their white teeth and dark sparkling eyes contrasting with their long black hair falling luxuriantly over their shoulders. If it is not too bold to say, I believe they probably possess all the coquetry and teasing arts of their white counterparts.

It was a short and easy trip down the Mississippi and to the Indian village of Kaposia. It lay just a few miles south of St. Paul, situated on a small piece of bottom land between the bluffs and the river itself.

On the Mississippi Between Kaposia and St. Paul

"Welcome to Kaposia," announced Dr. Thomas Williamson upon my arrival to the thriving Indian village.

"Thank you," I replied as I pulled myself up out of the canoe and onto shore. "I cannot express how grateful I am to be here."

"And we are grateful to you," said Dr. Williamson expressing the sentiment of the Indian people.

As I stepped forward to ceremoniously shake hands with Dr. Williamson, I took a quick look around to gather my first impressions. I was immediately impressed. It was a charming little village with probably three hundred souls and half as many lodges. The village appeared comfortable and quiet with men lounging, women toiling and children playing.

"This is my home," declared Dr. Williamson as he turned to usher me toward the lodges.

Dr. Williamson, whom I had not met until this day, appeared to be in his early to mid-fifties. His hair was clearly receding from the forehead but remained starkly black. His face was stern but resolute and weathered. It seemed to reflect years of patient toil thereby adequately representing his moniker as the Father of the Dakota Mission.

Dr. Thomas Williamson

"Tranquil," I uttered almost involuntarily.

"Indeed," responded Dr. Williamson. "That is an adequate word for this place."

As Dr. Williamson and I drew closer to the village I could see that it was made out of two types of lodges, one apparently being a summer lodge and one a winter lodge. The summer house is not much unlike a log cabin. It is square in shape with a slanted roof reaching nearly to the ground. The walls are the framework of saplings tied together and covered by interwoven pieces of bark. From the entrance there hangs a long piece of buffalo hide. Just above and outside the entrance there extends about eight feet a shed or flat roof supported by posts unhewn. This would appear to function as a shady retreat for the inhabitants during the hot afternoon hours. The winter lodges, or tipis, were much different. The tipi was formed by many long poles which were pegged in a circle and then leaned and tied together at a central point above the ground. The poles were covered in buffalo hide which were anchored to the ground and a flap was cut to allow the smoke of their fires to exit. Looking on, the tipi had a very practical and cozy appearance. Seen all together, the houses were arranged in rows with the tipis intervening here and there, pleasantly varying the angularity and ruggedness of the long succession of Indian lodges.

"Why do they call it Kaposia?" I asked.

"It means *the lithe people*," Dr. Williamson answered quickly and plainly. "The name was bestowed upon this band because of their skill at the Indian game of lacrosse, the success of which depending largely upon swiftness."

"I see. What brought you to this place, Dr. Williamson?" I asked curiously, though it may have been an imposition.

"That could be a long story," replied Dr. Williamson with a coy smile.

"I am quite interested," I returned, trying to indicate that I would not mind a long tale. "This is a curious place to me. The frontier is like a different world."

"Indeed," agreed my companion.

"When did you arrive and from whence did you come?" I prodded.

"I was not the first to come," he began as we found a quiet place to sit. "Certainly there is a long list of missionary work throughout the history of the new world. But among the Dakotas of this region it began in 1834 when two brothers, Samuel and Gideon Pond, arrived at Fort Snelling. These two young men came all the way from Connecticut and though they were not ordained ministers, they were devoutly Christian and wished to enlighten the Indians and save them from impending perdition. The Pond brothers settled among Cloudman's village at Lake Calhoun where they not only preached Christian theology, but implemented farming as well. They also recognized the need to put the Dakota language into written form. Until then the Dakota language existed only in speech."

"Is that so?" I interjected with astonishment.

"Yes," answered Dr. Williamson. "The primary goal of the missionary became the translation of the language. For this we owe much gratitude to the Pond brothers. They were the first to assign letters to the Dakota language. By living with the Indians, both brothers gained a mastery of the language and within a few years Samuel Pond completed a small grammar and dictionary of three thousand words."

"Amazing that they could accomplish such things," I said in earnest.

"They made our work possible," commented Dr. Williamson. "I arrived a year later in May of 1835 having come from Ohio. As a young man I was not a minister, but I have always felt a deep devotion to the gospel and the sharing of its message. I began as a medical doctor having graduated from Yale in 1824. I practiced medicine for nearly ten years before I decided to study theology. I felt a deep compassion for the Indians of the frontier, but at the time I had a young family and I did not wish to uproot them or to endanger them in any way. But Providence had other plans and I lost my dear children."

"You have my deepest sympathies."

"It was a great trial," acknowledged Dr. Williamson, "but it was also a great blessing. It has worked to strengthen my faith and that of my wife, and we have never once regretted our decision to do the work we have been called to do."

I nodded in return.

"I worked with the Pond brothers," continued Dr. Williamson, "for just over a month before I was given my assignment. So, in summer 1835, I and my wife, Margaret, were sent to Lac qui Parle to prosecute the teaching and civilizing of the eastern-most Dakota bands.

"Civilizing?" I asked. "I have heard this said, but what do you mean?"

"I mean exactly that," returned Dr. Williamson. "Not only have the missionaries here sought to Christianize the Indian, but we have recognized their poor and wretched condition and we have sought to provide them with a better way of life. We seek to implement farming, to provide education, and to build for them real frame houses. We wish to end their ways of indolence and squalor and to usher them into modern society."

"I see," I said hesitantly, being somewhat confused by the idea that Dakota way of life was somehow offensive or unacceptable, but also remembering the views Mr. Sexton had expressed earlier.

"That is what makes the upcoming treaty so important," explained Dr. Williamson. "Not only does it open up this vast and productive land to settlement, but it will concentrate the Dakota onto a reservation where we can teach and provide them with all the instruments of civilized life."

I did not reply.

"You will see."

"What happened at Lac qui Parle?" I asked trying to return the doctor to his narrative.

"Nothing of real consequence," he replied quickly. "I established a mission there and Margaret started a school.[17] The first few years were exceptionally challenging. In these years I dedicated myself to learning the Dakota language. After just two years I could comfortably teach to the Dakota in their own language. Furthermore, I set about translating the gospels into Dakota which I have since achieved. If nothing else was accomplished, this I feel has made it all worthwhile."

"Have the Dakota been unreceptive to Christianity?" I asked.

"It has been an uphill climb," answered Dr. Williamson. "You have to understand that the Indian is devoutly religious and set in his spiritual ways. In addition to this barrier, the white man's example has not to any great extent been a healthy example of Christian ideals. This, combined with the language barrier, has made it exceptionally difficult to earn many converts. But I remain steadfast as I have always."

"Your work is admirable," I said in response. "But why did you leave Lac qui Parle?"

"That is simple, really," replied Dr. Williamson as he showed the hint of a smile. "I was invited."

"Invited?"

"Certainly. Actually it was a good sign of progress. Some of my converts from Lac qui Parle made their way to Kaposia and reported the good work

---

[17] In this novel, very little is shared about the women who were an integral part of this history. For more on those women who played an important role, see Dakota Soul Sisters by Lois A. Glewwe. Lois A. Glewwe, *Dakota Soul Sisters: Stories of the Women of the Dakota Missionaries*, http://dakotasoulsisters.com.

that had been done. Little Crow, the newly appointed chief of the Kaposia band, wanted this good work among his people and thusly invited me to open a school and mission. Things having deteriorated at Lac qui Parle, and wishing to bring my family closer to civilization, I accepted gladly."

There was a pause in the conversation and we both observed that it had become dark.

"I understand that you brought your sketchbook," noted Dr. Williamson.

"Always," I replied while patting my hand against my satchel.

"Very good," said Dr. Williamson as he stood up. "For now we should retire. Tomorrow will be an eventful day and you cannot draw in the dark."

"I couldn't if I tried."

The following day, free to do as I pleased, I decided to take a stroll through the village and see if I might procure sketches of the Dakota people. As was my usual practice I decided to sketch my sitters unawares and without reference to their permission or disinclination. In this method I had met with varying degrees of success. Some of the Indians upon discovering my purpose found it most laughable—they had never seen themselves as a drawing and found it curious, showing no signs of objection. Others showed a stoic indifference while still others coldly declined being sitters. There were other Indians who observed my drawings with a sort of superstitious awe or just plain amazement. While making a sketch of a tepee a crowd of women, dogs, and youth collected around me. From among them I heard curious gasps and grunts while I translated the image onto paper. Later in the day, while attempting to sketch an old woman, I received a large portion of Dakota vocabulary of imprecations and expressions. This woman was not pleased and somehow believed that by acquiring her portrait I might obtain some powerful and mystical influence over her.

Despite some negative reactions, it was most pleasing to me to observe and record Dakota life. Women were at work sewing moccasins and dressing children's hair while gossiping with friends and watching their babies. Men lounged in the shade either sleeping or sipping smoke from their pipes. Meanwhile children chased their dogs and laughed and played in the most carefree manner. Dakota life appeared good here, the midsummer months being a time of rest and relaxation.

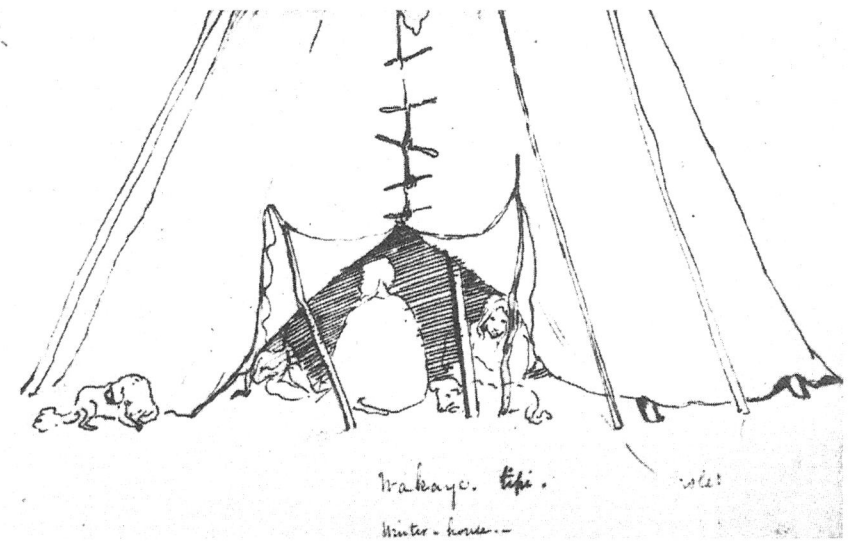

Dakota Winter Lodge

Dakota Summer Lodge

"Mr. Mayer!" I heard my name called. "Mr. Mayer!" came the voice again as I turned to identify Dr. Williamson approaching.

"I see you are making friends," said Dr. Williamson lightheartedly.

"More or less," I replied. "Some have taken kindly to me, others wish to take no part in my artistic endeavors."

"You are foreign to them, just as they are to you. I think you'll find that the Dakota are a most welcoming and hospitable people."

I nodded.

"Speaking of which," continued Dr. Williamson, "you have been invited to join Little Crow in his lodge."

"Very good," I replied, though I was exceedingly nervous to accept the invitation. I had no idea I would be so quickly led to the headman of the Dakota. I felt less than worthy.

"He is a friend of Captain Seth Eastman, a sketch artist I believe you are familiar with," explained Dr. Williamson. "Let us go now."

I entered the lodge slowly with the doctor entering just behind me. I immediately observed the cool and comfortable feeling inside the lodge. Inside, the light from the sun was intermittent in nature, reaching through the gaps in the lodge and stretching forward in unbroken rays of pure light. Before me were three Indian elders all seated cross-legged atop a buffalo robe on the floor.

"Taa-yaa ya-hi," said the elder in the middle which I could only assume meant *welcome*. The elder spoke several more Dakota words as he stretched his open hand forward as if inviting me to sit. I looked back to Dr. Williamson to confirm this notion and he nodded while giving the same motion with his hand.

"Welcome to Kaposia," said the elder in the middle, speaking in English this time. "I am Taoyateduta, spokesman of the Dakota people," he said in a dignified tone. "To the whites I am known as *le petit corbeau* or Little Crow."

I immediately observed that Little Crow was not only dignified in tone, but also in manner and dress. It seems that before meeting with me, he wanted to ensure that he was dressed in a manner befitting of his rank. He was in a full robe with a small blanket covering his arms and shoulders. On his feet were moccasins thereby leaving only his face and hands exposed. On his head was an elaborate and colorful headdress made of various materials. It was decorated by a colorful band around his forehead with many long and light colored strands extending from the top. From the back and sides of the headdress were woven and fringed multi-colored cloth that reached forward over his shoulders and onto his arms. The entire piece was most elaborate and impressive. I next noticed Little Crow's long, dark, and wavy hair which fell nicely over his many intricate necklaces. His face appeared mature, but not old. I figure he must have been about forty-five years of age. He looked dignified, determined, and somehow he looked as if he was filled with intelligence. All of this combined to make it overwhelmingly apparent that I was in the presence of an important man.

"Pleased to meet you," I replied softly as I tucked my legs beneath me to sit more comfortably. "I am Frank Blackwell Mayer, an artist from Baltimore."

"You come many lengths and crossed many rivers to be here," stated Little Crow in his broken form of English. "Balt-i-more," he sounded out.

"Yes," I replied quickly. "My journey was long and my home is far."

"Your home," repeated Little Crow. "There are many like you? There are many pale-face—they all come this way?"

"Not all," I explained. "But there are many and they are expanding across this land."

"You, artist?" asked Little Crow as he moved his hand through the air as if he were painting.

"Yes, I am a sketch artist," I replied with a nod. "I wish to draw pictures of you and your people. I want to record the images from the signing of the treaty."

"Yes, you record image," nodded Little Crow. "You record me?" he asked as he pointed to himself.

"Yes, I would like to draw your portrait."

"You record me," confirmed Little Crow. "Later."

"Of course," I replied.

"Now let us join together in the pipe," Little Crow said as he pushed his pipe forward.

Like his headdress, his pipe was also very elaborate. It was long, so long in fact that it could be smoked from the mouth while the bowl rested against the floor. The shaft was carved from wood. From the mouthpiece extending down was an intricate, patterned design. Attached to the design were several feathers, quills, and some horse hair, which were attached at the base and hung toward the floor. The bowl was made of a highly-polished red stone. This, as I would learn, was quarried from a place sacred to the Dakota Indians.[18] Inside the bowl was a material known as Kinnikennick. It is made up of various kinds of bark mixed with tobacco. I found the smell of it to be quite agreeable. It was clear to me in this moment that smoking the pipe among friends was a rather important and even necessary part of Dakota culture.

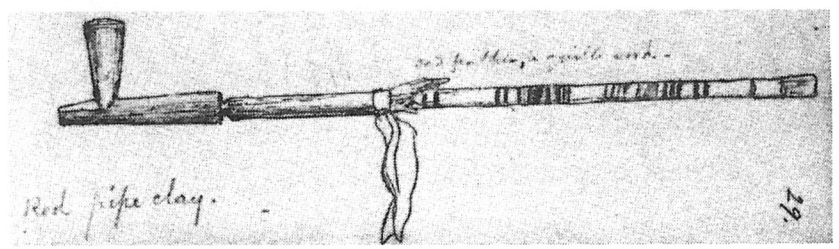

Red Clay Pipe

"You, young man," commented Little Crow as he pointed toward me.

"Yes, relatively so," I answered him.

"Your youth is as . . .," he struggled to find a word. ". . . is as many fox pelts."

"Oh," I replied in realization of what he meant to express. "It has value."

"Value," Little Crow repeated. "I am old. I cannot change world. World changes me. You are young. You change world. You help my people."

"Yes," I nodded politely.

Little Crow did not respond and little more was said. We sat in silence as we passed the pipe.

I am not sure exactly what Little Crow meant, but I left his lodge that evening with a feeling of reverence and awe. I began to wonder what might become of his people in the coming years and just what my role was in that future.

---

18   This place is known today as the Pipestone National Monument in southwest Minnesota. It remains sacred to the Dakota Indians.

Kaposia Village

Chapitre quatre

———=•(())•=———

"Fort Snelling sits atop a bluff with an amazing view of this bdote. It is sacred because it is here that the Mdewakantunwan Dakota creation story places the origin of our first people, where thousands of years ago our first ancestors were created from the land."

-Waziyatawin Angela Wilson,
In the Footsteps of our Ancestors

*R*ing, ring, ring.
"What is that ringing?" I asked Dr. Williamson.
"That is the school bell."
"Oh, the school," remembering that Dr. Williamson had mentioned the school at Lac qui Parle earlier.
"Yes," he explained. "My wife Margaret is teaching today. I will teach tomorrow."
"Teacher! Teacher!" came the call of a young Dakota. "Are you coming to school today?" he asked in perfect English as he went streaking by.
"Not today, lad," Dr. Williamson shouted after him. "Behave well for the misses."
The boy came to sudden halt, he turned.
"Who is that?" he said pointing his finger at me.
Dr. Williamson answered by scolding the boy in the Dakota language. "Hurry off to class," he then commanded in English.

The boy lowered his head, not ashamed, but frustrated, and continued toward the ringing bell.

"He seems very bright," I commented with surprise.

"That is Takoda, an orphan boy and a very bright young lad, but he forgets his manners. I care for him, but he is rather independent."

"Takoda," I repeated with curiosity.

"It means Friend to Everyone. It represents him well. He was so sad after losing his parents to disease, but he has overcome it well and he is now much more cheerful and jubilant. Though I have never been able to tell him what to do."

I laughed at the thought.

"Do all the children attend class?" I asked, wondering to myself if all the Dakota children were as capable as this young boy I had just come across.

"No, most certainly not," replied Dr. Williamson dejectedly. "Attendance is our greatest hurdle. We have but five or six students at any given time."

"Is that so? I wonder why?" I thought out loud.

"For whatever reason," explained Dr. Williamson, "some of the Native peoples have a prejudice to advancement, believing somehow that it is destructive or immoral. But also, the schemes of traders keep students away."

"Traders? How so?"

"Many of the traders believe it is in their best interests to keep the Dakota in ignorance," answered Dr. Williamson. "As long as the Dakota fail to understand and comprehend the new way of the world, the traders will be able to exploit such ignorance."

"How foul!" I said in disgust.

"Yes, yes," agreed Dr. Williamson. "It is one of many obstacles we contend with. But we must be patient and continue our work."

I nodded in a conciliatory fashion, not knowing how to express my sympathy.

I did not remain long at Kaposia, but before departing I was fortunate enough to witness the men prepare for a hunt. It was quite an ordeal that included loquacious speeches and extensive costumes. I took the opportunity to draw several of the hunters as they appeared like knights of old as fit for fray as feast. But I admit that in drawing them the rapidity of their motions and the prejudice against my art militated somewhat against my success. I bid a fond farewell to Dr. Williamson having been much pleased with my visit.

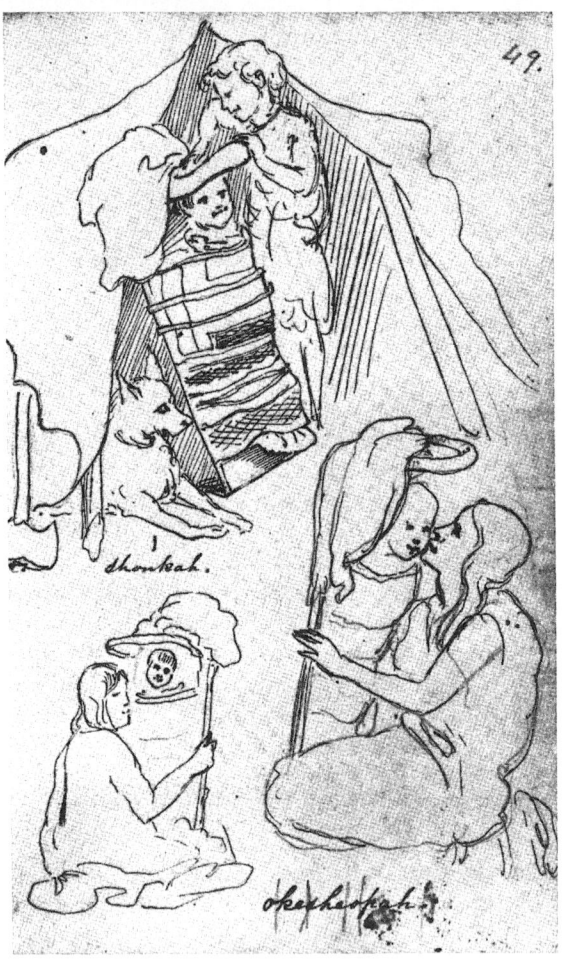

Dakota Children at Kaposia

Preparing for a Hunt

Like my trip down the Mississippi to Kaposia, so too was my trip back to St. Paul. I was shuffled into a canoe along with two Dakota women and a young half-breed boy. I placed myself opposite one of the women but soon learned that this was a breach of etiquette. Rather I was told to turn my back on the ladies so as not to observe their gestures and expressions. I was content then to lay relaxingly in the canoe and enjoy the scenery of the surrounding country. Moving upriver, we stayed in the quiet waters near shore moving swiftly and lightly underneath the overhanging willows. There was no talking among the occupants of the canoe, just the sounds of the cool and calm breeze against the dangling leaves and the persistent splash of the paddles against the water. The river had swelled from summer rains, making it seem as if we were passing through a forest canal where trees abound, some being curled by lightning, and where driftwood of immense size had escaped the forest and found its way over the falls which lay several miles ahead. Eventually we emerged from this enchanting scenery and into the broad and rapid river until finally reaching St. Paul, where I was once again among the voyageurs, Yankees, French and Indians with their peltries, notions, oxen, and pipes.

I then traveled upriver to old Fort Snelling, the military post at the time. I call it "old" because it was a long running frontier outpost, having been established in 1819. It was the first settlement of any kind west of Prairie du Chien and stood alone for many years as a desolate and lonely frontier post.[19]

"Mr. Steele, I presume," I said to the distinguished-looking man who came out to meet me as I arrived at the landing.

"Yes," he replied positively. "Franklin Steele, fort sutler."

He reached forward to shake my hand. "I trust you received my letter."

"Certainly, I did," I replied with a nod.

"I'd like to introduce you to my wife, Miss Anna Barney, also of Baltimore."

A dashing young lady appeared from behind Mr. Steele and held out her hand in a manner befitting an eastern debonair.

"Charmed," I stated.

She bowed gracefully, but had nothing to say.

"I presume your travel to the fort was without incident?" insinuated Mr. Steele.

"Yes, of course," I responded. "I have come to quite enjoy my canoe trips along the Mississippi."

---

[19] In 1805, U.S. Army Lt. Zebulon Pike negotiated the sale of 100,000 acres of land at the confluence of the Minnesota and Mississippi Rivers with an agreement that the United States could build a fort there. This is where Fort Snelling was eventually built. It should be noted, however, that of the seven chiefs present, only two signed the treaty. Also, for the land which was valued at $200,000, the United States paid just $2,000. Finally, it is unlikely that the Dakota understood the document that they were signing. "Minnesota Treaties," *The U.S.-Dakota War of 1862*, http://www.usdakotawar.org/history/treaties/minnesota-treaties.

"They do provide a restful spell," agreed Mr. Steele. "Allow me to welcome you to Fort Snelling. No trip to Minnesota would be complete without visiting the place where it all began. But I can tell you more as we make our way to the garrison. It is a long walk from the landing."

"Of course," I said politely, and before I knew it, two young officers ran over to collect my belongings.

"It is quite an imposing site, this old fort," noted Mr. Steele.

I had to agree with the post sutler. Looking up from the river the garrison appeared castle-like and impenetrable. Situated high upon a bluff at the confluence of the Mississippi and Minnesota Rivers, Fort Snelling appeared to watch over the entire region. It was built with a light, sand colored stone with a great round tower that expressed its dominance over the surrounding area.

"It is beautiful. I very much enjoy the varying size and colors of the stone that fit together in such unique manner to create the wall," I commented.

"Yes," agreed Ms. Barney who decided to join the conversation, "but terribly boring."

"Excuse me?" I replied.

"Oh, Anna," objected Mr. Steele. "Do not be so rude in front of our guest."

"I don't mean to be rude," argued Anna. "I simply mean to say that little goes on here. Look around, all you see are Indian tepees. And the soldiers spend all day training for what, I do not know."

"I understand," I responded sympathetically. "Being from Baltimore myself I can see how thoroughly different this place is."

"Well, regardless of what my wife says," chided Mr. Steele, "Fort Snelling and its surrounding country has provided us with great opportunities. One merely needs to seize them."

"Spoken with confidence," I noted.

After climbing the long, ascending hill alongside the fort we arrived at the front of the sutler's store which was operated by Mr. Steele. Above the door was a large wooden sign which read, *The Best Stocked Store in the West.*

"That is not just a saying," declared Mr. Steele. "It really is the best stocked store in the West."

"Remarkable," I said in an effort to be polite.

Anna scoffed.

"I have made quite a name for myself here in Minnesota," bragged Mr. Steele with his head held high. [20]

"I don't understand," I said quizzically as I began to wonder how a fort sutler could become so successful. "You must have other ventures beyond your role as sutler."

"Oh, indeed," exclaimed Mr. Steele. "I began as the fort sutler, but my profits have come through lumbering. After moving here in 1838, I quickly realized the potential of the lumber industry in this region. As soon as I could I opened a few sawmills and the profits soon followed. Today I am a partner in the Mississippi Boom Company and the Rum River Boom Company, the two largest lumber firms on the frontier. Not only that, but a few years back I purchased Nicollet and Boom Islands and platted the town of St. Anthony. I have built a sawmill at the falls of St. Anthony and business is good. Just wait," he said excitedly, "in a few years the town of St. Anthony will be bursting with people and industry just like St. Paul is today. They will be two great sister cities."

"I see now how you have come to stock your store so well," I admitted.

"It has required much foresight and shrewd dealing, but yes, the lumber industry has been good to me," declared Mr. Steele with a satisfied smile.

"Perhaps we should show Mr. Mayer to his quarters," interrupted Anna as if she had heard enough of her husband's pretentiousness.

"Yes, of course," agreed Mr. Steele. "Where are my manners?"

"It is quite all right," I said softly.

"You will be staying with Mr. Philander Prescott. He is a bit of a curmudgeonly old man, but is hospitable enough."

"I should be pleased to stay with him," I said as Anna directed me toward Mr. Prescott's cabin. I followed her lead.

"Mr. Prescott?" politely called Ms. Barney as she stood in the doorway of his home. "Mr. Prescott?"

---

[20] According to historian David M. Delo, "A combination of frontier opportunity and personal drive for acquisition of profits enabled him (Mr. Steele) to become a highly successful entrepreneur." David M. Delo, *Peddlers and Post Traders: The Army Sutler on the Frontier*, (Helena, Montana: Kingfisher Books, 1998), 87.

Before us sat a stout man with spectacles and a round face hunched over his ledger.

"Mr. Prescott, Mr. Mayer, the artist from Baltimore, has arrived to the fort," Anna said gently.

Mr. Prescott looked up, his eyes squinting and his head tilted down in order to peer through and above his spectacles.

"Very well," said Mr. Prescott as he turned back to his ledger. "You may show him in."

Ms. Barney directed me inside the small, organized cabin. Mr. Prescott remained in his place, head lowered and pen in hand steady at work.

"Make yourself at home," encouraged Anna, sensing my discomfort. "Someone will come by tomorrow to show you around the grounds."

"Very good. Thank you, Ms. Barney," I replied.

Still feeling a bit uncomfortable, I took a look around my newest shelter. It was a homely little cabin that was similar to any I might find on the frontier at this time. To the front was the door and two windows. Piled to each side were various materials. To the left was a rifle angled neatly within the frame of the window and to the right was a stool and butter churn. To the back was the kitchen with table, wood-burning stove, and various pots and utensils strewn about. Above the kitchen was a loft with an angled ladder leading toward its opening. Outside was a small, but impressive-looking garden. It grew corn, carrots, and potatoes and looked to be well taken care of. Just beyond the garden I could see an outhouse, a farm building and a small barn.

"Where shall I stay?" I finally decided to ask.

"The loft if you please," said Mr. Prescott, pointing his finger but not lifting his head.

"What is your position at the fort?" I asked, trying to make conversation.

Mr. Prescott made no response. I waited, but then turned to go toward the loft.

"I am the superintendent of farming," explained the curmudgeonly Mr. Prescott as he finally raised his head from his ledger.

"Have you been a resident of this country long?"

"Quite," he said with a grunt. "I was a young man when I came here in 1820. The fort had not yet received its moniker, but was known then as Camp New Hope."

"Wow!" I responded. "Over thirty years then."

"I never intended to stay this long," continued Mr. Prescott who had begun to speak more naturally.

"What happened?"

"I fell in love," he said with a smile. "She was the daughter of a Dakota Chief and we were married in 1823. I have since that time become ingrained in this community."

"How so?" I asked, hoping the elderly man would elaborate.

"Stay here a few days and you will see," replied Mr. Prescott. "I have many visitors."

"I see. Toward what purpose?"

"Toward many purposes," answered Mr. Prescott appearing somewhat irritated. "I host prayer morning and night. I conduct business. I teach and help the Dakota with their studies."

"You are integral to this place," I stated.

"Perhaps I am," returned Mr. Prescott with a furled brow. "For me, it has become commonplace."

And with that Mr. Prescott returned to his ledger.

Inside Prescott's Cabin

"Mr. Mayer," said a fine-looking old gentleman who came to meet me at the entrance to the fort. "I am Agent Nathaniel McLean. I will be your guide at the fort today."

"Pleased to meet you," I said habitually.

"Have you enjoyed your visit thus far?" inquired Agent McLean.

"It is a learning experience, indeed," I answered in the most polite but honest manner possible.

"Yes," replied Agent McLean with a hearty laugh, "it takes some getting used to."

I smiled in response.

"Well, let me begin by telling you a little about myself and my role here," stated Agent McLean as he ushered me through the gates and across the parade ground. "Have you much understanding of the Indian System in Minnesota?"

"I cannot say that I have," I admitted. "I came here to observe the Indians and the negotiations, but some background knowledge would largely benefit my understanding."

"Well, let me explain," said Agent McLean. "Across this great nation the Indians have been categorized and separated by region. Each region is appointed a superintendent and it is therefore defined as a superintendency. This region is known as the Minnesota Superintendency. Within this region there are three agencies: the Chippewa, the Winnebago, and the St. Peters, which includes all of the Dakota Indians."

Agent McLean spoke not with eloquence but with an effusive sophistication. He looked to be in his sixties and probably spent a long career in politics. He appeared genuine in his role, as if filled with integrity.

"Each agency is then appointed an agent. I am the agent for the St. Peters Agency. As an agent, we are required annually to report to the Superintendent who is then responsible for reporting to the Commissioner of Indians Affairs in Washington. The Commissioner maintains, monitors, and regulates each superintendency through the Bureau of Indian Affairs."

"So it is a political hierarchy," I said, trying to make sure I understood.

"Yes," affirmed Agent McLean. "From the Bureau of Indian Affairs, to the superintendencies, down to the agencies.

"And what is your role as an agent?" I asked.

"I oversee the Sioux—also called the Dakota," he answered quickly. "My tasks are many and varied and difficult to precisely define. They can vary greatly from one day to the next. First and foremost, I must observe and report upon the condition of the Indians within my agency. I must regulate trade and other transactions and interactions between the whites and the Indians. I must direct and supervise agriculture. I must oversee the schools and missionaries. I must attempt to maintain peace and order between the Indians themselves. And I must enforce treaties and other legal charters making sure that all terms are being observed and adhered to."

"That is an incredible list of responsibilities!" I said with astonishment. "You have a big role to play on this frontier."

"I am responsible for much that goes on here. Essentially, I am the intermediary between the United States Government and the Dakota Indians."

"Interesting," I commented in order to show that I was attentive.

"What is your impression of the fort?" asked Agent McLean, changing the topic.

"It is remarkable," I said honestly while looking up and down the grounds in front of me. The grounds were formed in a diamond shape with the northern corner stretching out to the edge of the river bluff. The center of the grounds were clear and open but with clearly worn and well-traveled paths. Along the perimeter was a tall and what seemed to be impenetrable stone wall. On the north and west sides were long, narrow buildings that appeared to be the barracks. They were two stories tall with wooden porches stretching across the entire front. On the east were more barracks, but these were less narrow and must have been the officer's quarters. To the south were various buildings such as the hospital, schoolhouse, and barn. Throughout the grounds were other buildings of various size and shape such as the batteries, sheds, and latrines. There was also a well from which to obtain water. To the southern corner, and well above the rest of the fort, proudly waved the American flag. All together I must admit that though the fort appeared imposing from the outside, from the inside it appeared to be rather simple.

"It is truly remarkable," agreed Agent McLean. "This post has been here many years and until now it has been far beyond the reaches of civilization. It is a world all its own."

"I am learning that," I said while considering my already numerous experiences here. "What is garrison life like?" I asked, remembering Ms. Barney's comments from earlier.

"Dull," he replied quickly. "For the soldier at least, it can be quite dull."

"How do you mean?"

"The days, I'm afraid, are filled with monotonous drills and tedious routines," explained Agent McLean. "Each day begins at dawn with the sounding of the reveille followed by the roll call. This is followed by chores such as sweeping the grounds, feeding the horses, and attending to the gardens. After chores the soldiers have their breakfast and then a second roll call. Then various tasks are performed. Sentinels are posted to stand guard, various detachments are formed for reconnoitering and foraging and other such military-related tasks. At three o'clock in the afternoon a third roll call is called, followed by dinner. And the meals, I will add, are just as monotonous as the routine. After dinner various maneuvers are gone through and orders are read. Finally, before lights out, the arms are placed in the arm-racks, the horses attended to, a final roll call endured, and the bugle call sounded."

"It is the same every day?" I asked.

"Virtually the same," replied Agent McLean. "There is very little excitement at a frontier post such as this. The soldiers, in fact, delight in any opportunity to go into Indian country."

"Winter must be even worse for the soldier," I added.

"Quite," agreed Agent McLean. "In winter isolation at the fort is almost complete."

"But you must stay occupied with your assorted responsibilities."

"Oh, without question," quickly blurted the Agent. "My role does not follow the monotony of the frontier soldier."

Agent McLean paused and tilted his head in thought. "Let me show you something," he finally said.

Agent Mclean, who suddenly looked younger and more invigorated, pointed to the northern corner of the fort and began steadily walking that way. I followed.

As we walked I began to recognize the activity going on around me. There were groups of soldiers painting the barracks, some were drying out and folding laundry, and several stood guard at various posts. Around me also were numerous sounds and smells. I could hear men at labor in the gardens and all the way down at the landing I could hear the call of boatmen to the shoremen. I inhaled and suddenly noticed the rich perfume of fresh baked bread. Also, along the soft summer breeze came the spring-like aroma of a recent rainfall.

"This is the half-moon battery," explained Agent McLean as we arrived at the point of interest. "But that is not what I wish to show you," he said, climbing the steps to the top. "Here."

I reached the top and looked out upon the confluence of the Mississippi and Minnesota Rivers. Not only could I see the merge of the two great rivers, but I could see for miles in any direction what appeared to be a pristine and endless forest. In front of me and across the river were numerous tepees with Indian women and children milling about as smoke bellowed steadily upward from their fire pits. In the river were canoes, some coming and some going, all of them moving gracefully through the water. In the far distance to the east I could make out the burgeoning city of St. Paul. From my vantage it looked minute and insignificant when made relative to the vast, lush, and beautiful region that surrounded it. To the far west I could see several pristine and shining lakes, one of which was Lake Calhoun. I knew this lake had supported the life of the Dakotas for many years and now supported rest and recreation for the soldiers at Fort Snelling and other wearied laborers to this region.

"The confluence below you is called Bdote by the Dakota Indians," said Agent McLean, breaking my momentary trance. "It is the center of Dakota spirituality and history. It is the place where they believe their people began. Where life itself began."

"Standing here I can sense its life-giving aura."

"Whether or not life began at this spot, it is the focal point of all people, business, commerce, and history in this region," continued Agent McLean. "For many years it acted as a gathering place where leaders of multiple tribes would negotiate and make critical decisions. Here is where I must keep watch of everyone and everything that passes through. Not a single boat may pass without inspection. Not a single wayfarer may enter this region until we obtain the truth in regard to their conduct. But even under my watchful eye, things have deteriorated so."

"In what manner?" I asked.

"For many years now the Indians have become starving and sick and, unfortunately, exploited. We have tried to make improvements in education, farming, and livelihood, but we have met with little success. Our intentions and our efforts are far too often thwarted either by ignorance, idleness, or avarice."

I listened intently and was very curious about what the Agent had to say.

"It is to be deeply regretted that, while the masses of our population will compare favorably with other communities for intelligence and sobriety, there are some always found on our frontier whose only livelihood is to sell whiskey and strip the poor Indian of his earnings and the pittance allowed him by the government, giving in exchange that which makes him miserable. That is what makes this upcoming treaty so important—so necessary."

I looked quizzically at the Agent, urging him to elaborate.

"Its efforts are twofold," continued Agent McLean, taking my cue. "First it will act to separate the growing population of whites from the Indians. It will create a distance that will afford the Indians the opportunity to improve their condition without those annoyances and adverse influences which prevail while living in close connection with a white population."

"And the second?"

"The second being that by concentrating the Dakota Indians within the same vicinity we create an effective means of providing a proper and economical superintendence."

"By placing them on a reservation," I said, seeking clarification.

"Yes," replied Agent McLean. "By creating a common center we can establish more effective schools, missions, farms, and other mechanisms acting for their benefit. A more wholesome discipline can be exercised among them, disorderly conduct promptly punished, all war parties checked before they have ripened into action. I fervently believe that the treaty is liberal to the Indians, advantageous to the United States, and vitally important to the peace and prosperity of Minnesota."

I thought on this for a moment, not sure what to say or whether to respond at all. Agent McLean seemed so sure of his hypothesis and he was much older, wiser, and politically experienced than myself. I felt as if I was expected to readily agree with the agent and others like him without giving the matter any thought. But something felt wrong.

"What of the Dakota way of life?" I asked skeptically.

"It will become extinguished. It has to," replied Agent McLean in a rather matter-of-fact tone. "That is one of the goals of the treaty. It is designed to create lasting impressions upon the Dakota youth so that as they grow up, their habits and pursuits may be changed. By the time their annuities expire, they might become incorporated into the state as citizens."[21]

"But must we destroy their culture in the process?"

"It is a savage way of life that cannot survive in these modern, industrial times. We wish to improve upon their simple and wretched condition and usher them into the civilized world. Dear boy, you must trust the powers that be."

"Powers?" I questioned. "Like the president?"

"Well," responded Agent McLean slowly, "Millard Fillmore is one of those powers."

"And where does he stand?"

"He seeks the protection of all Indians and all whites. He knows that the best way to do this is through the reservation system. He has seen the errors our policy when we forcefully remove the Indians and he does not blame them if they retaliate. But the president, like myself, believes it is in the best interest of the Native peoples to be placed on reservations where they might engage in agriculture and rely on their labor instead of the chase for means of support."

"What do the Dakota want?" I asked in a humorless tone.

"It does not matter what the Dakota want. It is what is best for the country."

It was clear to me that Agent McLean and others like him had all the right intentions. They seemed genuinely inclined to create a better, more prosperous future. Still, that didn't make it right. He was now the third

---

[21] The sentiments shared here were those shared by Nathaniel McLean himself in his annual report to the Commissioner of Indian Affairs in 1851. United States Office of Indian Affairs, *Annual Report of the Commissioner of Indian Affairs, for the Year 1851*, http://digital.library.wisc.edu/1711.dl/History.AnnRep51, 171-173.

person I had encountered who had expressed this notion of civilizing the Indians. I had met the Indians at Kaposia and found nothing to indicate a lack of advancement or quality of life. Until now, my knowledge of the frontier extended only as far as what I heard in stories or saw in the paintings of Seth Eastman and my tutor, Alfred J. Miller. But to be there, to meet people, both Indian and white, gave me a new perspective, though it was one yet to be developed and understood. I never meant to become intertwined with the people or politics, but I could not ignore the curiosity and conflict inside me.

I had much trouble getting much sleep that night. Truly, my accommodations were rude. As I lay in that loft, I considered how since my departure from the east coast my accommodations steadily declined. Here I stayed in this small and dusty apartment where there existed the accumulated cobwebs of many years, enhanced by the stale smell of kinnikinnick smoke which invaded my condition. Kinnikinnick being a combination of bark and leaves and the preferred pipe substance of the Dakota and frontiersman alike. Add to this the incense of unwashed utensils rising from the kitchen below me and the want of ventilation and I was left with an inescapable desire to be returned home where I might once again enjoy a modest level of comfort. But such is not the case as all those well-traveled know. Rather, travel works to illuminate and enhance personal perspectives on our own circumstances. And so having stayed in an unfamiliar loft, a buffalo robe at my side and a tent roof to shelter me from the pelting rain, I am humbled to learn how others live and are happy. Such was my stay with Mr. Prescott. Not ideal by any means, but filled with life and genuine sincerity. I laid there and pondered all these things.

Soon I would depart for the Traverse des Sioux.

Chapitre cinq

———◆———

"From the negotiation of these treaties it is believed a new era is to be dated in the history of the Dakotas—an era full of brilliant promise."
— Alexander Ramsey, Annual Report of the Commissioner of Indian Affairs, for the Year 1851

I found myself unexpectedly aboard the *Excelsior* on its way south toward the Traverse des Sioux, a trading post and Indian village about seventy-five miles distance from Fort Snelling. I say unexpectedly because the steamer arrived a day early. As a result, the twenty-five dragoons assigned to escort the guests on board were unable to ready themselves in time and the boat departed without them. The boat carried the men of the Treaty Commission, hence the reason for the escort. The commission included several important political figures, the foremost being Alexander Ramsey, the Governor of the territory and the Superintendent of Indian Affairs. The Treaty Commissioner was the honorable Luke Lea from Mississippi who is the current Commissioner of Indian Affairs in Washington. Also aboard as a part of the Treaty Commission was Henry Sibley, the most well-known and successful trader throughout the territory; a Mr. Ashton White of the Home Department; Dr. Thomas Foster, secretary to the commission; Mr. W.C. Henderson; Mr. Richard Chute, who represented the interests of the W.G. and G.W. Ewing Trading Company; and finally Mr. Hugh Tyler of Pennsylvania, the commissariat to the commission. Along with the commissioners were a variety of men and equipment, which included Indian traders; men of French, "half-breed," and American blood; a delegation of the principal men of the Kaposia band; and the tent furniture, buffalo robes, blankets, rifles, moccasins, and other provisions. All these things packed in the boat made it an eclectic array of people, materials, and interests, all prepared to determine the future of Minnesota.

As I journeyed with these prominent figures, ambitious traders, and hopeful Indians, I wondered just how inevitable that future was. By the looks of it, this treaty, this momentous occasion was only a matter of time, regardless of the players involved. In any case, I looked upon this disparate crew of men and interests as something to behold. I now considered myself privileged to be a part of it, but I also felt shameful. I did not feel like I had earned this privilege. I was too young and too disconnected from the outcome of all this.

"It is a marvelous place to be, is it not?" commented a man as he walked up beside me on the rail of the boat. The man spoke with a drawl that was lengthened and slow. Evidently, he was from the south.

"It is remarkably pleasant," I said as I turned to look at my new acquaintance.

"Reminds me of home," he said longingly as he peered out across the river. He was a young man and appeared to be about my own age. His features were strong but were made more delicate by his youth. He had wavy brown hair that covered his ears and a still-maturing beard that seemed to grow directly down and toward his chin. The way he looked, the way he sounded, somehow made it seem as if he belonged in a region such as this.

"Where is home for you?" I asked on cue.

"Grew up in Mississippi," he answered in his musical way of speaking. "I spent much of my youth on the river."

"I can imagine," I replied.

"Yep, just like home," he said as he continued to admire the river around him. "I am Ashton White," he said after a long pause. "I am the clerk to Commissioner Lea."

"Pleased to meet you," I said politely. "I am Frank Mayer."

"I know," he said quickly. "You're the artist from Baltimore. Everybody knows that the way you carry your sketchbook around."

"I would suppose so," I said with a smile as I realized just how true that statement was.

"I might like if you could sketch me a portrait sometime. I figure we'll be together in camp a few weeks."

"It would be my pleasure."

"I am a bit of an artist myself," said Mr. White enthusiastically. "Perhaps I could draw a portrait of you."

"I would like that," I said honestly. "Though it might trouble me to sit still for too long."

"No, it won't take long at all," contended Mr. White. "Not long at all."

"Very well," I replied trying to hold back my grin.

There was a long silence as we both enjoyed the intermittent and calm summer breeze which found its way along the side of the boat.

"You are now living in Washington City?" I finally decided asked.

"Yes," answered Mr. White. "As the clerk to the Commissioner of Indian Affairs I live and work in the capital, with the exception of necessary travel such as this."

"Of course," I replied quickly, but then paused to think. "Since arriving in Minnesota, I have learned that the Indian treaties are much more complicated than the buying and selling of land."

"Oh, yes," Mr. White agreed willingly.

"This treaty is no different, I presume."

"Not at all," Mr. White agreed once again. "You have to understand that there are varying interests involved."

"Being here has made that apparent," I said.

"You have the government which wishes to expand its territory and increase its resources," explained Mr. White suddenly sounding less like a southerner and more like a politician. "You have the settlers who seek land, opportunity, and prosperity. You have the traders who wish to collect on their debts. You have the trading firms who also wish to collect on their debts and increase their now dwindling markets. And finally the Indians who wish to obtain fair compensation for their rich and bountiful homeland."

"I did not recognize how complicated it was before I came here."

"It is perhaps more complicated than you know or than I can explain," admitted Mr. White. "Even the southern slave states have a vested interest in the outcome of this treaty."

"How can that be so?" I queried.

"Well," responded Mr. White, "if this treaty is signed and ratified it will inevitably lead to the creation of the state of Minnesota. The southern slave states will undoubtedly oppose this in order to avoid an unequal balance of slave versus free states in the federal government."

"That makes perfect sense now that you mention it," I said, feeling enlightened. "It reminds me of the major compromise made in Congress just last year."

"Exactly," replied Mr. White with a smile. "For years Congress has been debating this slave issue and whether or not to admit new territories as slave or free. With The Compromise of 1850 they admitted California as a free state, but will allow future territories to decide for themselves whether to be slave or free."

"I never thought of such things," I said with a nod of acknowledgement. "But I can see now why this treaty is a matter of national interest."

"Indeed," responded Mr. White. "But it gets even more complicated. Consider also the selection of the Associate Commissioner to this Treaty Commission," continued Mr. White.

"What of it?" I asked.

"It was a long and highly debated contest," explained my companion energetically. "There was a clash of interests between the American Fur Company and the W.G. and G.W. Ewing Trading Firm. Both firms favored the appointment of candidates that represented their interests. In other words, a candidate that could help them earn the most profit from this treaty. The American Fur Company favored Hugh Tyler, while the W.G. and G.W. Ewing firm favored Richard W. Thompson of Indiana. In the end Luke Lea was selected. This decision was favored by Henry Sibley and the American Fur Company not because it represented their interests, but because it eliminated Thompson from contention."[22]

---

[22] The contest for treaty commissioner lasted for several months and at one time or another each of the interests believed that it had secured the appointment. After the appointment of Lea, Henry Sibley wrote a letter to Lea expressing his satisfaction that he (Lea) was to serve on the treaty commission and assured him

"I never knew there was so much at stake."

"A treaty is by no means a simple process, especially one of this magnitude."

"You mentioned Henry Sibley," I said with some curiosity. "I have heard his name several times and I gather that he is a prominent figure in both the trade and in politics. Is that true?"

"Quite true," replied Mr. White. "This new territory owes much to Mr. Sibley. As a delegate from the Territory of Wisconsin, Sibley fought hard to represent the interests of the people of this region and he helped pass the bill that established Minnesota as a territory.[23] Now he is working to expand the territory and eventually establish Minnesota as a state."

"And now?"

"Pardon me?" replied Mr. White, in need of clarification.

"Does he hold political office now?" I asked.

"Indeed," answered Mr. White. "Now he is a representative of the Minnesota Territory's at-large congressional district."

"And what about his role as a trader?" I continued with my questioning.

"Sibley is a trader first and foremost," replied Mr. White. "He came to this region as a young man, having moved from Detroit. He studied law, I believe, but sought a more stirring and active life. He took up work as a clerk for a mercantile house in Sault Ste. Marie and eventually became a partner with the American Fur Company. That is when he was relocated to their headquarters at Mendota. Since that time he has established himself as the most prominent trader in this region, building profitable and trusting relationships with the French, the Americans, and the Dakota. He

---

of his "hearty cooperation." On the other hand, Dr. Thomas Foster was greatly displeased writing, "Since Tyler was defeated, I have several times wished the whole thing was postponed [indefinitely]." Folwell, *History of Minnesota*, 277.

[23] When Wisconsin became a state in 1848, it left the people living west of the St. Croix River in unorganized territory. Therefore a meeting was organized in the city of Stillwater on August 26, 1848, which became known as the Stillwater Convention. The convention adopted the proposal of creating Minnesota Territory. Henry Sibley was voted as the delegate to visit Washington and represent the proposed territory. Ibid., 237.

is known and liked by all throughout the territory. Even Governor Ramsey is his close personal friend. The Indian chief, Little Crow, too."[24]

"He seems to be more dependent on the outcome of this treaty than anyone," I noted.

"For him, yes," replied Mr. White. "He also happens to be Franklin Steele's brother-in-law. So you can imagine, between the Governor, Mr. Steele, the Indians, the American Fur Company, and his own political ambitions, there are many substantial influences tugging at Mr. Sibley."

"I might suppose so, Mr. White. May I call you Ashton?"

"Of course," replied Ashton with a pat on my back. "Don't worry yourself too much over the particulars of this treaty. Just enjoy this beautiful land the way it is, before it all changes."

"You're right, if I can help myself."

"I should leave you to your sketchbook," said Ashton kindly. "I will see you in camp, Frank."

"See you in camp, Ashton."

---

[24] Sibley was known and respected by the Dakota of Minnesota. His first wife was Dakota and he understood and appreciated the Dakota culture and spoke the Dakota language. He had become friends with Little Crow which included many hunting expeditions. His Dakota friends referred to him as Wapetonhonska (the Long Trader) in reference to his size and his fur trading profession. Micheal Clodfelter, *The Dakota War: The United States Army Versus the Sioux, 1862-1865*, (Jefferson, North Carolina: McFarland and Company, Inc., 1998), 50.

Ashton White

We arrived to the Traverse des Sioux on June 30. It was a lovely place where the prairie gently rises from the river and undulates until reaching the distant and more level prairies to the west. Our arrival was marked by a grand presentation which was given by the Kaposia Indians. As we neared the Traverse des Sioux, the Indian men assembled themselves upon the hurricane deck. All men were in full regalia with eagle plumes and turkey beards, deer tails and horse tails, and so forth. As a compliment to the village we were nearing, the group of assembled and attired Indians began singing in chorus. They bellowed their brave song in unison making deep, guttural and lasting sounds that, when sung together, were strong and reverberating. With the end of every stanza a whoop and yell was given which echoed over their audience. The song went on for many minutes repeating the same low, choral, melodic tune. It was an unexpected display of Dakota tradition and solidarity. As they sang, the landing below us became filled with the Dakota Indians of the Traverse des Sioux. They too began to whoop and yell. After several minutes Little Crow stepped forward and hushed the song. With the interpreter at his side, he began to speak.

"Brothers and sisters," he called out in his native Dakota tongue. "We are grateful and happy to gather at this crossing," began Little Crow, looking eloquent and fit for speech making. "For more than a generation we have become separated, weak, starving and sick. The buffalo of the prairie have gone and the deer and fox have hidden themselves. In the hot season we cannot feed ourselves and in the cold season we cannot keep ourselves warm. We suffer from want and sickness. Our land, once infinite as the sky, has become as small as the bear's den. No longer do we live like our fathers, soaring free as the hawk or running wild as the wolf. The white man has come and is too numerous to count. He brings us gifts, but his gifts deceive us. He gives us vows, but his vows are broken. Now he wants our home. He wants the river that gives us life. He wants the trees that give us shade. He wants even the dirt so that he can make it grow. Now we come together to trade with the pale-face. He wishes to trade for our land. He wants to take the place where our children were born and where our ancestors learned to hunt. Where our fathers took their first steps. Let us honor our ancestors and remember when they counted coup against the Ojibwe to protect our homeland.[25] Let us not trade freely like the bee when he makes us honey or the flowers when they give us beauty. Let us treat now, asking what we need, that like the vibrant sun, the green prairies, and the rushing river, we too will be strong. Now we gather in unity, brave Dakota. Let us remember our traditions and join in the gifts of our white neighbors. This is a time to be remembered when we come together to live as our ancestors once did, to save our people, and to give our children and seven generations following our children the same abundance we once had."

Little Crow dropped his head and retreated among his brethren. Immediately there followed a chorus of shrieks and yells. The sounds though, were not those of sadness or resentment, but sounds of joy and

---

[25] Counting Coup is a sign of prestige and valor during battle. In particular, it refers to the touching of a living enemy. This was the highest honor and for it the warrior received the right to wear a single eagle feather, standing upright on the back of his head. Amos E. Oneroad and Alanson B. Skinner, *Being Dakota: Tales and Traditions of the Sisseton and Wahpeton*, (St. Paul: Minnesota Historical Society Press, 2003), 65.

jubilation. They rejoiced in each other and the future they wished to create. For me, it was a candid moment to look upon.

With the pageantry complete, soon men began departing the steamer along with hordes of equipment and supplies. Camp was set up quickly and efficiently. The tents were pitched, the flag was raised, and every preparation was made for a stay lasting two weeks. Once camp was set up an ox was given into the hands of our butcher who divided it, surrounded by eager-eyed Indians, evidently much in want of food. Meanwhile, I was sought out by Little Crow who, being attired in his regal manner, wished to fulfill his promise and sit for his portrait. I was much pleased that the Dakota Spokesman kept his word and allowed me to capture his image. He looked in fact much like he had in his tent at Kaposia. He wore a rich headdress with a profusion of weasel tales that fell from his back to his shoulders. Two small buffalo horns emerged from atop the headdress while emerging below were ribbons and a singular ornament of strings of buckskin tied in knots and colored gaily. Little Crow sat still and calm, like a statue. Once again I felt privileged. It was an honor be there and to behold him in this very moment of history.

Chief Little Crow

It was an attractive little camp, commanding a view of the Minnesota River, the trading and mission houses, and the surrounding country. The camp was occupied by the commissioners and their officers and a motley collection of Frenchmen and half-breeds, traders, interpreters, voyageurs, and trappers. There were surprisingly few Indians, only those bands living at Traverse des Sioux and Little Crow's Kaposia band who traveled with us. This was on account of the exceptionally wet weather which had flooded the streams and sloughs and rendered travel in this wild country quite difficult. Thusly, we were forced wait for the distant bands to arrive. As for the Kaposia band, they were considered as especially our friends, and their tents were pitched nearby, creating a more intimate experience. It also seemed to reveal a superiority of the lower bands over the upper bands. Not in power or influence, but in condition and manners, the upper bands assuming a wilder character.

"Hello!" came the voice of a young Dakota boy as I was sitting down to make a sketch of the camp.

"Hello," I replied. I recognized him as the boy I encountered at Kaposia.

"What are you doing?" he asked curiously as he settled himself right beside me.

"I am drawing."

"Drawing?" he exclaimed in a friendly but confused tone. "What is that?"

"It is hard to explain," I began, trying to think of a suitable answer. "If I use this tool," I said holding my pencil in front of me, "and this paper, I can recreate the images I see by pressing the pencil to the paper." I then began to draw a tree.

The boy looked at the tree and then at the paper. He looked again. And again.

"Wow!" he shouted. "Let me try."

I handed him the pencil and paper and he began to make lines.

"Don't press so hard," I advised seeing that the pencil would break.

The boy was fully engaged, almost astonished, though his drawing could not be categorized as any particular shape.

"You're the school boy from Kaposia, are you not? Umm…Friend to Everyone."

"Takoda," he answered, still trying to draw the tree. "My name is Takoda."

"My name is Frank."

"This is too hard," Takoda declared, and he pushed aside the pencil and paper letting them fall hard to the ground. Having lost his interest he got up and sprung away.

"Good bye Takoda," I called, but he did return my farewell. He just kept running off to some other amusement.

Before my first day in camp was complete, I was invited to meet with Red Iron, chief of the Sisseton Dakota living at Traverse des Sioux. I welcomed the opportunity just as I had welcomed every opportunity thus far.

"Ho," said Red Iron as I came upon him in a seated position.

"Ho," I replied and seated myself across from him. He had a very kind expression about him and skin darker than most Indians I had met. He looked to be old in mind but not so much in body. His hair was long and dark, braided on each side and hanging down over his shoulders. He wore a head band with two long goose feathers extending high above the back of his head. His attire was fairly simple and consisted of a calico shirt, several stringed and beaded necklaces and a plaid, fringed blanket. There was nothing from what I could see that distinguished him as a chief.

"You are the artist who comes to learn about Dakota people?" asked Red Iron in rather clear English.

"Yes," I replied. "I wish to make a record of the frontier before it is gone."

"Before it is gone," Red Iron repeated, though not in a questioning tone. He paused and looked away. "I am Mazasha, known to the pale-face as Red Iron, chief of the Sisseton band that lives at Oiyuwega."

"Oiyuwega?" I asked curiously, barely able to pronounce the word.

"That is the Dakota word for this place. It means "crossing" in your language. It was named Traverse by the men who trade for furs. This is an important place to the Dakota. For here our ancestors created an ancient trail from the flat grasslands where the sun sets to the endless forests where the sun rises. It is not only important for the Dakota, but for all who wish to go into the country to the west. This is where they must cross."

"It is a magnificent place," I commented politely and truthfully. "Minnesota is a beautiful and rich region and I can understand why it is sought after."

"It is our homeland. But it is being taken away from my people," said the chief softly.

I saw that Red Iron was in distress, but I did not shy away. "May I ask, do you oppose the treaty?"

Red Iron looked at me, his eyes dark but gentle. "I am not the Dakota I once was. I no longer follow the buffalo or migrate with the fawn. I feel the winds of change and it carries me along. If my people are to survive, they too must change. We are poor and have nothing to eat, but the white man has plenty. His fires are warm and his tepees keep out the cold. I fear this treaty because we must sell our hunting grounds and the graves of our fathers. We must sell our very own graves. But to do otherwise would be to create our own graves. I think we must accept the treaty or the winds of change will blow us away."

"That does not seem just," I stated adamantly.

"The white man knows no justice," replied Red Iron calmly. "He makes promises he does not intend to keep. He says things he knows to be untrue. His greed is not like his thirst or his hunger; it cannot be quenched. He is not satisfied to share the land, he must have it all, giving nothing in return."

"I did not know these things before coming here. I lived in ignorance. Is there nothing that can be done?" I asked.

"You are young," noted Red Iron. "I did not mean to incite the innocence of youth through my words. Your presence is enough. Do what you came to do and record my peoples. Use your crayon and create our likeness and represent our land. Capture it in its last moments, before it is gone forever. That is what you can do."

Red Iron slowly got up, nodded, and walked away. I gave no farewell and thought on his words. I felt conflicted, but I knew his wisdom was greater than my own.

The next day was characterized by a competitive game of Lacrosse. This was a game that was unfamiliar to me, but one in which the Dakota were expertly skilled. The Kaposia band were particularly adept at this game, so they sent out a challenge to the resident Indians. The challenge was accepted and the entire event created quite a spectacle. First the stakes were drawn, for no competition was started without something to be won and something to be lost. The stakes included a variety of goods, some of which were very valuable: materials such as guns, saddles, and even horses. These were assembled and placed at the spot where the game would begin. Alongside the stakes sat the old men and judges of the contest. Once the stakes were set the boundaries were drawn and the competitors readied themselves.

To prepare for such a game the Indians stripped down to a breechcloth and adorned their heads in every variety of fanciful manner. The hair, too, as if part of the regalia, was greased, plaited, and tied back with the aid of feathers, ribbons, streamers of red cloth, and bands of richly worked embroidery. It was arranged with care in the great variety of manners which the imagination suggests. But their outfits were not nearly complete. In addition to all this, a collar or necklace was added along with bracelets or armlets. And their breech-cloth was by no means simple. It was attached to the waist by a cincture to which was added some pendant ornament of feathers, furs, and cloth. Some of the men included feathers or sleigh bells, all of which contributed greatly to the effect of motion as they ran. Completing their regalia was a variety of paint and clay applied to their faces and bodies. This dress, or rather want of it, displayed their elegant figures to the greatest advantage and on no occasion did the Indian appear in so suitable and tasteful an outfit and one so perfectly in harmony with the occupation in which they were to engage.

The men, now prepared for competition, sallied forth to the grounds now surrounded by eager spectators. A ball was tossed high in the air and the game began as the competitors battled for the small, round object. Each player was equipped only with a stick, his lacrosse, which appeared similar to that of a shepherd's crook. The crook at the end of the stick was used to pick-up, carry, and throw the ball. The goal of the game was to use one's stick to throw the ball beyond the boundary of one's opponent. But this was not made easy. The ball was often knocked loose by the opponent who attempted to disrupt and deny the ball carrier from ever throwing the ball. Once it was thrown it flew an incredible distance high through the air so that it could hardly be seen. Ambitious eyes watched for the ball's falling point whereupon they descended almost instantaneously. They fought and scuttled over the ball until finally one player had broken loose, alluding his pursuers. He advanced as far as he could safely carry the ball without risk of dropping it to an opponent. Then, standing a half mile from where the competition began, he hurled the ball beyond the horizon and over the boundary of his foes. He turned to the crowd which roared in excitement as he raised his stick and encouraged their adulation.

The game continued like this for many hours, no man showing any sign of exhaustion. I watched in awe at the physical endurance and prowess of the Indian. One can have no idea of the physical powers of the Dakota Indian until witnessing such an impressive display of athleticism and strength. His form so graceful and his movements so swift and powerful as he runs, vaults, springs into the air and courses from one end of the prairie to the other. I tried to capture these images in my sketchbook, but their movements were so quick, so constant, I could not properly resemble the brilliant setting for which I was witness.

With the game won the stakes were divided and the victors off to celebrate. The losers, though withdrawn, did not become angry or take offense to any rough treatment. The afternoon now waning, I set back to my tent satisfied with the day's events. I contemplated my unique surroundings once more, finding myself grateful to participate in such a profound and incredible experience. Remembering also the words of Ashton White and Red Iron, who told me not to take this moment for granted.

 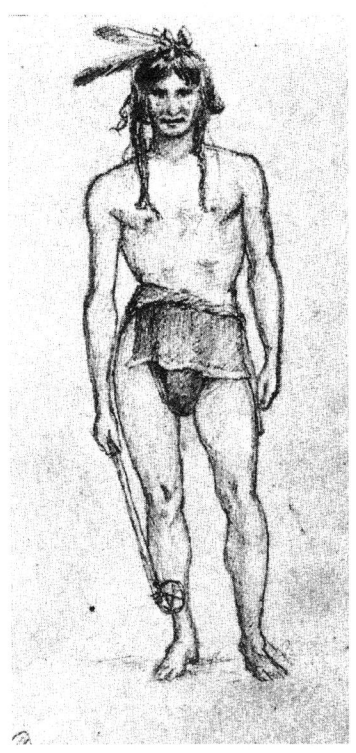

Dakota Ball Players

Chapitre six

―――≫《❂》≪―――

> *"I suppose a majority believe that we are expecting money to pay for the labor we do for them, and that our hope of getting it hangs upon the expected treaty. This is, of course, an exciting topic; everything connected with the making of a treaty is deeply interesting."*
> – Reverend Robert Hopkins, Letter from June 27, 1850.

Last night tested the efficacy of our tents as a heavy storm came upon us abruptly. The wind and the rain pelted the sides of our shelter making it seem as though it might collapse. All hands went immediately to hold the tent poles in place as the storm raged and a constant force of wind pressed itself against the walls. It felt as if we had become a sailboat in a tempest just trying to stay afloat. But the tents proved strong as they leaked not nor collapsed under the intense pressure. For this we considered ourselves fortunate. The storm was so fierce that I can only assume we will never again receive such a harsh blow.

Camp life is by no means a hardship as one might suppose. Surrounded by this picturesque and beautiful country we breathe the pure air and enjoy the calm breezes. To look out and see nothing but the rushing river, the green, luxuriant forest, or the tranquil and unending prairie, one is put at ease. With the urgency of everyday living gone, life becomes serene and without the constant measures brought upon by societal wants or expectations. Here we place a mattress to the ground, cover it with a blanket and enjoy peaceful rest and good-natured company. The day is passed in visiting, reading, interaction with the Indians, watching the ball-plays or dances, and a succession of surreal and novel scenes. At night we enjoy talks by the camp fire given by frontier and Indian subjects. Often we witness an Indian dance or listen to any variety of English, French, or Indian music. Combined together, the music makes camp life oh so lively. At one moment I hear the voyageur song, so light and airy, so graceful, and in the next I hear the Indian drum, so monotonous, but well suited for the dance. Its reverberating beat can be felt to the core. This constant mixture of music and cultures has created such a joyous and happy atmosphere; it is not something I will easily forget.

Camp Life at Traverse des Sioux

Like the traders, the French *voyageurs* took a particular interest in the results of the treaty and so they were well represented in camp. I found it quite interesting to observe their character. The voyageurs were especially acquainted with camp life having spent the greater part of their lives under such circumstances. For he is a man unlike any other, his job being rather unique. His name means simply "traveler," for that is what he does. The job of the voyageur is to trade goods with the Indians in return for furs, or to capture furs themselves. The furs are then brought east where they are sold and shipped to areas along the East Coast and Europe. But this task is not easy. In order to obtain the coveted furs, the voyageur must travel many miles through remote and unchartered territory. To do this, they travel by canoe. With all of their goods and supplies the voyageur daily traverses the rivers of North America traveling hundreds of miles to the next trading post. The freight they carry is heavy and their routes often dangerous. But the voyageur presses on day after day, taking little time for rest in order to stay ahead of his competitors. He does, however, seem to be rather fond of the pipe, this being his only respite.

Most voyageurs are short and quick with broad shoulders and massive arms from repeatedly paddling their loaded canoes.[26] Their clothes, like their backgrounds, show a mixture of French and Indian styles. The majority wear a short shirt, a woolen cap, a pair of deerskin leggings which reach from the ankle to just above the knee and are held up by a string secured to a belt above the waist. The thighs are often left bare while they wear a breech cloth in the style of the Indian. Finally they wear a pair of deerskin moccasins without stockings on the feet.

But perhaps most unique and most distinct about the voyageur is his character. The voyageur, though loud and vulgar, carries himself with refinement in his bearing and his speech. For no man but the voyageur seems so happy and carefree. This he demonstrates most often through song. Whether paddling or portaging or gathered around the campfire, the voyageur is always singing. Songs are simple and joyful and easy to sing along to. The songs are utilized to help the voyageurs maintain a steady rhythm while they paddle hour after hour and day after day. Over and again their songs are repeated until they permeate into the very being, the very culture of the French voyageur. It oozes from his every pore. The annals of history may forget this product of the upper frontier, but have no doubt, the French-Canadian voyageur played an instrumental and long lasting role in the development of North America.

---

[26] It was a necessity that voyageurs be small and quick. According to historian Grace Lee Nute, "A Canadien, if born to be a laborer, deems himself to be very unfortunate if he should chance to grow over five feet five, or six inches—and if he shall reach five feet ten or eleven, it forever excludes him from the privilege of becoming a voyageur." Nute, *The Voyageur*, 14.

Several days in camp had passed as we were waiting for more Indians to arrive. I was relaxing upon a tree stump when a new stranger approached me.

"Are you excited for tomorrow's events?" asked the man who I suddenly realized was the missionary at Traverse des Sioux.

"An Independence Day celebration is only fitting," I responded casually as if we were already friends.

"It is actually too good to be true," returned my newest companion.

"What, exactly?" I asked.

"The entire program," he answered. "Have you not seen it?"

"No, I have not."

"Well, it includes music, prayer, a reading of the Declaration of Independence, a procession, and a dinner fit for a king," he said in a cynical tone.

"A king you say?" I replied sarcastically.

"Truly," he answered with a quick nod.

"It will be a grand occasion, one befitting the event for which we are gathered."

"I suppose you are right," answered the reverend. "You must forgive any cynicism on my part. Perhaps I have been out here too long."

The reverend was a good-looking man. Square jaw, deep blue eyes, blond hair, with a sort of innocence that made him appear quite young.

"I don't believe we have met," I decided to interject.

"Oh, pardon me," responded the reverend with an attractive smile. "I am the Reverend Robert Hopkins. I am the missionary here at Traverse des Sioux along with the Reverend Alex Huggins."

"Pleased to meet you," I responded as I reached to shake his hand. "I am Frank Mayer," The reverend tried to interrupt but I raised my hand and would not let him, ". . . resident artist. I am aware that everyone knows."

"Indeed," replied Reverend Hopkins with a laugh. "I have seen you with your sketchpad."

"And I have seen you with your gospel," I replied amusingly.

"I suppose we are even then."

"I suppose we are," I said lightheartedly, though in the back of my mind I was curious about the reverend's earlier cynical remarks. "Do you think we are being treated too well?" I prodded. "After all, the food is plentiful, the company is amusing, and the setting is surreal."

"Surreal to you, perhaps," noted Reverend Hopkins. "You have to understand that I have been here for many years. This is not just some leisurely occasion, but my appointment and my work."

"I understand," I replied, acknowledging the reverend's perspective. "How long have you been at work among the Dakota?"

"Not as long as some such as the Reverends Riggs and Williamson," he responded, keeping his eyes strangely fixed upon my own. "I came from Ohio in 1843. I was appointed by the American Board of Commissioners for Foreign Missions and stationed at Lac qui Parle. I was soon after transferred here and I was officially ordained in 1848."

"Forgive my insensitivity, but why have you dedicated your life to these Dakota people?"

"That is a question I have come to ask myself," answered Reverend Hopkins with a sigh. "When I came here, I was filled with enthusiasm for the preaching of the gospel and its saving message. But my enthusiasm has waned and my work seems almost futile."

I listened intently and politely as the Reverend expressed his situation. I tried to be a comforting ear, if nothing more.

"I have dedicated my life to saving souls," continued the Reverend, "but I feel as if I have produced no visible results. The schools remain unattended and the Dakota men and women are skeptical of our message and our intent. Even those among them who desire to know the Word are discouraged by those who don't understand our message."

"Discouraged?" I asked.

"Yes. In order to prevent those who desire it from attending the public worship of God, threats are sometimes used and occasionally executed. But more generally, scoffs and ridicule are made use of, and as their language is peculiarly adapted to such a purpose, these means are very effectual."

"That is rather unfortunate," I said sympathetically.

"Even so, that is not what has got me so down," explained Reverend Hopkins. "I have heard reports circulating about us—about the missionaries."

The reverend raised his hand to his head and let out a long and dejected sigh.

"What kind of reports?"

"I suppose a majority of the Dakota believe that we are expecting money from this treaty. They believe that we wish to profit from the negotiations. This is distressing because nothing could be farther from the truth. I am and always have been a dedicated servant, wanting only to share the message of the gospel. I am of pure heart."

"I can see how that might be disheartening," I replied.

"I can only hope that this treaty changes things. That it gives us the tools to both protect and encourage our Dakota brethren. You must forgive my doubts and discouragement at this current moment."[27]

"Your duty is not to be scorned; it is one of interminable value. Coming from my more narrow perspective, all I can say is that you ought put aside your discouragement for now and enjoy this memorable occasion. For nothing can be gained in worry."

"Well spoken, young man," replied Reverend Hopkins with the return of his pleasant smile.

"Are you not to give the prayer before the procession tomorrow?" I asked.

"Certainly, I am," answered Reverend Hopkins. "For now I shall ponder on that. Be well Mr. Mayer, and continue to create your sketches."

I waved good bye, grateful to learn more about the people and mindsets of those involved here.

On Friday, July the fourth, tragedy struck. It was morning when we were all startled by a horseman riding into camp and announcing, "Hopkins is drowned!" We were all devastated and had a difficult time coming to terms with the news. Just the night before he had been among us with all of his pleasant manners. How quickly things can change. He had gone early in the morning, as his usual custom, to bathe in the river. When he did not return for breakfast with his family, a search was made.

---

[27] Reverend Hopkins claimed that the Dakota "people are wholly indifferent, if not averse, to the calls of the Gospel; and we can succeed in but a few instances in inducing them to hear it." He believed that it was "impossible" for him to "answer the expectations of the churches entertained of missionaries," writing that at times he just wanted to "Fly away and be at rest." Linda M. Clemmons, *Conflicted Mission: Faith, Disputes, and Deception on the Dakota Frontier*, (St. Paul: Minnesota Historical Society Press, 2014), 140.

His clothes were found upon the river bank, but his body could not be discovered. A net was stretched across the channel in hope that it might collect the body in its downward course. It was not for three days, when a terrible storm arose, that the body of Reverend Hopkins was discovered. Peal after peal of thunder called him from his grave and he emerged, a ghastly object covered with the mire and filth of the treacherous stream, his hands clenched in agony and his limbs stiffened in death, yet tranquil was his face, as though a prayer had passed his lips with his breath.

A kind-looking Indian and a voyageur lifted his grimy remains from the still turbid water. He was wrapped in linen and placed in a canoe to be brought to the widow's home. He was followed by a silent procession of spectators, French, Indian, and American, all wishing to give their respects to the noble missionary. His body was brought on shore where an old woman bent over him and started weeping convulsively. "Oh my son! My son!" she exclaimed. "He had pity on me, he fed me, he clothed me. . . ." But this was all I could hear as her tears smothered her words. She had lost a friend. People blame the Indian for having want of feelings, but this woman was Indian. So too were others around her who wept.

Soon the body was placed in a casket, the lid lowered and the nails driven. The casket and its contents were lowered respectfully into the ground, the widow too grief-stricken for tears. A silent chill. A hymn was sung, a prayer was made, and finally the dirt thrown over the top of the coffin lid.

For several days the mood in camp took on a somber tone. But life continued on while new and various occurrences transpired, ever and always shedding a new and different light on these unique circumstances.

Every day that passed brought with it more and more Indians arriving from the south and west. On July fifth alone there arrived two hundred Sisseton along with the well-known mixed-blood trader and guide Joseph LaFramboise. It was not unusual to witness a constant stream of Indians finding their way into camp with their baggage behind them carried in ragged wooden carts, drawn by ponies, or dragged upon poles. By this time the total number of Dakota Indians present had surpassed one thousand. The camp now presented a much livelier appearance, almost like a burgeoning city. Everywhere there was activity. Women gathered in gossip, men lounging in the shade, dogs barking, children playing, voyageurs singing, traders playing card games, and at all times canoes coming and going from the landing. Scattered along the prairie one could see white tents with pointed marquees of the early style next to any number of square wooden lodges. The entire Traverse had become a melee of sights, sounds, and interactions.

As a special guest in camp I was also given special privileges. One such privilege was being invited to meet the young Indian maiden named Winona.

"This is the lodge of Rdamahnee or the Walking Rattler," explained the campmaster Mr. Alexis Bailly as we approached the lodge together. "Here lives Winona, the natural daughter of an officer of our army and an Indian woman. We'll go in."

There seated on a mattress covered in a neat quilt sat the most beautiful Indian woman I had yet seen. Her face was pure and unblemished with kind and soft features. Her cheeks were rounded and her lips full. Her eyes were dark and piercing, matching her rich black, silky hair. Parted at the center, her dark hair seemed to flow gently down her scalp and softly over her ears, where it was pulled together in unison and plaited until falling neatly over the curves of her shoulder. As she stood to greet us I could see that she was tall and slender and all together graceful.[28]

---

[28] Nancy McLure lived with her grandmother in the Sisseton Dakota village at Traverse des Sioux. Her father, Lieutenant James McLure, was stationed at Fort Snelling from 1833 to 1837. In the latter year he was transferred to Florida where he died in 1838. Nancy's Dakota name was Winona, which means "the first born female child." Heilbron, *With Pen and Pencil*, 168.

Winona or Nancy McClure

The meeting was pleasant and our hosts were hospitable. But throughout the entire exchange the young Winona kept her head low and her eyes fixed to the floor. She spoke English well, but her excessive modesty prevented her from speaking much, answering only with downcast eyes and a nod of affirmation or denial. She had been visited by most of our camp, the rarity of her beauty being the attraction and the purchase of moccasins the supposed object.

The next day, July 11, was the wedding of Winona to David Faribault, a young trader of half-breed descent. The wedding took place about noon on what was an eventful day. The ceremony was attended by nearly all in camp and several friends of the parties to be married. Assembled beneath the commissioners' marquee were the bride and groom, their relatives, the Governor and the Commissioner, and several notable voyageurs and Indians, along with Mr. Alexis Bailly, the Magistrate who read the service. It made for a picturesque and novel scene.

The groom stood still, large and handsome, while the bride, fresh and young, seemed to tremble and blush as the service was read. The announcement of marriage was made and a salute of lemonade corks, there being no champagne, quickly followed. All attending joined in song and joyously celebrated in hilarious harmony the union of these two young people. A hearty dinner was served along with the subsequent toasts and speeches. Joseph LaFramboise was the first to make such a speech.

"Gentlemen," he bellowed out with a glass held high. "I appear here under somewhat extraordinary circumstances." He paused and turned to the commissioner. "We thank Colonel Lea, the able and sagacious head of the Indian Department for the special favor he has shown us in coming so far to see us; the Indian and the white man alike, and we trust that he and Governor Ramsey will treat us to a good treaty."

He paused again and looked over the assembled guests. Mr. LaFramboise was an older gentleman and acted as a trader, interpreter, and guide in the region for many years. He was well known and respected and had ties with nearly all present for the negotiations.

"I cannot express just how important this treaty is," continued the old trader. "I have been with the American Fur Company since 1823 and I have been trading in this region since 1833. I have taken part and been witness to the changes for the whites, the traders, and the Indians. The value of the fur continues to decline whilst the needs of the native Indian continues to rise. Our debts climb but competition does not allow us to cut off credit. The immoral trade of alcohol also causes problems. It further indebts the Indian while bankrupting the good and moral traders who abide by the law. The days of the voyageur have passed, the Big Woods no longer flourish with game, and the white encroachment will only persist. A treaty is our only solution. A treaty is our only chance."

Mr. LaFramboise sat down fully satisfied with having said his piece. The responses varied. There was no applause, just some claps, some stomps and a few shouts of "Ho!" from the Sisseton Indians present. Mr. LaFramboise's speech was followed by none other than the Commission of Indian Affairs, Colonel Luke Lea.

"Gentlemen, I also appear under somewhat extraordinary circumstances," called out the commissioner as he stood tall and erect. "Placed at the head of that department which has under its care all the red children of the Great Father, it is a departure from the ordinary course of things that I have been dispatched here by him in effecting a treaty with the Dakota nations."

All was silent and everyone listened closely to the commissioner's words, even the Dakota, many of whom could not understand.

"But, gentlemen," he said projecting his voice in the manner of any great orator. "There was a reason for my coming, which I think well to mention to you, who live and whose interests are among the Dakotas, or who are connected with them by ties of blood."

There was a sense of anticipation among those gathered, knowing the power and influence the speaker in front of them wielded.

"The Dakotas are not unknown to their Great Father," continued Commissioner Lea. "Though so far off, their Great Father thinks of them kindly and affectionately, and he wants to do what is best for them, and he wants them to do what is best for themselves. When their Great Father, therefore, learned that the Dakotas desired to sell their lands, that the game had nearly all disappeared from it, and that hunger and starvation, like wolves, were often in their lodges, he concluded to show them and their nation particular respect by sending to treat with them one of his principal officers, who being near him, knows his mind. This is the reason I have come over two thousand miles to meet them here in council and help to treat with them for their land."

There was a pause, but all remained silent. Commissioner Lea had yet to conclude his remarks.

"He has no wish," he said speaking of the aforementioned Great Father, "I have no wish, and I am sure my friend Governor Ramsey has no wish to take any advantage of them in any way. Nor, in the provisions of the proposed treaty, do aught what is fair and just both to the Indians and their friends, to red man and white man. I trust we will have no difficulty in making the treaty when we once get into council," said Commissioner Lea as he began to soften his tone. "Though I regret the delay which the weather and other causes has subjected us to. But I am confident that when the treaty is complete, its ultimate results will ameliorate the condition of the Dakota Indian to a gratifying degree and will likewise open a magnificent country to the improvements and refinement of civilized life, dotting the banks of this beautiful river before us with thriving towns and bustling cities, and these broad and fertile plains, with cultivated fields, glowing firesides, and happy homes. These are the grand objects of my mission among you and I therefore give you long life, prosperity and happiness to the Dakota nation."[29]

An applause immediately followed as Commissioner Lea returned to his seat among the other guests. The address was interpreted by Mr. LaFramboise and was received well by the Indians who were crowded on all sides. Throughout the speech they nodded their heads and voiced their customary form of acquiescence with "Ho's" of assent and approbation.

There were numerous toasts and sentiments given throughout the remainder of the reception. Some toasted to the health and well-being of the couple, others gave their general satisfaction for the treaty negotiations and their gratitude toward all of the important officers present.

The Wedding of Nancy McClure and David Faribault

The day's events were not complete without a long-standing Indian tradition in which the newly wed bride held a feast for all of her young, unmarried friends. The tradition began with a long train of Dakota men and women, arrayed in their best, and headed toward the commissioner's

---

[29] These speeches were recorded by James Goodhue, editor of the Minnesota Pioneer, and published by historian Thomas Hughes. Thomas Hughes, *Old Traverse des Sioux*, (St. Peter, Minnesota: Herald Publishing Company, 1929).

Ceding Contempt

marquee. Here they formed a circle and entertained the commissioners and others present with a dance. Within that circle gathered the unmarried guests. On one side of the circle sat the young women and on the other sat the young men while at the very center was a large red stone. It was apparently painted red for the occasion. Each unmarried guest stood and touched the stone one by one as a way of accepting their invitation and acknowledging their solitary status. Soon afterward a crier announced the beginning of the feast and he proceeded to divide the food which consisted of flour cakes and tea. All present heartily enjoyed the traditional event as men and women conversed and laughed. Jokes were played and stories were told and the mood was one of grand amusement.[30]

The tradition, as I soon learned, is connected with the Legend of Maiden's Rock. According to this legend a young Indian woman was first accused of lying about her solitary status and then told she must marry one whom she did not love. The maiden felt so scorned that she threw herself from the highest rock overlooking Lake Pepin. The story is well-known among the Dakota and remembered through this traditional feast.[31]

Among the merriment of the evening I noticed a man, middle-aged, who sat alone at a table, feverishly writing in his notepad alongside the light of a candle.

"Why not join the festivities?" I asked, breaking his solitude.

"Festivities," he said with a growl, "are for youth. I am busy."

"I beg your pardon," I replied courteously. "But surely you can partake in a few moments of celebration."

"Mister . . . ?" The man looked up, waiting for me to give my name.

"Mayer."

"Mister Mayer, I am certain there are enough people in celebration. I am here on business and I have no time such matter. I am James Goodhue, editor of the St. Paul Pioneer newspaper and I have much to report. There are matters of far greater importance than a frontier wedding." He scoffed and began writing again.

---

[30] This tradition is known as the "Virgin's Feast."
[31] For a full account of the Legend of Maiden's Rock see *Voyage in a Six-Oared Skiff to the Falls of St. Anthony* by Stephen H. Long. Stephen H. Long, *Voyage in a Six-Oared Skiff to the Falls of St. Anthony in 1817*, (Carlisle, Massachusetts: Applewood Books, 1860), 24-26.

"I did not mean to be rude," I replied. "May I ask what matter of interest you are reporting on now?"

"If you must," Mr. Goodhue sighed. "Events in Cuba are broiling again and it is my duty to write an editorial."

"Cuba?" I questioned, urging Mr. Goodhue to elaborate.

"Yes," responded Mr. Goodhue, now looking up from his paper. "Narciso Lopez, who has already attacked Cuba twice, is planning another attack. He wishes to capture Cuba for the United States and then bring it into the Union as a slave state."

"Yes, I recall the previous attacks," I responded. "Do you think he will succeed?"

"I do not," answered Mr. Goodhue. "He does not have the support of the federal government."

"Interesting."

"If you don't mind, I'd like to get back to my work. You…you can get back to your celebration."

"Of course," I replied with a polite nod. "I am sure I will see you in camp again soon."

As I walked away I felt perplexed about the atmosphere of the camp. Here was a man reporting on events far and wide, meanwhile the camp celebrated a new union among the somber tones of a life recently lost. It was a great mixture of people and perspectives. I also began to consider just how important was this marriage. It was more than just two young people, but the knitting of cultures in order to become one stronger, unique frontier culture. It exhibited the importance of our gathering at the Traverse des Sioux. It showed, for all to see, the people involved and the necessity of making a treaty for each party included, whether it be the Dakota, the whites, the mixed-breeds, or the United State government. But it did nothing to alter or remove my own growing skepticism. The words I heard from Commissioner Lea were the same words I had been hearing for days, words that made the treaty sound too good to be true, as if there were no drawbacks whatsoever. As I continued to observe the camp and the multiple circumstances occurring at any one time, I can rightly say that the commissioners were losing no opportunity of conciliating the bands that were present and informing themselves of their condition and expectations. In the same way the traders continued to almost bait the

Dakota into believing that the treaty was an opportunity that could not be missed. They suggested that to reject the treaty would be the end of the Dakota people and culture. But I was beginning to believe the opposite. Or, that no matter the results of this treaty, the outcome for the Dakota would remain the same. I did not actually know the truth of the matter, but it just appeared as if the commissioners and traders were far too eager to complete and sign this treaty. What, I wonder, were these men out to gain and what exactly might the Dakota lose?

Chapitre sept

"The effect upon the Indians is obvious. Instead of being civilized, they would be degraded and extirpated, and the benefits of the perpetual investments would go to a few cunning half-breeds, or their white assignees. Such are some of the objections to the Indian Territory on the St. Peters."
- Major Joshua Pilcher, Superintendent of Indian Affairs, 1838-1843, speaking about the failed Doty Treaty of 1841

"They are calling it a 'Traders' Paper.'"

"Traders' Paper?"

"Yes," answered Mr. Ashton White, who had become somewhat of a friend and confidant.

"Who?" I asked, feeling confused and bitter. I wanted to know what was happening behind the scenes and if in fact the Dakota were being exploited.

"The traders of course," answered Ashton in an almost argumentative tone. "Men like Alexis Bailly, Hercules Dousman, Alexander Faribault, Henry Sibley, and Joseph Brown."

"So what does this mean, this Traders' Paper?"

"It means that should this treaty be signed and ratified, any funds awarded to the Dakota could be directly appropriated to the traders, in order to pay off Indian debts," explained Ashton. "But the claims, as far as

I can tell are grossly inflated. And even if they are not, the Dakota should decide when to pay their debt."

"Can the traders do that? Can they add a document to the treaty?"

"I don't know," said Ashton with a shake of his head, debating the matter to himself. "I mean . . . no. According to the law they cannot, but the traders are smart and savvy and may find a way around the law."

"What law?" I asked.

"An act of Congress," specified Ashton, "that requires annuity funds to be paid directly to the chiefs or heads of families or individuals as entitled. But I cannot imagine how the Dakota would agree to give up payment directly to the traders. I saw their claims; they were more than $400,000."[32]

"My goodness, Ashton!" I said with astonishment. "Without that money, the Dakota would be ruined! While making the traders considerably wealthy."

"I know," agreed Ashton.

"But as you said, the Dakota would never agree."

"Not knowingly," replied my concerned friend. "But as I also said, the traders are savvy. Especially Joseph Brown."

"Who is Joseph Brown?"

"He is Henry Sibley's right hand man," answered Ashton as he began to calm down. "Or at least that is the best way I know how to put it. Like Sibley he is a prominent trader, but also a prominent politician. As a matter of fact, he has been in this region longer than almost any other white man, having begun his time as a private at Fort Snelling in 1820."

"Wow," I added. "He must be well associated with all people living here."

"Surely," continued Ashton. "He has kinship ties with the Dakota through marriage and he has at various times been a trader, farmer, lumberman, Justice of the Peace, and Congressional Delegate. He began his political career in 1838 when he was appointed Justice of the Peace for Crawford County in Wisconsin. A few years later he was elected a member of the Wisconsin Territorial Assembly."

"He is a man of many trades," I commented. "I can see why he would carry much influence in these negotiations."

---

[32] According to accounts filed under oath with Governor Ramsey, the traders' claims totaled $431,735.78. Folwell, *A History*, 283.

"And that is not all," said Ashton. "Much is owed to Joseph Brown for effecting the organization of Minnesota as a territory. It was him who established the Stillwater Convention."

"Stillwater Convention?"

"Yes," answered Ashton as he continued to explain the people and contexts of the treaty negotiations. "When Wisconsin became a state, it left the people of the St. Croix River Valley in unorganized territory. But Joseph Brown orchestrated a meeting or convention of sixty-one self-appointed delegates who signed a petition requesting the formation of Minnesota Territory. It was his initiative, along with Henry Sibley's ambition, to fight for the petition in Washington that forced legislation to create Minnesota as a territory."

"He must be quite shrewd, this Joseph Brown," I added. "I am surprised that I did not know of him."

"Indeed, he is shrewd," replied Ashton. "Which is what worries me so about this Traders' Paper I have heard them discussing. If there is a way to approve such terms, I am certain Joseph Brown can find it."

"What shall we do?" I asked.

"I am not sure there is anything we can do, Frank. It is a matter far outside of our own hands."

Ashton may have been right. Perhaps we could not do anything to right these potential wrongs. I did not know, but I would wait and watch.

It rained often in camp. Almost every day we were visited by a storm. It had become quite an inconvenience, there being not enough sunlight to dry things out. Clothes and other materials were made heavy with water leading men to joke about their blankets' ability to soak up moisture. But to the Indians it was no joke. Some had suggested that we had made the gods angry by holding the treaty negotiations. They feared that the *Thunder Bird* had come to wreak havoc on the camp and that the gods must be appeased in order to put an end to the violent weather. For this purpose, a Dakota man named Walking Thunder stood before his people and made a speech.[33]

"This high water is unusual," the young man announced with a strong, carrying voice. "The Great Spirit does not smile. He growls at us. Something does not suit him."

The people listened carefully, for they were all concerned about the constant storms, but more so over the prospects of their future. They feared what might happen if they signed the treaty.

"Our young men cannot hunt," continued Walking Thunder. "The powder in our rifles is wet. It will not burn. We kill no game, nothing. We have little to eat and we are very poor. Our ribs may be counted like the poles of a lodge-frame, through the skin. Corn will not grow without sunshine and if we have nothing to eat, we must starve."

The Dakotas present began to audibly grumble.

"We do not like so much rain; it is more than there is any use for. Our tents are soaked with water. It pains us to have our women loaded down with wet baggage when we travel. We cannot bear it."

The moans and grumbles from the Indian crowd turned to *ho, ho's* of accession.

"It may be the steamboats drove this flood up the river when they came," suggested Walking Thunder. "But we do not know and they brought us beef and corn. There is too much thunder and rain and sharp lightning. We want more beef and less lightning. They say the great Thunder Bird has dashed his wing upon the head of the Blue Earth River and broken open a fountain, out of which comes this freshet. It was whispered to me in a dream that we ought to have a round dance this afternoon."

Ho! Ho! came the shouts of agreement as the Indians seemed very pleased with this suggestion.

"It may save us much thunder and lightning and rain. If our Great Father wants to buy our land, we will talk to him about it at the proper time. There is no hurry. We will attend the round dance this afternoon and try to allay the Storm Spirit. The wing of the Thunder Bird must be broken."

---

[33] This speech was recorded by James Goodhue, editor of the Pioneer. Hughes, *Old Traverse des Sioux*, 47-48.

The Dakota reacted with shouts and grunts of approval as they beat their chests and thrust their lances in the air. Soon they scurried off and readied the dance.

The site for the dance was about a half-mile in back of the river on the open plains. All in camp were in attendance including the commissioners and near a thousand Indians. The spot for the dance was a large circle, probably large enough for a circus. At each of the four points of the compass was constructed an arbor made out of birch branches. The arbors were rudely constructed arches tall enough only for a man to sit, with the exception of the entrance. At the center was a sapling and from it hung the image of a large bird which had been cut out of a piece of bark. This image was meant to represent the Thunder Bird. In the same way there hung a smaller representation of the Thunder Bird from each of the four arbors. Also at the center, and in front of the sapling, sat the medicine man. His face was blackened and his head was covered with tufts of interwoven grass. Between his legs sat the Indian drum and at his side was the Indian flute. He was to act as sorcerer, uttering incantations and regulating the dance though music and song.

The dance commenced as the sorcerer beat his drum. Scores of finely dressed dancers rushed through the gate and into the circle. They moved in a circular procession, bouncing up and down to the beat of the drum. As they danced excitedly they hooted and hollered and made all kinds of frantic noises while their faces had the liveliest expressions. This carried on for fifteen or twenty minutes, the only respite being when the sorcerer played his flute.

The dancers exited for a brief interlude and upon returning they were accompanied by many horsemen. Like the dancers, the horsemen were gaily dressed in a fantastic array of blankets, sashes, feathers, and beads. The cavalcade of dancing continued as the sorcerer beat his drum and sang his high pitched, shrieking tune. The horsemen raced around the dancers at incredible speeds as their blankets and hair streamed behind them, whipping through the air. The music quickened and so too did the dancers, who continued round and round like a whirlpool.

Next there entered into the circle the Indian boys and girls. Just as their adult counterparts, they danced excitedly, waving their arms and raising their voices. The entire scene became an indistinguishable melee of bodies and movement and sound. It was a virtual feast for the eyes, a gala for the senses.

Suddenly the dance halted. All participants froze as if directed by a switch. The music stopped. Only the heavy breathing of the once-active dancers could now be heard. But within moments the silence was broken and the audience was startled by the discharge of several rifles. The Thunder Birds, all five, had been cut down instantly. A cheer arose. Not a happy cheer, but an eager one. So ended the round dance and with it, perhaps, the rain. It was a thrilling exhibition, possibly the most stunning I had ever witnessed.

The Thunder or Round Dance

Having been among the Dakota for several weeks, I had learned a little about their history and arrangement. As a tribe, the Dakota consist of seven bands known as the Seven Council Fires. The bands are closely related in language, culture, and origin and still bound together in alliance for mutual protection. The word *Dakota* literally means an alliance of friends. (As for the word *Sioux*, which they are frequently called, this is an outsider term credited to a French corruption of the Ojibwe word for snake.) Over time the seven Dakota bands began to stretch out across Minnesota and into areas west reaching as far as the Rocky Mountains. The seven bands are named as follows: Tetons, Yanktons, Yanktonais, Sisseton, Wahpeton, Wahpekute, and Mdwekanton. While their languages are closely related, the Teton speak Lakota and live furthest west, while the Yankton and Yanktonais speak Nakota and live across the western plains. Finally, the remaining four bands speak Dakota and reside near the Minnesota River. Together the four bands within Minnesota are called the Santee. And even within the Santee the Sisseton and Wahpeton are known as the upper bands while the Mdewekanton and Wahpekute are known as the lower bands. The purpose of the Treaty of the Traverse des Sioux is to first treat with the upper bands and then to treat with the lower bands residing at Mendota.

The political organization, if there is any, seems to be democratic in the truest sense. All bands have a chief or headman, but he holds no direct influence over the political decisions of the band. Rather, every important decision is made in council together and no decision made outside of council is considered binding or valid.

I cannot say for certain the population of the Dakota Indians, but they probably number somewhere close to 25,000 souls, with the number in Minnesota being much less, perhaps several thousand. The entire white population throughout the territory is probably not more than 6,000. What is certain is that the Dakota Indians are a large tribe with an immense territory with each band somewhat distinct and yet somewhat the same as the others. Some live among the woods and hunt deer, others reside around the lakes and fish, while still others roam the plains and follow the buffalo. But all Dakota appear to be a ranging people not desiring to be confined by any one place or region. They are adventuresome at heart. Though when necessary, as has become the case this summer, they come together to unite and share in their related traditions and background. As an outsider, this is the best description I can give. To know better would be to consult a Dakota himself.[34]

---

[34] For this information I consulted several sources. Hughes, *Old Traverse des Sioux*, 54-55; Amos E. Oneroad and Alanson B. Skinner, *Being Dakota*, 5; Doane Robinson, *A History of the Dakota or Sioux Indians*, Volume 2, (Aberdeen, South Dakota: News Printing Co., 1904), 19-27.

"These buffalo gnats and mosquitoes are the most terrible annoyance," declared Ashton as we sat down to our evening meal. "Must we swat at them all day?"

"I have found it nigh impossible to sit and rest for a moment," I commented. "To do so would be to invite their swarming, uninterrupted attack."

"I just hope the people downriver will not entertain the opinion that we are enjoying a life of extreme luxury and enjoyment," added James Goodhue with a hint of derision. Mr. Goodhue was in a much livelier mood than he had been when I had met him before.

"Can you imagine," laughed Ashton, "if your friends and colleagues considered this some holiday?"

The men, still growing in number as they gathered at the table, now laughed heartily.

"Oh to be envied," said Mr. Goodhue sarcastically, "while sleeping out of doors amongst the savages while eating this pilot bread," he said, poking at his less than appetizing food. "Why, it is harder than the horn of thunder."

The men laughed in unison once more.

"Mr. Goodhue, Mr. Goodhue," repeated Ashton as he tried to control his bemusement. "Mr. Goodhue, watch."

Ashton now had the attention of the entire table as he slowly picked up a biscuit with his fork, then immediately it fell to the table with a slam.

The men waited with anticipation for our jester to explain his gag.

"Oh, what pain," exclaimed Ashton as he held his wrist in false agony. "I have sprained my wrist severely just trying to raise this biscuit to my mouth."

The men broke out in an uproar of laughter.

"We shall have to take one of them down with us and have its specific gravity compared with that of platinum," shouted Mr. Goodhue over the laughter. His comment added to the amusement as the men convulsed with uncontrollable glee. Even I found myself clutching my sides to keep them from splitting.

"I do not think I can look at another beef tongue or sip down another bowl of watery soup," continued Mr. Goodhue as the laughter slowly began to die down.

"A capital amusement," said Ashton. "It feels good to laugh over our present discomforts."[35]

"If only they had ratified this treaty the first time," mentioned Mr. Goodhue. "Then there would be no need of us gathering here today."

"Pardon?" I asked. "What do you mean, the first time?"

"Ten years ago they met at this exact place," clarified Mr. Goodhue, looking at me under the brim of his worn and dirty top hat. "Have you not heard of the abortive Doty Treaty?"

The men were no longer laughing, but intent on devouring their food, disagreeable though its flavor.

"I was merely a child living in the high society of Baltimore," I asserted. "I have no such knowledge."

"Well," said Mr. Goodhue with a bite of his heavy biscuit. "Allow me to enlighten you on the subject."

I too began to eat my meal, not completely interested in the stories of the arrogant man across from me, but not completely disinterested.

"For years, politicians and reformers had been advocating the creation of a permanent Indian territory," explained Mr. Goodhue, despite the fact that his mouth was full. "They sought to move all the Indians living across the northern and western plains into this territory with the hopes that once the Indians adopted the ways of the white culture, they might be granted statehood."

"Here, in Minnesota Territory?" I asked.

"Yes," replied Mr. Goodhue with a pause to swallow and take another spoonful of soup. "Here and points north and west. Reformers believed that this northern region had a growing season that was too short for cultivation and therefore had no use for the farmer. Nothing would grow, or so they argued."

"So they sought to give it to the Indians?"

---

[35] James Goodhue did not seem to enjoy his time at Traverse des Sioux, writing on July 13 that "our sufferings have not been light." He further stated, "I hope the people down the river will not entertain the opinion that we are enjoying a life of extreme luxury and enjoyment; for it would be truly annoying to combat buffalo gnats and mosquitoes here amongst the savages for a month sleeping out of doors and feeding upon tough beef and pilot bread, without even the poor satisfaction of being envied." Hughes, *Old Traverse des Sioux*, 51,53.

Ceding Contempt

"The Indians did not farm, thusly it seemed reasonable."

We both paused here trying to eat and drink for a moment.

"The man assigned to orchestrate such a territory and such a treaty," continued Mr. Goodhue, "was James Doty, the governor of Wisconsin Territory."

I nodded and allowed Mr. Goodhue to continue.

"Everything appeared good. The new territory carried with it the advantage of consolidating the tribes such as the Winnebago, the Sac and Fox, the Potawatomi, the Ottawa, the Chippewa, and the Dakota at a time when Iowa and Wisconsin had just become territories and settlement of these regions was at its height. Furthermore, the potential territory benefited the traders by creating a sort of "fur trade preserve," while allowing traders to settle claims through payments in the treaty."[36]

Mr. Goodhue was now talking at a good pace with his eyes down and his fork in full service of his overworked mouth. I continued to listen, though I found the man comical.

"The treaty negotiations were held right here in 1841 and they went smoothly, with much less difficulty than these negotiations thus far."

"Which haven't even started," added Ashton, expressing a degree of annoyance.

"So the treaty was signed," I said thinking out loud. "Then whatever happened to this so-called Indian Territory?"

"Signed, yes. Ratified, no," answered Mr. Goodhue who finally looked up from his food. A smirk began to form on his face. "The measure failed ratification in the Senate by a vote of 26 to 2!" he noted as he started laughing.

---

[36] As the fur trade era came to an end, its agents moved into the more lucrative opportunities of land speculation, timber sales, and mining. Those who did not, relied heavily on the provided for claims through treaties. After the Doty Treaty failed ratification, Joseph LaFramboise, a trader in the region since 1823, wrote to his cousin, "I just received note that it is not completed which is a great concern to me and all who I deal with . . . I don't know what we'll do to subsist . . . they (furs) have no value. If I had known things would turn out as they now have I would have abandoned the whole affair." Janet Timmerman, *Joseph LaFramboise: A Factor of Treaties, Trade, and Culture*, (Master's Thesis, Kansas State University, 2009), 59-60.

"26 to 2!" said one of the men in astonishment as others reacted with a bit of a giggle.

"Why did it fail so utterly?" I inquired curiously.

"Manifest Destiny, my lad," answered Mr. Goodhue in his pretentious sort of way. "The fervor of expansionism. The belief that it is the white settler's destiny to march unopposed across this entire continent claiming all of the land as his own."

"Yes, yes," I replied with a nod. "This Manifest Destiny has only been intensified since then."

"Precisely," replied Mr. Goodhue as he, like a dog before a puddle, slurped the soup from his bowl. "After winning the Mexican-American War in 1848, the United States added millions of square miles of territory. Texas, New Mexico, California, all brought into the Union. Nothing can stop us from gaining all lands between the Atlantic and Pacific Ocean," said Mr. Goodhue confidently.

"Then why go through this entire treaty process at all?" I asked, discovering for myself the potential futility.

"Why I say," began Mr. Goodhue with the same smirk as before, "so they can torture us with water-downed soup, biscuits too heavy for a lamplighter, and corn so often the very sight causes us to wretch!"

The men laughed uproariously once more, caught up in the moment, in the enjoyment of a good joke and a hearty laugh. And who could blame them, living at this time and in this part of the world? A touch of haughtiness is almost required, perhaps for their own self-preservation. But I took a step back as I am wont to do, being young and somewhat disconnected with this place in the world. As the men laughed and enjoyed each other's company, I pondered once more the fate of the Dakota people. As I had discovered, they were a unique people rich in culture and tradition. They were, for me, inspiring in the way they lived so close to the land, taking what it gives gratefully and respectfully. They observe the animals and seem to know them intimately, studying their every move and learning what the animals can teach them. The Dakota imbue every object with a spiritual existence or mysterious power. Not ignorantly, but deferentially. Even the sky is sacred. When they look up at the stars and see the wavy cluster of the Milky Way, they see their ancestors traveling along the road to the spirits.

Yet I sit here among the whites, the French, the mixed-bloods, the Dakota, all wanting prosperity. And I have learned of things such as a Traders' Paper and Manifest Destiny and I fear that the future looks bleak for the Dakota. Who could stop or alter this unyielding force of progress and change? Who even would be an advocate for this once-thriving culture now begging for each and every meal? I wonder, what will become of my portraits and sketches. Will they be mere relics of a time gone by, a time lost to the ages? Will this important place that has been my home for the past several weeks even exist, or will it be forgotten? Perhaps there can be no answer. Perhaps only time will tell, and only history will decide.

James Goodhue, Editor of the Pioneer

Chapitre huit

"Give us the capital of more men, more people, and we will vivify, infuse the breath of life into, the dead capital of millions of acres now growing only prairie flowers."
—Alexander Ramsey, 1860 inaugural address as Governor of Minnesota

The time nears now. Finally, after much delay, the last of the Sissetons expected to participate in the proposed treaty have arrived. The day is bright and beautiful and the rain visits us no more. The summer air feels good in my lungs.

"Are you here to help us?"

I turned to see the young Takoda. He had snuck upon me quickly in his usual manner.

"Do you need help?" I replied.

"These men are going to take our homes. I don't want to lose my home."

Takoda did not appear sad. He looked to be—lost.

"They will give you a new home," I said, trying to be of some comfort.

"I know better," said Takoda as he kicked the dirt. "Nothing ever happens the way they say it will."

"It's okay, Takoda," I said, again trying to comfort the boy. "These men want to help you and all the Dakota."

"They don't!" Takoda shouted in a very sudden fit of anger. "And neither do you!" Takoda ran off into the woods, visibly upset.

I was struck by the young boy's reaction. He was clearly smart, but not yet mature. For him, the results of this treaty were very real and very important. I was sad to see him hurt.

Upon a knoll, in an opening between the leafy forest trees, the United States Commissioners met to treat with the Upper Bands of Dakota Indians. Underneath an arbor constructed with large branches and decorated with green boughs was placed a raised platform where negotiations could take place. On the left, seated at a table, were the commissioners. Beside them were the secretaries and reporters, and in front of them, seated on the ground below, were the traders, half-breeds, and spectators. Behind them, just a few feet beyond the arbor, the American flag was hoisted, looking fresh and new with its newly added thirty-first star to represent California.

To the right, opposite the commissioners, sat the chiefs of the Dakota nation who formed a semi-circle. They appeared most attractive, dressed in their finest regalia. Behind the chiefs stood and sat all types of Dakota, young and old, superior and inferior in rank, grouped tightly together in hopes of hearing and understanding the deliberations from both sides.

In the small, intervening space between the U.S. commissioners and the Dakota chiefs stood the interpreters, prepared to effectively transfer the meaning of one language to another. Also in that space, alongside the interpreters, was a barrel of sugar water, a favorite beverage among the Indians during the hot summer days.

Finally all was ready and negotiations were opened with the lighting of the pipe by the Camp Master, Mr. Alexis Bailly. Silence and dignified postures characterized the assembly as the pipe was passed to each of the commissioners and then on to the chiefs, each taking a few whiffs in succession.

Then stood Alexander Ramsey, Territorial Governor of Minnesota, and the Council was opened.[37]

"You chiefs, warriors and headmen of the Sissetons and you chiefs, warriors and headmen of the Wahpeton," announced Governor Ramsey in

---

[37] The negotiations for the Treaty of the Traverse des Sioux were recorded by James Goodhue and printed weekly in the *Minnesota Pioneer*.

a tone directed at the Indian chiefs, but loud enough for all to hear. "We are glad to meet you here today and we have been waiting a long time for you."

Governor Ramsey paused and allowed the interpreter, Reverend Stephen Riggs, who seemed very capable, to translate.[38]

"We are here as representatives of your Great Father, the President of these United States, Millard Fillmore," continued Governor Ramsey. "We are pleased to have the opportunity of conversing with you, his red children. Your Great Father has often heard of the distressed condition of yourselves, your wives, and your children, and having a warm heart for you all, he is anxious that something should be done to mend your condition."

The Governor spoke plainly, describing the treaty at its most basic level, apparently believing persuasion was still necessary.

"For this purpose, he has sent us to confer with you, the principal men of both bands, to see if something cannot be done for your improvement and real welfare."

As the words were translated, the Indian chiefs appeared stoic, nodding ever so slightly but remaining still and quiet. The Governor continued his monologue.

"The Great Father has learned that you have broad lands up here. He has been informed that there is little or no game on these lands and that for your purposes as Indians, they are of little benefit to you, while he has many white children who could improve them. Thus while he has not quite as much land as his white children can use, he has plenty of money and goods, while you his red children have much more land than you need. He thinks therefore an exchange could be made between you to your mutual advantage. To show you how important he considers this matter, he has sent one who stands near him and sees him daily and to whose charge he

---

[38] After coming to Minnesota from Ohio in 1837, Stephen Riggs and his wife Mary spent forty years living and working with the Dakota Indians. Reverend Riggs translated the bible into the Dakota language and also published a Dakota dictionary and grammar book. In 1856 he established the Hazelwood Mission and Republic, a self-governing Dakota community that acted as an agricultural and educational center for Christian Dakota. "Reverend Stephen and Mary Riggs," *The U.S.-Dakota War of 1862*, http://www.usdakotawar.org/history/reverend-stephen-and-mary-riggs; see also Stephen R. Riggs, *Mary and I: Forty Years with the Sioux*, (Boston: Congregational Sunday School and Publishing Society, 1888).

has committed the care of all the Indians, to confer with you and to see if a proper exchange cannot be effected. As such, you will listen to him and regard what he says. From my knowledge of him, I can assure you that he as well as your Great Father has nothing more at heart than the prosperity and welfare of the red man equally with the white. He will now explain to you the wisdom of your Great Father."

With that Governor Ramsey took his seat and gave the floor over to Commissioner Lea, the man he had so justly introduced. Commissioner Lea then stood, ready to address the council. Like Governor Ramsey, he appeared dignified, dressed with a jacket, vest, and neck tie. He was small in stature, but had a strong voice and a stern face.

"Chiefs, headmen, and warriors," he began ceremoniously. "You all no doubt understand the general object of your meeting together. The country you possess here is of comparatively little value to you, and your Great Father wishes to buy it of you. He thinks it would be to your advantage to sell all as far west as Lake Traverse, running up to the Red River of the North, and down to the Western border of Iowa, all that you own east of that to the Mississippi River."

This was the first geographic description I had heard of the land that was to be purchased. I admit to knowing little of the geography, but it was not hard to imagine that this was quite an extensive area of land.

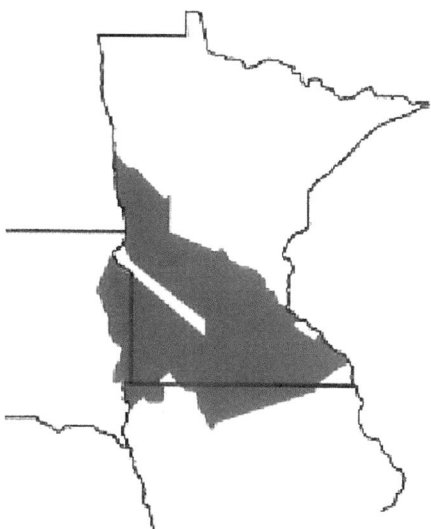

Land Ceded by the Dakota in 1851

"But while he proposes to buy so much of your country," continued the Commissioner speaking calmly and easily, lacking no patience, "it is no part of his purpose to deprive you of a home. Your Great Father would not consent to our making any arrangement with you whereby you would be deprived of a comfortable and sufficient home for yourselves and families. He expects to give full compensation for all of the land he purchases from you. If you are willing to agree to the terms we are instructed to propose to you, we doubt not it will be better for you and your prosperity. Should you agree to sell this land, a portion of it will be set apart for the future, a permanent and common home of you all."

There was a pause here. The Indians sat still silent, still stoic. I looked up to watch a hawk, high overhead, peacefully gliding along the river valley, never once flapping his broad, feathered wings. It looked to be completely free, and alone in the sky. I was sad to turn my head away when I heard the Commissioner speak once more.

"We think from all the information we have been able to obtain," continued Commissioner Lea like a lawyer pleading his case, "that if you had a country provided for you high up on the Minnesota River, where the farms and improvements I have mentioned could be made, it would be much for your good. Once collected there you would be less exposed to the bad influence of the white man," he stated, referring to the whiskey sellers, "then if you should remain where you are. In your new country an agent would be sent to reside among you, to look after your interests. Your Great Father is not only disposed to secure you a home sufficiently large and good, but he is willing to give you much in addition; enough he thinks to keep you comfortable in the future. There are many other tribes of red men, who, like yourselves, once owned a large country. It was of little use for them, and they were poor, so they have sold out to their Great Father, receiving therefore goods, provisions, and money, with many other things of substantial value. Those tribes are now happier and more comfortable and every year growing better and richer."

Could this be true, I wondered? Or was Takoda right—was this just another method of persuasion? What were the intentions of these men and did they really believe the Indians would profit?

"In connection with the home which will be set apart for you as I before mentioned, your Great Father intends to place farmers among you, to teach and help you cultivate the soil, so you will not have to depend upon the chase, which is becoming every year more unsafe and unreliable for your support and subsistence. He expects, likewise, that in a few years you will all have comfortable houses to live in, that your children will be taught to read and write as those of the white people, and that you will not only have corn in plenty, raised by yourselves, but cattle, horses and other animals. That you will have both provisions and clothing sufficient to keep you from starving or freezing."

After so much talk there was still no reaction from any in the crowd of Dakota Indians. Commissioner Lea may as well have been alone on that stage, speaking to none but himself. Perhaps the Dakota were as skeptical as I.

"If you agree to go to this home which is provided for you," continued Commissioner Lea, "removal will be expensive. But your Great Father has thought of this. He will give you enough money to bear the expenses thither, to supply you with provisions for a year afterwards, and to settle and arrange your affairs before you start. Your Great Father will take care to have the farms opened, schools established, and blacksmith shops erected and carried on for your benefit. He will also have medicines and physicians provided so that you may be properly cared for when sick. You will not only be taught to raise corn and potatoes but he will also have mills erected to grind into flour for you the grain you may raise. In a word, should you be willing to sell your lands, your Great Father will provide funds for farming, education, and other matters conducive to your happiness."

There was a pause here followed by a change in tone as the Commissioner finished his remarks.

"We have now made known more particularly than you had been previously advised. We have perhaps said enough today for you to think of until tomorrow, and let me repeat, and I wish you to consider, that it has been said for your welfare."

Commissioner Lea took his seat while the Indian chiefs conferred among each other. Not giving them much time, Governor Ramsey raised his voice to speak.

"We desire that the chiefs and principal men," explained Governor Ramsey, "should get together, after we adjourn, talk over these matters among themselves, and make up your minds and meet us here again tomorrow, ready to go on with business."

"If there are any among you," immediately followed Commissioner Lea, "who want to speak tonight, we will hear him now; if not, you can come prepared to talk to us in full tomorrow."

Everyone looked to the chiefs, awaiting their reply. Not a word was spoken, just a wave of the hand and it was determined that council would adjourn until tomorrow.

There was no argument and quickly all those gathered began to disperse. I don't know why, but I expected there to be more. It seemed too simple, too casual for an agreement of this magnitude. There was no debate and no complicated forms or detailed laws. Just a long list of assurances given by the U.S. commissioners. Was this so worth the trouble in gathering on this remote frontier all these people and interests?

I looked around and found Ashton White, apparently unneeded and uninterested in the proceedings. He was far away, having raised a kite greatly to the amusement of the Indian children. A crowd had gathered, laughing and playing, amazed at the kite as it soared higher into the pure ether. They cared not for the future. Only for the simple pleasure of a moment's wonder. But I wondered if Takoda was among them. His reaction still worried me.

The setting for the second day of negotiations was identical to what it had been the day before. Commissioners to the left, chiefs to the right, interpreters in the center. The preliminaries too, were the same, with the peace pipe passed slowly around.

"Chiefs, Headmen and Warriors," addressed Commissioner Lea as he opened council about noon of that day. "We met you in council yesterday and we are happy to meet you again today. We hope you are all in good health. You have no doubt considered the subjects we brought to your notice yesterday, and we shall now be pleased to hear what you have to say in regard to them."

There was a long, awkward silence. None of the Indians appeared ready to speak and I began to wonder if they would speak at all. Finally the silence was broken by a Sisseton who was called The Orphan by the whites.

"I listened to your talk yesterday, and heard it all," began the old chief who appeared tired and slumped over. He spoke in Dakota, slow and quiet, his words translated by interpreter Joseph Campbell.[39] "But I do not see any of my young men here. My thoughts are turned toward my young men who are behind, and I should be glad if you thought the same way. On looking around yesterday, you said you were glad to meet and shake hands with us, but I am sorry you are not willing to wait to shake hands with those who are behind. That is all I have to say."

The Orphan sat down and awaited the commission's response. Governor Ramsey stood and very calmly began his reply.

"Say to the chiefs, that we are very sorry indeed to hear no other reply than the expression of a wish for further delay. We have now been here three long weeks, doing nothing. When we reached this place three weeks ago, we expected to find you already here. We were disappointed, but the respect we had for you, induced us to grant you all this time."

The Governor was frustrated, but he did not speak in a tone or manner that expressed frustration. He directed his words at the interpreter staying calm and collected, but I knew how badly he wanted this treaty to be negotiated smoothly.

"We know, moreover, that the business we came on was of the most vital consequence to you and your people for generations to come. But there must be an end to delay sometime. We came here with provisions we supposed sufficient to carry us all through this council. But we see it fading away very fast, and you know there are no farms in this country where more can be obtained when our present supply is exhausted, as it will be in a very few days."

It seemed as if Governor Ramsey was done speaking, but when no response was given or no acknowledgment made he continued his remarks.

---

[39] Joseph Campbell was at this time a newly appointed interpreter having been preceded by his father Scott Campbell. Joseph was of mixed-blood and could speak in several languages including English, French, Dakota, Menominee, and Ojibwe. He and others like him were essential in facilitating all types of relationships and communication between whites and Natives throughout the frontier period. For more on Joseph Campbell and his role see *Grace at Spirit Lake* (Colin Mustful, 2014).

"Nor is this all," he continued, now in a more urgent tone. "The representative of your Great Father who was sent here from Washington has pressing business which calls him back to that place, and before he goes he has to meet with your friends, the Mdewakantons and the Wahpekutes, in council below. He has no time to spare, and I think that after he has given you more than three long weeks, it is unfair to ask him to stay any longer. We feel very sorry with the chief, that his young men are not here, but if they did not come for six months, would he want us to wait for them still?"

The Governor was noticeably upset as he dropped his fist to the table. He was speaking on behalf of the entire commission.

"The question is a simple one. It is whether you will sell your lands and get in return what will make you comfortable for many years, or whether you will continue to starve in the midst of a wide country, almost destitute of game, and, therefore, valueless to you," stated the Governor bluntly. "If you think you should make this exchange, say so, and the formalities and details as to what you should receive and how, we can no doubt agree upon easily."

The Orphan, while seated, finally produced a response.

"I understood some person was out to meet my young men who are on the road," he said quietly like he had before, "and sent them back. That is the reason I feel so bad about it."

"It is not absolutely necessary that all your people or all your young men should be here," answered Governor Ramsey quickly. "The government only requires the chiefs and principal men and they are generally present. Your young men will understand that you requested us in open council to wait for them. Besides, those behind will share in all the annuities and benefits accruing from the treaty equally with those that are here, and when they learn this they will not complain."

Governor Ramsey now returned to his method of persuasion by trying to soften the Indians, perhaps fearing a deal would not be reached.

"And when our business is finished, we may be able to send them something which will satisfy them with all that has been done. But at any rate, they can have no great cause to complain sharing alike as they will in all the benefits arising from the treaty."

Sleepy Eye, probably the oldest and most revered among the chiefs present, now stood to speak.

"Fathers," he said addressing the commissioners. "Your coming and asking for my country makes me sad, and your saying that I am not able to do anything with my country makes me still more sad. Those who are coming behind are my near relatives, and I expected certainly to see them here. That is all I have to say. I am going to leave and that is the reason I spoke."

Unexpectedly, before the words were even translated, the Indian chiefs arose and left the council. Confusion ensued as the commissioners looked with disdain upon the departing chiefs while loud cries were lifted up by the young Indian men watching on the outskirts.

"As our provisions are short and they seemed undisposed to talk or treat," said Governor Ramsey to the other commissioners, but loud enough for all to hear. "We shall stop the issue of rations to them for the present."

"You wish for us to withhold their supply of food," clarified Commissioner Lea.

"Yes," answered Governor Ramsey, still directing his speech to the other commissioners.

"Interpreter," directed Commissioner Lea, urgently but not impetuously. "Proclaim that we desire to understand distinctly whether they wish to have any further talk or interview with us about selling their land."

There was a pause as Reverend Riggs shouted these words to the departing chiefs.

"If they wish so in earnest, they need to say so," continued Commissioner Lea. "If not, they need to say so. We are in this last case as ready and willing to come to a conclusion and go as they are. They must let us know by this evening if they are serious in wishing to treat. If we do not hear from them to that effect, I will leave for below early tomorrow morning."

The chiefs paused and turned, but then continued on toward camp. The other Indians, men and women, whooped and shouted, encouraging the display of indignation and contributing to the general sense of confusion and dismay.

"Strike the flag!" ordered Commissioner Lea angrily. "Strike it! And have it retired from the council ground. I want the Dakota chiefs to know we are serious."

The commissioners, traders, voyageurs and half-breeds alike looked distraught and frustrated. Their expectations had been high but were suddenly deflated. They objected among themselves, creating even greater commotion.

"Get the boat ready for departure in the morning," continued Commissioner Lea with his orders.

"But shall we give up on negotiations that easily?" returned one of the secretaries.

"Haven't any worry," replied the commissioner, who now appeared confident among the dozens of dejected and discouraged men. "It's all part of the show."

My heart dropped and my focus turned inward. *It's all part of the show* he said, as if so many lives, and so much at stake, was little more than a part in a play with a predetermined conclusion. How could he be so callous to a people so genuine, to a people so much in need?

As I watched the commissioners and secretaries dismantle the council grounds, I too felt dismayed, exhausted by weeks of watching, waiting, and taking in so many new and different surroundings. But I knew this was not the end, only the beginning. Callous though the commissioner may have been, I felt assured that he was right—that this was just an act and that the negotiations would go on. It couldn't end like this.

Chapitre neuf

"The Indians are all prepared to make a treaty when we tell them to do so, and such a one as I may dictate . . ."
-Henry Sibley to Pierre Chouteau, Jr., and Company,
November 3, 1850.

Toward evening, a council of Dakota Indians met and spoke with the commissioners. I was not privy to this conversation, but the results were obvious. The commissioners halted all means of preparing for departure and rations were directed to be issued as usual. It seemed the Indians decided that they wished to continue negotiations.

I was neither happy nor sad with this result. I was just as unsure what might happen if the treaty was not signed as if it were. Frankly, my future did not hinge upon the outcome. But my time here had enamored me with this region and fascinated me with its aborigine population. I feared exploitation lie in wait for the Dakota if they signed the treaty. But if they did not, then what? I feared they would be overrun by industrious settlers and enterprising businessmen, which was a course, if taken, that might leave them with nothing. If the treaty was signed, at least they would still have a home and hope for a future, though it might be a future devoid of their long-established cultural traditions.

As this turbulent day came to an end, I put aside my thoughts and admired the unique qualities of camp life. Slowly the sun became low, the moon became high and twilight was enveloped by darkness. The wistful sounds of the flute drifted softly through the air while young men, dazed with affection, sought to gain the attention of young maidens. In each tepee across the long-reaching, ever-flowing prairie, fires burned to give light within and produce smoke that might shield its occupants from the constant attack of the bedeviling mosquito. With that light a peculiar, yet lovely effect was created as the fires danced off the skin of the tepees and the cloth of their tents. This effect exposed their transparent qualities allowing the shadowy figures inside to show through the walls. Each figure bounced back and forth, here and there, reflecting the rising and falling flames. So shown the graceful silhouette of the frontier Indian as he smoked his pipe or the lonely traveler, who, by the light of the candle, penned a note to his wife back home.

The next day, like the one preceding it, was a beautiful and warm summer day. The morning air was refreshing and the glowing sun was comforting. I made a trip down to the river only to find my young companion, Takoda. This time, I sought him out.

"Takoda," I called softly, hoping not to scare him away. "Takoda, how are you?"

He looked at me. Not afraid, but not enthusiastic either. "I'm okay," he answered blandly.

"I didn't mean to upset you the other day," I explained.

"Oh," he said. "I'm just scared."

"Scared of what?"

"Like I said before," he began as if I should have known. "These men are going to take our homes. I know it is supposed to help us—that is what Reverend Williamson says—but I don't believe it."

"It's okay to be scared," I said comfortingly as I slowly placed my arm on his shoulder.

"My father used to tell me that to be Dakota was to be strong but gentle, brave but cautious, firm and true. But I don't know how."

"Your father would be proud of you. You are all those things."

Takoda did not reply. His face was held toward the ground his posture slumped as if defeated. He slowly turned toward me with a look of sadness which only a youth could express.

"You can help us. You can help the Dakota," he stated with a touch of eagerness.

"I came here to observe," I said nervously. "I don't know what I can do."

"Yes, I know you can help. We have been so poor for so long, we just need someone to speak up for us." Takoda's emotions had flipped from sadness to excitement.

"I...," I stuttered while searching my head for the right response. "I will do my best."

"Don't let them take our land and our money. Please," he urged now looking at me with hope.

Just then an announcement was made. It was barely audible, but they were calling for the negotiations to begin once more.

"I must go," I said to the young boy. "I will do my best, Takoda."

I parted from the boy, feeling nervous because I truly wished to help, but I did not know if I could. The boy had struck a chord with me. His lively and youthful spirit was engaging, while his adolescent like sadness heart-rending.

Negotiations were reopened on Monday, July 21, following a day of respite. The scene, again, was much the same. The crowd gathered, all packed tight and close to the stage. The commissioners and chiefs took their place and the usual preliminaries were followed. After a long pause, Chief Sleepy Eye arose to speak.

"On the day before yesterday when we conversed together," said the old chief, "you were offended. No offense or disrespect was intended. We only wanted more time to consider. The young men who made a noise were waiting to have a ballplay, and thinking the council over, arose, and as they did so, made the disturbance which we were sorry for."

This being all that he wished to say, the chief sat down, looking fine in his long buffalo robe that draped smoothly in regal fashion across his arms and legs.

"There was no particular objection to what was said," responded Governor Ramsey. "You had a right to ask for further time. Your leaving the council in the manner you did was objected to. But what you have said is received as a full explanation. The council is now again open for business, and we are prepared to hear anything the chiefs have to lay before us."

The chiefs and headmen looked to each other, and seeing that Sleepy Eye was not inclined, so stood Chief Opeeyahedaya, known to the whites as Curly Head.

"I am not speaking for myself, but for all that are here," began Curly Head in a clear and audible tone. "We wish to understand what we are about to sign, to know exactly the proposition made to us by the commission. The chiefs and people desire that you make out for us in writing the particulars of your offer for our lands, and when we have this paper fully made out, we will consult among ourselves, come to a conclusion, and inform you what it is."

Curly Head's request was more than reasonable. Until now I had not known the particulars of the treaty and I am not sure the Dakota had either. All that had been given were broad, general assurances.

"Very well," answered Commissioner Lea. "I have the preliminary terms right here."

Commissioner Lea then handed a piece of paper to Camp Master Bailly.

"You may read them aloud," instructed Commissioner Lea.

Camp Master Bailly took a few steps forward to position himself exactly between the chiefs and commissioners and then read aloud the terms of the treaty.

"The Indians cede to the United States," he said loud and clear in his slight French accent, "all their lands in the state of Iowa and territory of Minnesota lying east of a line drawn from the Red River to Lac Traverse and thence to the northwest corner of Iowa."

Camp Master Bailly, dressed neatly in a double-breasted coat, paused before giving the specifications.

"Number one," he announced. "The United States will set apart a suitable country for the Indians on the upper waters of the Minnesota River for their future home."

"Number two. An amount, say $125,000 to $130,000 will be paid to enable them to arrange their affairs preparatory to removal, to defray the expenses of removal and to subsist themselves for one year after their removal, part to be paid in money, part in goods and services."

"Number three. An annuity of from $25,000 to $30,000 will be paid to the Indians for many years, say thirty to forty years, part in money, part in goods and provisions, and part to be applied to such other beneficial objects as may be agreed upon."

Once Camp Master Bailly finished, and once the interpreter had translated, Commissioner Lea then followed.

"Before we trouble ourselves further in relation to this business, we wish to know certainly whether you intend to sell this country. Having made up your minds, we can then agree to terms."

I was uncertain why the Commissioner and Governor Ramsey were so aggressive when it came to a verbal commitment of selling lands. They seemed indisposed to negotiate the particulars despite the importance such particulars held in agreeing to sell such a large tract of land.

"When those sitting around here have seen this paper, had it explained to them, and talked it over among themselves, we will let you know our opinion in regard to it," rightly answered Chief Curly Head. "I meant to have said before that we wished to sell, and we will give you our country, if we are satisfied with your offers for it."

"If we do anything in regard to making a treaty here, it must be done quickly," asserted Commissioner Lea. "You are not women and children but men and chiefs, and ought to be able to act without delay, like men. We shall expect to hear your views decisively at our next meeting."

"We have made known to you our offer," immediately followed Governor Ramsey. "When you meet us again if you are not satisfied with our terms, you can inform us what it is you wish for your lands, and we will then take your proposition into consideration likewise, as you are about to do."

The Indians did not respond while the commissioners had nothing further to say.

"Council is thus adjourned," announced Camp Master Bailly.

The Indians spent the remainder of the day assembled on the upper terrace above the treaty grounds while messengers shuttled back and forth between the Indians and the commissioners. I sat alone nearby the tent of Henry Sibley, drawing my sketches and observing with curiosity the negotiations that continued throughout the day. I was also thinking of Takoda and the hope I had seen in his eyes.

"It's just business," said a man breaching my solitude.

"Excuse me?" I replied.

"I can see that you have taken an interest in the proceedings, in the negotiations," explained the man. "But I wish to inform you that it's just business. It's *all* business."

The man was young, probably in his early thirties. He appeared somewhat disheveled with wild hair and unkempt clothing. I recognized him as having been among the traders.

"I beg your pardon," I declared. "But I am not clear as to what you are referring."

"Do not be so coy," implied the man. "I have seen how you react and have taken an interest in the events here. You have become well-acquainted with the whites and Indians alike. You know more than you admit."

"Perhaps," I said. "But why lay upon me these accusations? What authority have you?"

"I meant no accusation," replied the man, who was clearly agitated by something other than me. "I just wish to reveal to you the truth of the matter. To spare you the trouble of seeking or concerning yourself over justice."

"Whatever do you mean?" I asked honestly. "Who are you and how does this concern me?"

"I am Richard Chute," he answered. "You have no doubt heard my name. I am a trader who represents the W.G. and G.W. Ewing Trading Firm of Indiana."

"Very well," I replied, "but I still do not understand your insinuations."

"It is understandable that you are naive, not having any interests in this region," Mr. Chute said coldly. "You have to understand that these negotiations have little or nothing to do with the future or well-being of the Dakota Indians. Business and politics are the only mechanisms at work here."

"I have been learning this," I answered respectfully, despite Mr. Chute's bluntness.

"Let me give you just one example," noted Mr. Chute. "I have been sent as an informer for the Ewings in an effort to break up the monopoly of the American Fur Company in relation to the treaty results. These are the real powers at hand. Not the Indians or even the government, but the trading interests. However, even I, backed by the power and influence of the Ewing firm, and in my underhanded position, can make no impact on the results of this treaty. I have not even received a hearing before the traders' committee. The fact is that Lea, Ramsey, and Sibley are thick as thieves and they will have their way."[40]

I was shocked at this new information. Perhaps not so much at its revelation, but by the fact it was so openly shared with me by someone on the inside. Mr. Chute, it appeared, had become jaded to the politics of the treaty negotiations and had lost all inhibition.

"That is extremely unfortunate," I replied. "But I still do not understand why you felt it necessary to tell me these things."

"I have a feeling you wish to stir things up," replied Mr. Chute unabashedly. "That you wish to be an advocate for some sort of justice. That you want to fight the powers that be."

"I have no such intentions," I answered defensively, though he was not accusing me of anything unscrupulous. "I merely wish to document the proceedings with my sketches."

"Not from what I can tell," returned Mr. Chute. "You have become too involved. I've seen you speaking with Mr. White, with Reverend Hopkins, Winona, even that young boy. You know more than you realize."

"That may be, but why can't there be a fair and just accord?" I asked, engaging my true ambitions. "Something that benefits everyone. One that not only appears fair, but is fair."

"Fairness is relative," answered Mr. Chute. "And besides, the results of this treaty are and always have been predetermined."

"Determined by who?" I interjected, though I had my suspicions.

"By the thousands and thousands of settlers pushing west onto any and all land they can find," answered Mr. Chute brusquely. "Let me tell you that if no treaty were signed, white men would force their way into the

---

[40] Richard Chute traveled to Minnesota from Indiana in order to represent the interests of the Ewing firm, but he immediately recognized that he was not in a favorable position. When Chute arrived in St. Paul, he observed that Sibley had "his stakes pretty well set," but he watched for an opportunity to get "a lick at the platter." In a letter to the Ewings in June, 1851, he wrote, "Lea, Ramsey, and Sibley are now as thick as three in a bed." Lucille M. Kane, "The Sioux Treaties and the Traders," *Minnesota History*, Vol. 32, No. 2, (June 1951), 74.

region anyway. Should the Dakota try and drive them out, some pretext would be found to send in troops. Not only that," continued Mr. Chute, confirming what I already knew, "but you must understand that this is just one of hundreds of Indian treaties. It follows a well-defined pattern of corruption and greed that always has and always will result in the exploitation of the Indigenous people."

I was saddened; I was speechless. With my sketchbook in my lap, I wondered now why I had even come all this way. Why had I been so wide-eyed and ignorant?

"Listen," said Mr. Chute, seeing that I had become distraught. "What you are doing here is valuable. Having become disillusioned myself, I just wish to warn you that there can be no changing the outcome here no matter how well-intentioned you may be. Rather, it is a political game, a game that can only be fought in Washington."

"In Washington," I said flatly, echoing Mr. Chute's statement.

Mr. Chute nodded in reply. He set his hand on my shoulder as he then peered across the open ground toward Mr. Sibley's tent where activity continued to flourish. "Best of luck to you Mr. Artist," he said after a long pause, and then walked away.

Sibley's Tent

After much behind-the-scenes negotiating that lasted all through the night, Council resumed at 7 o'clock on Tuesday morning. This council, though similar in format and appearance, was different than the councils that preceded it. There was a much smaller audience for what felt like an informal gathering that carried with it less merit. It occurred to me that this meeting was merely a formality; that the work had been done and an agreement had already been made. The purpose of today's meeting, I determined, was only to serve as a segue to the signing itself. Therefore attendance was low as everyone in camp waited for the more meaningful council that would take place the next day. Nonetheless, today's council was necessary and would go on.

"The council is now open and we are ready to hear from the chiefs their reply to our proposition submitted in writing to them yesterday," announced Commissioner Lea.

There was a long hesitation among the chiefs while they decided who would step forward to give a statement. Finally, the chief called Eyangmanee, known to the whites as The Big Gun, arose and placed into the hands of the commissioners a paper containing the terms upon which they would agree to sell.

"Fathers," said The Big Gun, "I desire that those young men around may live long to tell what I now say. We wish you to do as is written in this paper. Now, I have spoken."

The Big Gun, having done his task, turned and went back to his place among the chiefs. He appeared emotionless.

"I am glad you have come to the wise conclusion of making us an offer to sell your lands," Commissioner Lea responded. "We will look it over and as soon as we can draw up the necessary documents, we will meet again to complete our work and sign the treaty. We will have our goods and medals ready for those who attend on that occasion and who behave well."

The Dakota chiefs gave no response, but continued to sit quietly, adorned as they always were in their buffalo robes and headdresses of eagle plumes and weasel tails.

After a long and silent pause, Governor Ramsey decided to speak up.

"Your Great Father has proposed this treaty we are about to complete because he is your friend," he assured them. "Those who participate in it will be sustained by him. At any moment he can have soldiers without number here for the protection of his friends."

Governor Ramsey, having attempted to solidify the confidence of the Dakota, nodded to Camp Master Bailly so as to indicate that this was all he wished to say. The camp master then announced the adjournment of the council. Everyone present departed rather quickly without much talk, just the shaking of a few hands. And just like that, the council grounds were empty.

It was sometime later in the day, while the entire camp was at rest or leisure, when Ashton and I found solace along the gentle flowing river. Here the waters made the benign sounds of movement and the clouds floated pleasantly overhead.

"What is the real significance of the treaty signing?" I asked Ashton. "I feel as if it is only another part of the process, but I also feel like it is the most important part of the process."

"You are right," answered Ashton, in a slow, relaxed manner. "The only thing that matters right now is gaining the consent of the Upper Bands of Dakota Indians."

"But that doesn't mean the lands have necessarily been sold, right?"

"Right," answered Ashton supportively. "But in a way it does. Gaining these signatures is the greatest obstacle. Once this obstacle is overcome, all other obstacles should fall more readily."

"What obstacles, exactly?" I asked, still trying to understand everything that was involved in the Treaty of the Traverse des Sioux.

"Well, to begin," explained Ashton, "we will still need the consent of the Lower Bands at Mendota."

"And this will be easier?"

"Not necessarily easier, but more likely. The commissioners chose the Upper Bands first for a reason. They speculated that because the Lower Bands signed a treaty in 1837, selling their lands east of the Mississippi, they would more willingly sell again. And, seeing that the Upper Bands had already signed, they will be much more likely to sign as well."

"But without the signatures of both Upper and Lower Bands, the treaty is not valid?" I asked, though I was near certain this was the case.

"Right," replied Ashton. "The signatures at the Traverse alone would not be enough to complete the sale."

"I see," I replied with a nod. "And the other obstacles?"

"Ratification in Congress," answered Ashton straight-forwardly.

"Oh, like the Doty Treaty," I said, recalling the failed agreement I had learned about.

"Indeed," was Ashton's only response.

"Then why expect this treaty to become ratified?"

"To be honest," began Ashton, "there is no reason to expect that it will be ratified. It is a long and sometimes drawn-out process that will require lobbying on the part of Henry Sibley and others."

"Why might Congress strike it down?" I asked.

"That is up for conjecture," answered Ashton. "But I reckon the passing of this treaty would imply the addition of another free state to the Union. The state of Minnesota. That is something southern representatives do not wish to allow."[41]

"It would upset the balance of power," I asserted.

"Yes, but it may not matter," replied Ashton.

"Pardon?"

"The commissioners are confident that the necessity of the treaty will force ratification," explained Ashton. "They believe that the surge of settlers and the fear of retaliation by the Indians will force Congress to ratify the treaty because to do otherwise would be adverse and detrimental. Persuasion will be necessary, but the commissioners do not envision a failure to ratify."

"How interesting," I said. "I had no idea it could be so complicated. Yet, in some ways, it remains simple."

"Nothing can be simpler than this," replied Ashton facetiously as he dipped his feet in the water. "Lounging down by the river, water between our toes."

"I will miss days like this," I said wistfully.

"Tomorrow will be different," said Ashton with a sigh. "Tomorrow will be the day we've been waiting for."

---

[41] According to historian William Watts Folwell, southern senators did not desire to see an enlargement of the area of settlement in a new northern territory, which would soon be knocking at the door for admission as a state. Folwell, *A History of Minnesota*, 290.

Chapitre dix

"It is the greatest event by far in the history of the Territory, since it was organized. It is the pillar of fire that lights us into a broad Canaan of fertile lands. We behold now, solving views, the red savages, with their tepees, their horses, and their famished dogs, fading, vanishing, dissolving away; and in their places, a thousand farms, with their fences and white cottages, and waving wheat fields, and vast jungles of rustling maize, and villages and cities crowned with spires, and railroads with trains of cars rumbling afar off – and now nearer and nearer, the train comes thundering across the bridge into St. Paul, fifteen hours from St. Louis, on the way to Lake Superior."
-James Goodhue in the *Pioneer*, July 31, 1851

The day has finally arrived. The day set apart from all others, the signing of the treaty and the crowning moment in this region's history. Oh how marvelous to be witness to such a watershed event when the past and the future meet. On that morning even the sun aspired to observe this great accord as it slowly rose in the east and peered through the broken cloud cover. The air was crisp and the temperature was pleasant. It felt good to take a deep breath and revel in the natural beauty surrounding this spectacular oasis; this congenial sanctuary.

Everyone was busy on that fine morning. The Dakota gathered in cliques, preparing for the event. All of them, men and women, were regaled with paint and feather and appeared stunning, like the Greeks and Romans of ancient times. The commissioners had busied themselves with putting the finishing touches on the treaty documents. Meanwhile the agents, secretaries, and missionaries had collected all sorts of goods to be placed near the treaty grounds and delivered as presents to the Dakota. Even the traders, voyageurs, and half-breeds had huddled together to discuss last minute business and to make future deals and arrangements. I observed all this with awe and satisfaction, knowing just how unique, brilliant, and significant it was.

By noon all was ready. The flag was hoisted, the stage was set, and the clouds had given way to the full radiance of the summer sun. Everyone took their seats. The commissioners, once again behind a table on the raised platform. The chiefs and headmen assembled upon benches opposite the commissioners. In between was a podium where upon lay the official treaty documents. In and around the treaty grounds were hundreds, if not thousands, of spectators crowded in every direction. And beyond them, in the distance, was a myriad of tents and tepees, of plants and trees, all contributing to the novel and picturesque scene that was the signing of the Treaty of the Traverse des Sioux.

After a grand smoke from Commissioner Lea's magnificent Eyanshah pipe, council was opened.

"Chiefs, Headmen, and Warriors," announced Commissioner Lea in his usual manner. "Our anxiety to make a treaty with you satisfactory to yourselves, has induced us, after much reflection, to agree to nearly all your terms."

Apparently, whatever happened during the behind-the-scenes negotiating process had favored the Dakota. I could not be sure if this was true, or just a clever way to make it appear that the Dakota had made a good deal.

"We have accordingly prepared a paper to be signed by you and ourselves," continued the rather staunch looking Commissioner. "It contains the provisions which you have asked us to consent. Nothing but our kind feelings toward the Dakota could have induced us to a treaty so favorable to them. No Indians under the same circumstances have ever made a more favorable treaty with the Government."

Again, I could not be certain just how valid Commissioner Lea's statement was. But I recalled the warnings of Mr. Chute and I remember the worries of Takoda and I remained skeptical.

"We hope when we make it known to the Great Father, he will be content with it," said Commissioner Lea referring to ratification in Congress. "Even though we have agreed to pay you more than he expected."

Commissioner Lea paused and held the treaty document high for all to see.

"We will now have it read to you," he announced. "And we hope there will be no difficulty hereafter in consequence of anyone not understanding fully what is done here today."

The treaty was then read aloud, in full, by Dr. Thomas Foster, secretary of the commission. Immediately thereafter it was read aloud again, this time in the Dakota language by the Reverend Stephen Riggs. All was silent during the readings with the exception of few crying babies and several barking dogs.

As near as I could tell the terms had changed very little from those read at the prior council. Essentially, the Sisseton and Wahpeton bands of Dakota Indians agreed to the sale of approximately twenty-four million acres of land in exchange for a sum of $1,665,000 and a reservation ten miles wide on either side of the Minnesota River stretching from Lake Traverse to Yellow Medicine. The money was not to be paid in full, but the bulk of it was to be set aside in an interest bearing account and paid to the Indians over a period of fifty years. The remainder, that was not set aside, was to be paid for several different purposes which include, but were not limited to, cash annuities, good and provisions, education, and the erection of needed enterprises such as farms, schools, and mills. Finally there remained a sum of $275,000 which, as the treaty stated, was given to the Indians so that they might comply with their present just engagements. This included the costs of removal, one year subsistence, and obligations they owed to the traders.

After the readings were finished there was a small commotion among the crowd, but this was mostly just the onlookers discussing with each other the terms of the treaty.

"We, the commissioners appointed by the United States Government," announced Governor Ramsey, "will now sign the treaty documents in duplicate. Immediately hereafter the chiefs and headmen will affix their signatures, also in duplicate."

After a long silence while the commissioners signed their names, the chiefs and headmen were called forward. One by one they arose from their benches and stepped forward to sign, each one appearing dignified and regal. As each Dakota signed, he was then presented with a medal, bearing the head of the President of the United States, which was placed around his neck.

It was at this point that I noticed something out of the ordinary, something that didn't seem to fit with the official proceedings. After each medal was presented, the Indian men were then pulled aside by Reverend Stephen Riggs and directed toward Joseph R. Brown.[42] Here, upon a barrel with a board laying across it, was another document which the Indians were directed to sign. *Could this be another copy of the treaty?* I thought. Or was it the so-called traders' paper I had heard Ashton talking about? As each chief was pulled aside I became more and more anxious. What were they signing, I wondered. Did the Indians themselves know what they were signing? Has no one else noticed this irregularity? Had I overreacted? I had to do something.

"Excuse me," I called out to the commission.

"Mr. Mayer," answered Governor Ramsey. "This is neither the time nor the place."

"I beg your pardon," I said cautiously. "But I wonder if the trader, Mr. Joseph Brown, could explain the document in his charge?"[43]

"I should rather not," said Mr. Brown in a stark manner. "It would only create a disturbance and the Dakota understand it anyway."

Governor Ramsey looked toward me and lowered his head ever-so slightly. "Let there be no more interruptions," he demanded.

The signing continued and one Indian after another was, seemingly, coerced into signing this superfluous document. I could only sit and watch, aghast at this apparent wrongdoing going on in front of me and

---

[42] According to Limping Devil and Sounding Moccasin, who had testified during the Ramsey Investigation, Reverend Stephen Riggs had "pulled them by the blanket" to the barrel where Joseph R. Brown held the pen for the signing of the second paper. Folwell, *A History of Minnesota,* 282.

[43] In reality this question was asked by Agent Nathaniel McLean. Ibid., 283.

all others present. I was stunned that no one else found this unusual, or at the very least, distressing enough to speak up in support of my request. Whatever the Dakota were signing, certainly it was not unreasonable to have it explained.

Meanwhile, as the procession of Dakota chiefs continued, several of them had valedictory remarks. But I was too distracted to pay much attention. I remember only Chief Curly Head who, when accepting his medal, took it from his neck and placed it over the head of a young Indian saying, "Fathers, I am an old man. This is my son. He will keep this for you." It was a graceful display of the perseverance of the Dakota spirit.

Commissioner Lea now addressed the council: "Friends and Brothers," he began. "We have now happily concluded the important business that brought us together. I told you at first that we were willing to give you a good treaty, and there is but one thing necessary for you to do, in order to feel hereafter that you have acted wisely in making it, and that is to be as honest and faithful in observing it on your part as the Government will be on its part. We are now about to separate, and I may never see you again. I came among you a stranger and friend. I leave you with the kindest feelings. The red man will always find in me a sincere friend. Having now finished our business, I bid you all an affectionate farewell."

Commissioner Lea raised his hand and lowered his head out of respect for the Dakota. His short farewell was met with grunts of approbation by the Dakota chiefs.

As if on cue, Governor Alexander Ramsey then rose to follow the Commissioner's remarks.

"You now have made a treaty," he bellowed out in his deliberate manner, "which I consider an excellent treaty for you. If you make a proper use of the good things it provides, prosperity and happiness in all time to come will be your lot. You and your children and your children's children will become surrounded with comforts to which you are now strangers, have enjoyments which your fathers never heard of, and possess advantages, physical and intellectual that will eventually place you on the same social platform of happiness occupied by your white brethren."

Governor Ramsey continued his speech summarizing and detailing the potential advantages of this treaty for the Dakota Indians. Never mind that he not once explained the advantages for himself and the white population of Minnesota. But as he continued, I looked around, not just at the setting, but at the various people I had the great fortune to meet since my arrival to Minnesota.

There was the great chief Red Iron, the old but kind looking chief who showed me wisdom through his compassionate acceptance of the changing world. I saw Franklin Steele, the confident and ambitious fort sutler and entrepreneur who welcomed me to Fort Snelling. There was also Thomas Williamson, the very gracious missionary who showed me around Kaposia and shared with me his story, his hopes, and his life's work. I also saw Mr. Nathaniel McLean, the Indian agent and longtime politician who shared with me his knowledge of the structure of the Indian Superintendency.

While looking at these characters, so-to-speak, and remembering so many others, I marveled at the eclectic nature of this place and period. So many varied roles and interest all coming from different backgrounds with separate motives and separate minds. But all come together in this one place and at this one time, it was amazing to me. And as for myself, to be yet another piece in this broad and diverse arrangement, I could not express my satisfaction and wonder.

"Above all things," I heard Governor Ramsey say as he continued his long-winded speech, "it is our desire you should be friendly and peaceful. And as you know your Great Father at Washington is the Father of all the Indians, he desires that they should act as friends and brothers towards each other no matter what name the nation may be. We have the goods and provisions here that we promised you after the treaty was over, and we will leave your agents to distribute them among you."

Governor Ramsey and the other commissioners quickly departed the treaty grounds. Also departing were the traders and voyageurs who, the treaty having been signed, likely had more business to discuss. But the Indians remained, crowded around the pile of goods to be distributed. Hugh Tyler and Agent McLean also remained as they began to hand out the presents to the anxious Dakota. The gifts consisted of blankets, cloth, powder, lead, tobacco, vermillion, beads, looking glasses, knives, trinkets and so forth.

I withdrew from the treaty grounds with mixed emotions. I was content to know that a momentous moment in history had been achieved and that I had been there to witness it. But I was concerned to think of the negative possibilities that may result for the Dakota Indians. I am not sure they had much choice but to sign the treaty. However, to be without options is usually to be without leverage which means they might easily have been exploited in this deal. The treaty, of course, appeared ideal for the Indians. A permanent home, annual payments, government assistance, but was it realistic? Would it lead to the cultural and community enhancement of the Dakota Indians, or might it breed and foster corruption while sabotaging the beautiful and enduring Dakota culture? What concerned me more, was the notion that outright deception took place in front of my very eyes with the signing of the paper at Mr. Brown's table. Though I was sure the Dakota owed the traders money, it appeared they were tricked into giving it straight out of the treaty funds. In which case, the money promised the Dakota Indians would pass straight from government hands into traders' hands. I needed to know more.

Signing of the Treaty of Traverse des Sioux

"They are meeting right now," explained Ashton.

"Who? The traders?" I asked anxiously, having met Ashton a few hours following the treaty signing.

"Yes," answered Ashton in a rather annoyed tone. "McLeod, Brown, Sibley. The committee of traders."

"What are they discussing? What was written upon the document that they refused to explain during open council?"

"Why do you wish to know so much?" retorted Ashton.

"If there was a wrong I believe it ought to be righted," I replied confidently.

"But I am merely a clerk and you are merely a sketch artist from Baltimore. There is nothing that can be done," answered Ashton.

"That may be," I replied somberly. "But I'd still wish to know. I'd still like to make a difference if a difference can be made. I have my reasons," I said, all of the sudden feeling obligated to Takoda who seemed to trust me so much.

"It is complicated," conceded Ashton. "The law states that the monies must be paid directly to the heads of families or individuals designated by the tribe in open council in order to comply with their present and just engagements. That is exactly what this document does. It is an acknowledgement by the Dakota of their debts, and a solemn pledge in open council to pay those debts directly to the designated individuals in said document. The issue that arises is whether or not this was truly done in open council."[44]

"Exactly," I quickly replied. "I don't believe the Dakota knew what they were signing. Had they known, they would have never agreed to it."

"It was a loop-hole cleverly discovered by the traders and I am not sure there is anything that can be done," replied Ashton in a calm tone this time. "It has become a legal matter now."

"But how can we stand by when such a blatant deception has taken place before our very eyes," I urged.

"Let's not concern ourselves over it right now," pleaded Ashton. "In time perhaps you can notify a lawyer and begin the legal process. But for now let us enjoy our last evening here in camp."

I sighed, remembering the words of Mr. Chute who, like Ashton, told me nothing could be done. At least not here and not now.

---

[44] This was called, "An Act to Regulate Trade and Intercourse with the Indian Tribes, and to Preserve Peace on the Frontiers," and its goal was to lessen or eliminate the influence of traders on the tribal leaders. Francis Paul Prucha, Ed., *Documents of United States Indian Policy,* 3rd edition, (Lincoln: University of Nebraska Press, 2000), 75.

"Remember when I told you that I was a bit of an artist?" asked Ashton, changing the subject. "Let me draw that portrait I promised you. It will take your mind off things.

"Well, I *could* use a laugh," I said sarcastically.

"Just sit still," replied Ashton with a wink and a smile.

Frank Blackwell Mayer

"Strike your tents and march away," was the announcement given early the next day. Soon all hands were engaged in some activity preparing for our departure. The last meal was had in the old house having been hastily dispatched. The remaining provisions of oxen, corn, flour, etc. were handed over to the Indians. All else was packed and quickly taken toward the boat landing. Before our departure the Dakota held a Buffalo Dance, but the men showed little interest. I caught a few glimpses and found it intriguing how these Indian men, adorned in buffalo masks, could so precisely imitate the natural habits of the buffaloes. Like all of the dances I had witnessed in the previous weeks, it was most entertaining.

Ceding Contempt

By noon our boat was loaded to capacity and ready for departure. We took what we could to eat. Whether it be a cold piece of ham between our fingers or a hard section of pilot bread upon a tin cup filled with river water, this would be our supper, dinner, and breakfast for each and all without discrimination as to class or status.

I searched and searched for Takoda, but could not find him. I felt as if I had let him down, having asked about the traders' paper, but having not succeeded in preventing its signing. I wasn't sure if I'd see Takoda again.

Homeward bound we were when we finally shoved off. Our mode of transport was a keel-boat—a long, narrow yacht with a permanent keel[45] designed and built for navigation of rivers. The bow was long and unsheltered while the stern was enclosed providing a neat little space for the oarsmen. There were about fifty souls aboard including traders, tourists, French voyageurs, and the commissioners. All of the men were light-hearted and appeared exceedingly happy to be going home, the signing of the treaty having been accomplished.

With Henry Sibley as our captain and the voyageur Henry Belland at the helm, our loaded keelboat skidded swiftly down the river. The men were jubilant while all united in full chorus of boat songs. Each man singing his tune and pulling his oar, it was both enchanting and resourceful as the thirty-some individuals rowed together as one. Meanwhile, others collected on deck joining in song or sharing in conversation or some other amusement to pass the time.

I was greatly impressed with the voyageur Henry Belland. He was a capable man in the prime of his days with a youthful, flawless face, and shoulder length, wavy brown hair tucked neatly below his sun-stained, wide-brimmed hat. He was an energetic and happy character who epitomized the French voyageur.

The son of Canadian parents who resided in Montreal, Henry Belland had traveled through the wilds of Canada, visited the frozen lakes of Pembina at the northwestern most corner of the frontier, and seen the trackless prairies of Nebraska. He was a true adventurer who carried with him the elegance of his French nature and the energy which distinguishes

---

[45] A keel is a long wooden structure attached to the bottom of the hull to provide stability.

the American pioneer. He was both strong and graceful, cheerful and generous, a true ideal in actual life. He was a man to be envied.

Henry Belland

The most gorgeous sunset shined gloriously off the clear river water while illuminating the horizon with attractive hues of red and orange. Soon darkness enveloped the fading colors and we welcomed the night with as much joy and ambition with which we had begun. We did not stop for respite but continued well past the midnight hour, the river appearing like a tunnel through the darkness. Those wrapped in buffalo robes and seeking slumber on the deck were sorely disappointed as the boat songs continued one after another as the oarsmen rowed to the rhythm of the music. All joined in with great spirit to songs like *Sparkling and Bright, Farewell to Moore, Lord Tom Noddy,* and the *Star-Spangled Banner*. But my particular favorite was a beautiful French song called *A la Claire Fontaine*.

I did not understand the words, but it had a charming rhythm and an effortless rising and falling flow. Over and over they sang:

Il y'a longtemps que je t'aime, Jamais je ne t'oublierai
(Long have I loved you, Never will I forget you.)

As the night went on we were joined by three Indian canoes which only added to the poetic allure of our travels. The accompanying canoes could narrowly be seen through the darkness but could only be heard as their paddles softly cut through the water and their war songs overcame our own. But every so often, like a firefly, the glimmer of their pipes revealed their location through the starlight. Like a patient companion the three Indian canoes stayed by our side, not out of necessity but out of the comfort associated with the absence of loneliness.

Finally, by noon the next day, we reached our long-sought destination of Fort Snelling. And though tired and hungry, we welcomed the final leg of our journey with repeating choruses of the *Chanson du Nord*. The song of the North. It was a fitting end, an appropriate finale to our treaty trip.

I can rightly say that I most thoroughly enjoyed my time at the Traverse des Sioux. Not one moment passed without the opportunity to fill my sketchbook with some novelty or some hint of the traditional Indian life, a life completely unknown to me before this memorable trip. What I could not capture with my pencil, I have committed to memory. Picturesque images and extraordinary people. In my mind these people will remain, surreal and brilliant. And though the treaty was not without its manipulation and scheming, an accord of great significance was met thoughtfully and peacefully. That is something I do not wish to underplay. What a great moment in the history of this region. What a great moment for which to witness.

But with that knowledge and appreciation, I could not overlook the sensation of guilt that grew in the pit of my stomach. I had before felt curious and apprehensive, but the jubilation and comradery of our return trip to St. Paul triggered within me more than just curiosity. Although I wanted to, I could not wholeheartedly partake in the merriment. For mine was a restrained jubilation. *What had we really done?* I thought. Something did not feel right and it weighed on me. Despite all previous warnings against it, I decided that I was going to investigate. Perhaps there was truly nothing I could do, but maybe there was someone else who could. I owed it to Takoda to find out.

Return from Traverse des Sioux

Chapitre onze

>―――《❖》―――

> *"Indian Treaties were made not at times and seasons appointed by government agents but according to the pleasure of Indian traders, half-breeds, and squaw men, and that their advice and consent could be obtained only by allowances for traders' claims and bonuses to half-breeds."*
> - William Watts Folwell, Minnesota Historian

On my return to Fort Snelling I was placed once again with Mr. Prescott and his unpleasant little loft. It was of no consequence to me after now having been so long away from the luxuries of home. The negotiations with the lower bands were not to begin until July 29, and thusly I had several days to myself. On the twenty-sixth I had an agreeable meeting with George A. Richmond, a Boston man I had met previously aboard the Excelsior. Mr. Richmond was a talented gentleman and I must say that I rather enjoyed the more refined company of another Easterner. The following day I attended drill of the troops at Fort Snelling. To my surprise, two-thirds of the men were foreigners and seemed rather uncouth. These young men had left their homes and families from places like Norway, Sweden, Ireland, and Germany, in hopes of establishing a farm and earning a living. They were unskilled and had little knowledge of the language or culture. For many, the military was the best chance. Nonetheless, it was interesting to observe the routine of frontier garrison life. The next day, July the twenty-eighth, I spent at St. Paul observing the Red-Rivermen, a caravan who had arrived from well north with their skins and peltries. It was quite a site to see and one I found most intriguing.[46] The annual event brought out the entire city as about one hundred ox carts arrived, laden with all types of goods for sale or trade. These included buffalo hides, pemmican (dried buffalo meat), peltries, fur, embroidered leather coats, moccasins, saddles, and so-forth. The men and women operating these ox-carts had traveled a distance of about four hundred fifty miles from Pembina, a settlement on the northern part of the Red River. Originally an English settlement, the people had mixed with the neighboring Indians and had become a population of mixed-breeds. They appeared to be a wild yet picturesque race who were hardy and athletic. They were almost exclusively employed as hunters and trappers, the buffalo being their favorite object of their pursuit. The women produced the most beautiful garnished work of beads, porcupine quills and silk with which they adorned leather coats, moccasins, pouches and saddles. They remained in the city a few days, unloading their goods, but once their exchange was complete, they returned to their secluded homes where nine out of twelve months they experience the intense cold of a northern winter. I think perhaps Pembina is the northern most settlement of any consequence in the United States.

---

[46] Mayer describes the Red River carts as "rudely made of wood, no iron being used in their construction, the fastenings and clamps being of raw-hide or pegs of wood. They are drawn by a single ox, or horse, in shafts and carry from eight hundred to a thousand pounds." Heilbron, *With Pen and Pencil*, 237.

Red River Cart

The time had come to treat with the lower bands of Dakota Indians. These were the Wahpekute and Mdewakanton bands which included Little Crow's Kaposia band. Although Little Crow's band had traveled with us to Traverse des Sioux they stayed only a little while and took no part in the treaty negotiations. They came only to show solidarity with their tribal brethren and to share in the government provided rations.

The lower bands were fewer in number than the upper bands, perhaps several hundred rather than several thousand. They are referred to as the lower bands because traditionally they have resided on the lower portion of the Minnesota River as it flows.

The meeting place for negotiations was the upper room of a large warehouse in Mendota, a settlement located across the river from Fort Snelling. It was an awkward selection for a meeting of this magnitude. Because it was so near the settlements of St. Paul and St. Anthony there was quite a crowd of spectators anxious to witness the opening of such a vast, lush territory. There was barely enough space for all to fit and the compactness created a tension and discomfort that was almost unbearable. Regardless of such, the commissioners were ready and the Dakota chiefs were present. The pipe was smoked and negotiations were opened.

"Chiefs, Headmen, and Braves of the Mdewakanton and Wahpekute Bands of Dakotas," said Governor Ramsey as he began the proceedings. "We are both gratified to meet you here today, pleased to have this opportunity to smoke the pipe with you, as an emblem of the good feeling and reciprocal kindness so long existing between the white people and yourselves."

Governor Ramsey continued his speech with the usual courtesies. It was nearly all the same as I had heard before. He mentioned the President as the Great Father to the Indians and made certain to state his good intentions toward them. He also noted that the land had ceased to have value for the Dakota and that a treaty would be mutually beneficial for the whites and the Indians. Finally, one bargaining tool he added, was mentioning the treaty with the upper bands that had already been agreed upon. None of this was news to me, but for many in the room it was the first time they had heard such remarks.

Governor Ramsey was followed, of course, by Commissioner Lea, though usually it was the other way around. Commissioner Lea gave the same predictable speech. It was a speech I had heard many times now.

"I salute you as friends and brothers," declared Commissioner Lea. "All of the Indians who know me, consider me their friend. Your Great Father at Washington, is himself the friend of the Indian, and he would not permit me to hold the high office I do, if I were not like him, your friend."

I feared it was all empty-talk. But what else might the Commissioner say? Negotiations were by definition a venue for persuasion. And so Commissioner Lea continued his calculated message. He noted the good home that would be provided for the Dakota and the goods and services that would come along with it. He suggested that living close together, on a reservation would unite the Dakota and make them a great people once more. When Commissioner Lea finished wooing the Indians, and the audience for that matter, he then began explaining the general terms of the treaty. They were, for all intents and purposes, the same as had been stipulated in the Treaty of the Traverse des Sioux but on a smaller scale. As I sat and listened, I wondered what Takoda would think of all this.

"You will need schools and mills, blacksmith shops and farms in your new home and a sum sufficient for these purposes will be set apart for you," announced Commissioner Lea as he stood confidently before all onlookers. "And to further aid and support you for a great many years, say fifty years, the payment for your lands will be so arranged that you will received about $30,000 annually."

The Dakota chiefs looked on patiently, all of them adorned in their finest regalia like their Sisseton and Wahpeton brethren. They appeared calm and in no haste or hurry. They also seemed to represent a stunning juxtaposition between the population that was Minnesota and the population that would be. Dressed in their feathers, paint, and fur, they looked as if they had come straight out of a storybook of past relics. Opposite them the commissioners were dressed with suit and necktie as if their manner of dress were some code to erase the past.

Commissioner Lea concluded his remarks by stating that he expected no answer from the Dakota. Rather, he handed them a document with the terms of the treaty and asked them to return tomorrow in order to consider and negotiate the proposed terms.

But before the council could adjourn, one of the Dakota chiefs arose. This was Chief Wabasha of the Mdewakanton band.

"Fathers," said Wabasha addressing the commissioners. "These chiefs and braves that sit here, have heard what you have said from our Great Father. I have but one thing to say to you and then we will separate for today. I was among those who went to Washington and brought home the words of our Great Father."

This struck me to hear that the chief had been to our capital. It occurred to me that this must have been in 1837 when the lower bands previously signed a treaty.

"Some of those here, were there also, and some who went are now dead. According to what our Great Father then said, we have some funds lying back in his hands. Those you see here around, are anxious to get that which is due them, before they do anything. That is all I have to say on this occasion."

Again I was surprised, not only learning that the chief had visited Washington, but that the terms of the previous treaty had not yet been fulfilled. It was obvious right away that the lower bands, unlike the upper bands, had experience making a treaty with the government. I was now interested to see how that would play out in the negotiating of another treaty.

"I have heard what you have had to say, with respect," answered Commissioner Lea. "The subject to which you referred, I have before thought of, it has not been forgotten by me. If we can come to an arrangement about other and more important matters, no doubt all can be satisfied in reference to the back money."

Chief Wabasha was apparently satisfied with Commissioner Lea's response as he calmly nodded his head in acknowledgement. After a brief pause he then rose to make one more comment.

"Fathers, I have one single thing to say and then I will go out. You came to speak the words of our Great Father, but it is warm in this place and we should like tomorrow to hold council in the open air."

"Very well," replied Commissioner Lea. "The commissioners will take your request into consideration."

I think everyone was relieved by Wabasha's final request, knowing that it was too hot and crowded in that warehouse room. Although the Commissioner said he would only consider the request, it was almost a forgone conclusion that he would acquiesce.

"This meeting is adjourned," announced Commissioner Lea who then beat his gavel.

The commissioners, I believe, expected a quick and easy negotiation, but before even the terms were discussed the Dakota put up opposition in regards to the 1837 treaty. Therefore the lower bands were not as willing to sign as the commissioners may have anticipated. Furthermore, the potential failures of the previous treaty may also have prompted reluctance on the part of the Dakota. I was curious to know just how advantageous or disadvantageous that treaty had been. Perhaps the lower bands' experience with treaty negotiations had made them keen to recognize the duplicity on the part of the commissioners and traders that I had come to suspect.

The negotiations were moved to a prominent hill called Pilot Knob and located southeast of the confluence of the Minnesota and Mississippi

Rivers. The hill offered a commanding and fine view of Fort Snelling, St. Anthony, St. Paul, and the two river valleys below. To the Dakota this place was called *Oheyawahi* or A Hill Much Visited. It was a sacred site where the Dakota had traditionally buried their dead. It was chosen as the place for negotiation by Chief Wabasha because he wanted a full view of everything the Dakota would be giving up if they chose to sign the treaty.

Valley of the Mississippi from Pilot Knob

A large arbor was constructed at the crown of the hill where the land levels off. Underneath was placed a stand and table for the Commissioners while seats, in the form of a half-circle, were placed for the Dakota chiefs. Once again the crowd was large and varied, but the setting had become much more pleasant than the day before. The sun was shining and a cool and comfortable breeze moved swiftly over the hill.

When all was ready, Commissioner Lea opened the council by greeting the chiefs and inviting their response to the terms presented the day before.

At length no one spoke. It appeared that the chiefs were not ready to give a response until, after several minutes, Chief Little Crow of the Kaposia band arose and spoke.

"Fathers, these chiefs and soldiers, and others who sit here, have something they wish to say to you, and I am going to speak it."

Little Crow appeared at ease and his tone was very respectful. It was clear to see why he was chosen as spokesman. Having succeeded his father and grandfather, it seemed leadership was in his blood.

"There are chiefs here who went to Washington and brought a good report concerning the settlement of affairs in the treaty there made, and they and we were glad. But it has not taken place as it was promised."

I was struck once again hearing that the previous treaty had not been fulfilled. Had Wabasha and Little Crow spoken truthfully?"

"These men sit still and say nothing," continued Little Crow while pointing to his brethren. "But you, fathers, are the cause of this being so. They speak of some money that is due them, but we have not seen the money. We desire to have the money laid down to us. It was money due on the old treaty, and I think it should be paid. We do not want to talk on the subject of a new treaty until it is paid."

Little Crow sat and allowed his words to be translated. Although Little Crow spoke with eloquence and respect, it was clear that he was adamant in his request. The Dakota wanted the money owed them before they would negotiate a new treaty. This seemed to validate my skepticism and I admit it made me feel satisfied.

"I have read the treaty to which Little Crow alludes," began Commissioner Lea with his rebuttal. "I find it there written, that the money he demands was to be expended under the direction of the President. Their Great Father thought it would be for the benefit of the Dakotas to apply that money to the education of their children. The Dakotas thought otherwise," said the Commissioner, now appearing slightly agitated. "An unfortunate difference of opinion. Your Great Father did not wish to keep back anything that was justly yours. He merely thought different in the mode of applying it. We regret that this was so and we are anxious now to make a treaty which will relieve them from this difficulty. We wish now to make a treaty that will be so plain that there will be no difference of opinion about it. And as I stated when we first met, when we succeed with more important business, we will be able to arrange satisfactorily the money matters."

"To get this money ready and everything arranged to pay it," added Governor Ramsey, "will take a good while, and we may as well, therefore, proceed with the treaty."

The commissioners were as reluctant to talk about the old treaty as the Dakota were to talk about the new treaty. Little Crow immediately fired back.

"We will talk of nothing else but the money, if it is until next spring," the great chief said staunchly. "That lies in the way of a treaty."

The commissioners were clearly displeased by Little Crow's insistence. They began to whisper among each other. So too did the audience creating an imperceptible chatter that was carried along by the breeze.

It had become apparent to me that this stalemate was caused by a particular stipulation in the 1837 treaty. In this stipulation, it was stated that $5,000 annually should be paid, in such a manner as the president should direct, for the enlightenment of the Indians. This became known as the education fund and for whatever reason, it had never yet been paid.[47]

"It is all very nice to talk about money," began Governor Ramsey in his response to Little Crow. "Money is a rather fine thing if properly used, but there is also some business to be done first, and besides it is in many boxes, and will take several days to count and put in order. In the meantime we can go on and complete the business for which we are assembled. You talk about money. We are willing to give it to you, as soon as we get through with this treaty. Now, if your people want this money, you know how to get it for them."

There was a long silence and then Commissioner Lea decided to break in.

"You can believe my words and the words of my brother," said Commissioner Lea, assuring the Dakota chiefs. "Your Great Father did not send me all the way from Washington to lie to you. We hope you are now satisfied in reference to the money. We now go back to the proposals for a treaty we have made you. If you wish to hear the proposals again, that can be done."

There was another long silence. The chiefs looked at each other and at the commissioners, but then back at each other. The tension surrounding talks slowly dissipated and it appeared that the issue of the money had been settled. But there was something else discouraging the chiefs. The warriors, standing behind the chiefs, showed disfavor in their expressions. There was

---

[47] Historian William Watts Folwell writes that, "the retention of the greater portion of this fund in the treasury is not easily explainable, but the suggestion is ventured that if could not be placed in the hands of missionaries of different denominations, in those days less tolerant in the good work of salvation." Folwell, *A History of Minnesota*, 285.

apparently a rift between the chiefs and warriors regarding what to do next. Finally, one of the chiefs whom we had not heard from stood to speak.

"I would rather be excused," he said nervously, "and that some other chief should speak. I am of the same mind with my friends here and I will sit and listen."

There was another pause. I was unsure what was going on, but the chiefs were quite reluctant to speak on the treaty.

"They are all chiefs and ought to speak," said a perturbed Commissioner Lea. "We met them as chiefs and thought they were all chiefs who would speak out what they thought."

Still no response.

"Say to the Dakota," said Commissioner Lea, directing the interpreter, "that as they seem to have nothing to say, we take it for granted they do not wish to sell their lands."

Commissioner Lea now spoke in a more somber tone, as if gravely disappointed.

"I hope they will not regret it. It grieves my heart, and I know it will make the heart of your Great Father sad, to know that they are disposed to act in a manner that is so little for your own good."

Commissioner Lea paused and looked coldly upon the chiefs.

"Say to them," he continued, "that we will meet them here tomorrow or at any other time they may desire."

The commissioners rose and quickly exited the treaty grounds much like Sleepy Eye had done during the earlier negotiations. The chiefs and warriors all remained as they were, seated and motionless. The crowd let out a muddled sigh, believing perhaps that this ended the hopes of a successful treaty. I, no longer being a novice, knew better. I could not be certain if or when the negotiations would continue, but as the previous treaty had taught me, I knew negotiations did not occur without some drama.

What concerned me most were the apprehensions expressed by the lower bands. The fact that the terms of the 1837 treaty had not been fulfilled, coupled with the knowledge of the traders' paper, assured me that no matter how necessary or beneficial the Indian treaties were, they were not without their perniciousness. I wanted to believe that our two cultures, white and Indian, could live side by side, and that in these treaties we truly had the better interests of the Dakota in mind. But the more I learned and the more I saw, the less likely this became. If not for my conscience, and the commands of the young Takoda, I might have let it go. But I couldn't. During the previous negotiations I had spoken up, but been rejected. I had to find another way to make a difference, but how, I wondered?

During the hiatus, temporary or otherwise, I decided to travel up river to visit the burgeoning little settlement of St. Anthony. This was the town described to me by Franklin Steele who owned much of the land.[48] Looking upon it myself I could see that it was destined to be a great manufacturing point. This was made obvious by the Falls of St. Anthony which provided some of the finest water power in the world. Standing about twenty feet high and stretching the entire width of the Mississippi, the falls presented a beautiful appearance. As the water rushed over the crest of the falls it displayed an amber color graduating into a snowy whiteness as it approached the rocks beneath. The falls were briefly interrupted by an island on the eastern half which extended about a half mile up the river. The island was covered in lush green foliage and rich pine forests. But the beauty of these falls was not what it once was and might soon disappear altogether. The western side remained untouched and the land was empty prairie, but the eastern side had been destroyed by saw mills above which were the homes and businesses of St. Anthony itself. The beauty of the falls, which must have been stunning when first viewed by the white settlers, might someday become entirely destroyed by the sawmills, dams, and logs.

"It's an amazing thing, isn't it Mr. Mayer?" I heard a voice behind me say. "The way we harness the power of the rushing waters."

I turned to see Mr. Richard Chute.

---

[48] Franklin Steele built a dam across the east channel of the Mississippi at the Falls of Saint Anthony in 1847, and in the next year he began operating a sawmill on the east bank. Settlement followed, and the village of St. Anthony, now a part of Minneapolis, developed. Heilbron, *With Pen and Pencil,* 243.

"I did not expect to see you again," I remarked graciously and without disdain. "Are you responsible for destroying the natural beauty of these falls?"

"Destroying?" he replied quickly. "This is not a source of natural beauty but a source of natural energy. It is an industrial nucleus and will become the focal point of a great city. This, Mr. Mayer," he said pointing toward the mills, "represents progress."

"Do you then have business interests here?" I asked. "I figured you for only a trader."

"The trade is declining, and will continue as such," he answered. "I must evolve just as the times do. Real estate, milling, and water power; that is where I will focus my attention."

"Is that all you see here?" I asked loudly and with a sudden tinge of anger.

"Indeed, yes," Mr. Chute answered with enthusiasm, almost sarcastically. "Look at that prairie to the west," said Mr. Chute pointing the open land on the other side of the river. "As soon as the Indians sign that treaty I will lay claim to much of that land and in a few years, when this city is booming I will make a fortune in real estate."

"Very ambitious of you Mr. Chute. Have you given up then on making your fortune off the Indians?" I said caustically, though wary of making such a direct allegation.

"Very good," laughed Mr. Chute. "Perhaps you are learning something after all."

"I know there is more to this treaty than meets the eye."

"Well, you are right," confirmed Mr. Chute. "I stand to gain nothing monetarily from the treaty. But there are many others who do. You see," explained Mr. Chute, "there is only so much money to go around and Mr. Sibley and his partners have their hands on all of it. Therefore I must move on to other ventures."

"But how can they get away with such things," I said not as a question, but as a realization.

"There might be something you can do," noted Mr. Chute.

"Yes, what?" I asked, wanting very much to know what this man might suggest.

"Since it is a matter of legality, it must be proven that the law was broken," Mr. Chute explained plainly. "I know a man that may be able to help you with that."

"Who?"

"His name is Madison Sweetser. He is a trader from Indiana and he is partnered with the Ewing firm. As a matter of fact, he is a brother-in-law to the Ewings. He is not presently in this territory, but I have received correspondence indicating that he will be here soon in order to establish a trading interest."

"And how might he bring to light the deception of the traders' paper?" I asked.

"I must tell you," warned Mr. Chute, "that the men you are dealing with have a lot at stake, none of whom share your integrity. Madison Sweetser may be able to help you, but his intentions will not be as saintly as your own."

"I understand," I said, acknowledging his fair warning.

"Sweetser, like myself, was rather dismayed when Richard Thompson failed to be named treaty commissioner. I presume Mr. Sweetser will be eager to do anything he can to spoil the intentions of Sibley and the American Fur Company. Plus, he is a savvy, charming, and intelligent man. He may not side with the Indians, but he will certainly side against Sibley."

This was more than I bargained for, I thought to myself. Yes, I sought justice for the Dakota and their defenseless situation. But it all bordered on deceit and trickery. What might happen if I got further involved? What might happen if I did not?

"Do you understand what I have explained to you?" asked Mr. Chute, interrupting my introspection.

"Yes," I said plainly.

"What will you do?"

"I will wait expectantly upon Madison Sweetser."

Chapitre douze

"We are constrained to say, therefore, that in our opinion the time has come when the extinguishment of the Indian title to this region should no longer be delayed, if government would not have the mortification on the one hand of confessing its inability to protect the Indians from encroachment, or be subjected to the painful necessity, upon the other, of ejecting by force thousands of its citizens from a land which they desire to make their homes and which without their occupancy and labor will be comparatively useless and waste."
- Luke Lea and Alexander Ramsey to A.H.H. Stuart, Secretary of the Interior, August 6, 1851

After an interval of several days, the Dakota chiefs called upon the U.S. Commissioners and informed them that they were ready to reopen negotiations. Both parties had ample time to review and adjust treaty terms so that they might be mutually beneficial. For this reason, an agreement was expected promptly and without haggling.

The negotiations resumed at Pilot Knob, the weather once again being pleasant and the crowd generous. The commissioners and chiefs took their places and all others gathered around tightly. The pipe was passed around and the negotiations were opened.

"The treaty has been prepared in pursuance of the terms agreed upon, and being now ready for signatures, it is best not to delay any further," proclaimed Commissioner Lea in his clear and dispassionate manner with which I have become all too familiar. "We will have the treaty read and explained so all can see it is a good treaty."

The treaty document was then handed to Alexis Bailly who read the terms aloud in English. He was followed by Reverend Gideon Pond, the missionary, who read the terms in Dakota.

The terms of the treaty, being called the Treaty of Mendota, varied little from the treaty signed at Traverse des Sioux. The only real difference was in the amounts of money named. In general terms, the Dakota agreed to sell their lands west of the Mississippi River in exchange for annual annuity payments amounting to $1.41 million. They also agreed to a reservation along the Minnesota River and bordering the upper bands. Finally, the Dakota were to be given aid and support in the forms of education, farming, and other goods and provisions. Now it was only a matter of whether or not the chiefs would sign.

As the terms were read there was a tug at my shirt. I turned to see Takoda's smiling face.

"Takoda," I said with a smile and a hushed tone. "What are you doing here? Who is watching over you?"

"I take care of myself," answered Takoda confidently. "I wanted to see what would happen today. I wanted to see why all these people came here."

"Very well," I said without objection. "Just behave yourself."

Takoda snarled sarcastically.

"The chiefs and principal men have had the treaty explained to them," declared Governor Ramsey once the terms had been read. "Have they arranged among themselves who shall sign first, or is it left to us?"

There was no response.

"Little Crow," called out Commissioner Lea. "You are revered and respected. You ought to be the one who signs first."

Little Crow did not answer. He simply remained still as if he had not been spoken to. So remained all of the chiefs. It was an awkward silence that created a palpable tension. The same undefined tension that existed when negotiations were suspended.

Finally, Wabasha arose slowly but firmly. All of the attention turned his way.

"You have requested us to sign this paper," he said meekly, "and you have told us that it is for our good. But I am of a different opinion. In the treaty I have heard read, you have mentioned farmers, schools, and physicians. To all these I am opposed. They and others who went to Washington and made a treaty, in which the same things were said, but we have not benefited by them. I want them struck out of this treaty. We want nothing but cash turned over to us for our lands. You have named a place for our home, but it is prairie country. I am a man used to the woods, and do not like the prairies, and perhaps some of us who are here will name a place we would all like better. When I went to Washington to see our Great Father, he asked us for our land and we gave it to him, and he agreed to furnish us with goods and provisions for twenty years. I wish to remain in this county until that time expires."

"You see, it is just as I said," Takoda pointed out as he was now at my side.

"What do you mean?"

"It's not for our good—the treaty I mean. Even Wabasha says so," explained Takoda being respectful not to talk too loud.

"Then why agree to the treaty?" I asked with honest curiosity.

"Because this is what the white man does to the Dakota," answered the boy, sounding more like a man. "They force upon us these things that we don't want. The previous treaty is proof of that. But our only other choice is to accept nothing and wait for the whites to force us out. We Dakota have no choice."

I was enlightened by Takoda's explanation. The Dakota knew the treaty was unfavorable, but also knew it was their best option.

I listened once again to the negotiations as the commissioners were prepared to respond to Wabasha.

"I expected to see a man who was chief, and was the friend of his people," replied Commissioner Lea who had clearly lost patience. "I expected to see a man who did not speak with a forked tongue. But we know he has been talking in a way that shows he is neither the friend of the white man, nor of the Indian."

As the Commissioner spoke I could not be certain how accurate his condemnation was, but in any case it was obvious that he wanted to stomp out any opposition to the treaty being signed today.

"We don't expect to be able to make a treaty to suit him. That would be impossible, for he wants none. Since I have been here, I have tried to inform myself in regard to your wishes, condition and wants. Now, you are all men, and have your peculiar notions about things, and you can hardly get two men to look alike upon the same proposition. It is impossible to get a treaty to suit all—what suits one won't suit another, but it is our wish to make a treaty to do you all the most good. We have thought upon this a long time, and we have written this in such a way as we think will be for your good. We have talked about the matter until there is no use of talking anymore. We have written this treaty and signed it, and it is now too late to talk of changing it. We couldn't make it any better if we tried."

Takoda looked at me with his deep brown eyes. "Don't you see, now they bully us. This is not a negotiation."

Takoda was very perceptive for such a young boy. Unfortunately, I think he was right.

"Will either of the principal chiefs sign the treaty?" asked Governor Ramsey referring to Wabasha and Little Crow. "Do they say yes or no?"

Again, silence and awkward tension. It appeared for the moment that confirmation of the treaty was quite doubtful. In a way I was pleased and hoped the Dakota would hold their ground. I felt as if no good could come from signing the treaty, but I also knew that to not sign might be even worse.

Finally, Chief Wakute of the Mdewakanton band stood to speak.

"Fathers, your counsel and advice is very good to Indians, but there are a great many different opinions, and it appears almost impossible to get an agreement though we have been consulting so many days."

The chief was adorned in all the usual regalia such as eagle plumes, weasel tails, beadwork, leggings and moccasins. But beneath his regalia, was a pensive looking man who spoke with patience and wisdom. His stature, though small, in no way limited both the power and dignity of his words.

"You have come with the words of our Great Father," he continued, "and have put them in this paper, but the Indians are afraid it may be changed hereafter. I say this in good feeling. But when we were at Washington, the chiefs were told many things which when we came back here, and attempted to carry out, we found could not be done." [49]

---

[49] On August 18, 1837, a delegation of twenty-six Dakota traveled to Washington along with Agent Lawrence Taliaferro. The Dakota were told that they would

Several of the Dakota warriors answered these words with *ho's* of approval. Takoda did the same. I was almost compelled to do it myself.

"At the end of three or four years," explained Chief Wakute, "the Indians found out very different from what they had been told, and all were ashamed. I hope when the people sign this treaty, you will take and deliver it to the President as it is. I am pleased with the terms of the treaty and the money that will be paid for our lands. I only wish that what you write will be the same as what you do."

Again the warriors seemed to approve of the chief's statement.

"I say to Wakute," answered Governor Ramsey, "that he is a man I always listen to with a great deal of respect. I am satisfied with the good sense he has always shown. He will understand then the difficulties in fulfilling the details of such a large and nuanced agreement. Every chief and warrior cannot be catered to individually. The terms are for the general good and are fulfilled in time as made possible to do so. What we have written is more than sufficient and will be carried out. You should understand this. A great deal could be talked about, but it is useless to say more. You must have confidence in us and in your Great Father."

Under what basis? I thought to myself.

"We might talk a month, and no business be done," finished Ramsey.

Wabasha then rose to speak. He asked the commissioners how or if the chiefs would be distinguished by the treaty. This had shown that Wabasha had apparently given up his earlier opposition.

Commissioner Lea was pleased and said that he was talking more like a chief than before. It seemed to be a turning point in the negotiations. And if it was not, what Wabasha said next certainly was.

---

be negotiating a peace settlement with the Sac and Fox, but once they arrived they learned that the true purpose was to sell part of their lands to the federal government. A deal was made and according to historian Linda Clemmons, "the Treaty of 1837 served as the turning point in government-Dakota relations, instead of the Treaty of 1851 . . . By 1851 the Dakota has already learned to mistrust the government and to question their ability to follow through with promises made during treaty negotiations." Linda M. Clemmons, "We Will Talk of Nothing Else: Dakota Interpretations of the Treaty of 1837," *Great Plains Quarterly*, (Summer 2005), 183.

Wabasha turned away from the commissioners and toward the Dakota warriors. There was a look of passion in his face and there was vehemence in his voice.

"You have said young men, that the chief who got up first to sign the treaty you would kill."

There was a slight gasp among the crowd.

"See," commented Takoda with a wave of his finger. "The Dakota don't wish to sell their land. Not only will we lose our land, but it will invite more white men to take other things from us as well."

"I'm sorry, Takoda," I replied almost involuntarily.

"It is this that has caused all the difficulty," continued Wabasha. "But it appears you have agreed among yourselves to sell the land."

The brother of Chief Little Six, also called Shakopee, replied immediately to the accusation.

"Wabasha has accused us of something we never thought of," he said adamantly in his native Dakota tongue. "The soldiers heard that the chiefs were making a treaty and they didn't like it, for the land belongs to the braves. Though we never spoke of killing the chiefs. The soldiers afterwards had got together and agreed to sell the land. They had told him to say so and he now said it."

"This being the understanding," said Governor Ramsey trying to calm the situation, "let the soldiers tell us which of their chiefs shall sign first."

Medicine Bottle, first soldier of the Kaposia band, said, "To the people who did not go to Washington, and had no part in the first treaty, to them belongs the land on this side of the river. There is one chief among us who did not go to Washington at that time. The soldiers want him to sign first. He has been a great war chief and has been our leader against the Chippewas. It is Little Crow. Him we want to sign first."

There was a brief silence as everyone looked toward Little Crow, or Taoyateduta, meaning His Red Nation. The chief held his head low as he collected his thoughts. It appeared almost as if he were in prayer or meditation. He arose, slowly, with his hand upon his staff and turned to face the warriors.

"Young men and braves," he said easily and confidently. "I did not choose my position among you. Though I was not with you at that time, I returned because it was right to do so. And when I did, my own brother shot me through the arm. Yet I did not turn and run. Like a mother to her cub, I could not run at the first sight of danger. I stayed, just as I do now."

It was eerily quiet while Little Crow spoke. Even the breeze halted periodically, allowing Little Crow's word to resonate.

"I am not afraid of anyone killing me. Though I should be the one to sign first and though I may be hunted, I am not afraid to die. For every man has to die sometime and he may die but once. The time when I die is not for my choosing and so I am not afraid."

"If Little Crow signs, there is no turning back," said Takoda as we both looked on with nervous expectancy.

Little Crow paused, and then turned and faced the commissioners.

"Fathers," he said, speaking effortlessly. "We have met like this before. We have talked many times. You say you want good things for my people. You say these things are for our benefit. But I look around and my people are poor and their children are starving. I do not see the good you promised us. For many years the Dakota flourished in this land. We lived without want or need relying only on the hunt to give us food, the rivers to give us water, and the land to provide us shelter. Now you say the land is of no use for us. You say we must live in one spot without moving and without hunting. Do the buffalo not migrate? Do the birds not wander from one side of the sky to the other? How can we, born of the land and made of the earth, be held in one spot? I do not understand the pale-face or where he comes from. But he is many and we are few. He is strong and has many tools and resources. He has many warriors. We have learned to depend on what the pale-face gives us. Without his tools and without his gifts we would melt away like the morning dew. I do not know what will happen to my people. Our ancestors are ashamed and our children are suffering. I agree to your terms because I see no other way. But I know it cannot last. Someday, when we have lost too much, when we can change no more, we will ask for our land back. And when we do, there will be no talk at all, no promises to make, or money to be paid. There will only be ourselves and the way we once knew. We will take it, the way you have taken it from us."

Little Crow, having finished his speech, sat down and waited for the commissioner's response. It was an impassioned and honest speech and one I think I needed to hear. Little Crow's words told me everything I needed to know about the unfortunate circumstances between the whites and the Indians on the Minnesota frontier. He also foretold of potential conflict if things did not change. I truly believed that is not what Little Crow wanted, but he knew someday that the Dakota might have to fight for their own survival.

"These chiefs make us feel ashamed by the way they talk all the time," answered Governor Ramsey as if he were greatly offended by Little Crow. "They seem to think we have come here as representatives of their Great Father to cheat them. The only encouragement we receive is from the warriors. They seem to understand us. We look upon them and have confidence that all will yet go right. But there is no agreement among the chiefs. No, they act like children and put their entire tribe at risk. We have made a good treaty and have given you all we can give. It is all that we can do."

Governor Ramsey was upset and annoyed. He did not wish to prolong the negotiations and he was anxious to acquire the Dakota lands.

Commissioner Lea's response was less impassioned but just as biting. "We have certainly talked about this business a long time," he said. "As long as will do any good. No man puts any food in his mouth by long talk, but may often get hungry at it. Let Little Crow and the chiefs step forward and sign."

Takoda covered his eyes and could not watch.

Seeing that nothing more could be done or changed, Little Crow arose and approached the table whereupon sat the treaty document. He did not look over his shoulder or appear intimidated in any way. He merely signed his name to the treaty and received his medal. He was followed, without provocation, by Wabasha. Then all of the chiefs and warriors followed in what seemed like an endless procession. Sixty-four Dakota in total put their names on the Treaty of Mendota and it was done.

"It is done," I said to Takoda.

The Commissioners exited, the crowd dispersed, and the Dakota received their gifts. As far as a traders' paper, I did not witness any such paper being signed at these negotiations. But I can only assume that a similar arrangement was or would be reached between the traders and the lower bands of Dakota Indians.[50]

---

[50] There was in fact a traders' paper signed in consideration to the debts owed by the Wahpekute band of Dakota. The allowance for traders was ninety thousand

"Can't you do anything to help?" asked Takoda who was nearly sobbing.

I was struck by this show of emotion. "Maybe. Maybe I can."

I quickly moved away. Out of the corner of my eye, I caught sight of Mr. Sibley. He was, of course, instrumental in the entire process of making these treaties with the Dakota. He was also the trader with the greatest amount invested, both financially and otherwise, in the result of these treaties. Though he was not a part of the commission, his presence was unmistakable. Having seen him now, alone, I sought to speak with him. He had the power and influence to change things. I was hesitant to approach such an important and revered man, but I decided I must.

"Pardon me," I said, but too softly for anyone to hear. "Pardon me. Mr. Sibley."

He turned and looked at me. Because of his important and renown status, this filled me with a moment of shock and regret. Was I worthy of his attention? It was too late to walk away.

"Mr. Sibley," I said as I drew close enough to shake his hand. "I am Frank Mayer, an artist from Baltimore."

Though he was a tall man, Henry Sibley was by no means imposing. He was slender and lanky. He appeared purposeful, but not in the sense of a destined leader. What he earned, he earned with his intellect and hard work, not with his might or brawn. His dress was business-like and his posture was too. He appeared like a man who knew his course and who would not be shaken from it.

"Pleased to make your acquaintance, Mr. Mayer," casually replied Mr. Sibley as he held out his long arm to shake my hand. "I have heard very many good things about you."

"Thank you, sir," I answered politely, still feeling quite nervous. "I'd like to congratulate you on this historic day. I know you have put much labor toward the consummation of these treaties."

"Thank you, Mr. Mayer, that is kind of you to say," he replied, though in a somewhat agitated manner as if he had somewhere else to be. "This is indeed the culmination of many years labor and is in fact now the beginning of many more."

---

dollars and it was signed by seven chiefs, soldiers, and braves. Folwell, *A History of Minnesota*, 284.

Ceding Contempt

"If you wouldn't mind," I said cautiously, "I have some questions regarding the treaties just made. I have observed many things throughout the past month and I am trying to further my understanding of those things."

"Certainly," answered Mr. Sibley with a blank stare. "This must be an entirely new world for a young man from Baltimore."

"Indeed," I responded quickly. "I wonder about the document signed at the Traverse des Sioux. The one I asked to be explained. I have come to understand that that document entitles the traders, such as yourself to a large sum of the Dakota's annuity funds."

Mr. Sibley's expression changed as he squinted his eyes and looked toward me ponderously. I had his attention now.

"That is a matter of fact," he answered plainly. "But of what consequence is that to you?"

"None, I suppose," I said truthfully.

"Then you are best to leave it alone," he said, almost scolding me.

"But is that not illegal based on an act of Congress which states that the money must be paid directly to the Indian heads of family?"

"Or individuals who they direct in open council," replied Mr. Sibley quickly and assuredly.

"But how can that be considered open council when they did not understand what they were signing?" I asked boldly.

"I am not going to argue such matters with you," he answered coldly. "You forget who I am and I don't think you adequately understand the circumstances."

"Enlighten me," I said, again being quite bold, but feeling exceedingly nervous.

"It is notorious that not a single man who has been engaged in the trade for any length of time, is not reduced to utter poverty or overwhelmed with debt, because none have been paid their dues by the Indians," explained Mr. Sibley in a fervent manner. "Debts so extensive, that our only hopes of collecting even a portion, are directly through an Indian treaty."

"Is there no other way," I said, "then to thereby impoverish the Indian. Might you not allow the Indians to pay their debts in their own way and in their own time?"

"Money passes through Indian hands like water," he said holding out his hands and spreading his fingers. "Our debts would not be repaid and our money would go into the hands of other merchants. I am not callous, I am merely conducting a business."[51]

"The system doesn't work," I alleged in a moment of clarity and realization. "The effect on the Indians, who collect communal rather than individual debts, is to encourage them to become more reckless and dissolute in extravagant expenditure. How can you prey on a system that exploits an entire culture?"

"I am a friend to the Dakota," said Mr. Sibley in a resolute, not angry manner. "Believe me that I and many of the traders would gladly have seen the white man's plow stop at the bank of the Mississippi, allowing the Indians to hunt and fish in their ancient homes in perpetuity. But that is not the case. Unfortunate though it may be, this is the system in place and it will not change. There was a time for the Dakota to flourish and live free, but that time is over."

"You haven't any right . . ."

"I must be going," said Mr. Sibley interrupting me. "It has been a pleasure to meet you, but I suggest you let things be. Especially in regards to the traders' document. I assure you there has been no wrongdoing."

Mr. Sibley quickly walked away and did not allow me to formulate a response. I believed what he said about the traders and their debts. I believed him when he said he was a friend of the Dakota. But something did not feel right at all. The traders, right or wrong, were using the treaty system to take advantage of the American Indian. And though Mr. Sibley was a business man conducting business, he seemed to be doing it in a mischievous and coercive manner that benefitted few and abused many.

I turned to find Takoda. He was there among the receding crowd.

"Don't give up, Mr. Mayer," he called out decidedly as if he knew something I did not. "Don't give up."

---

[51] It is true that Sibley's outfit had shown a loss since 1842 of at least ten thousand dollars a year, amounting to as much as thirty thousand dollars in some years. Writing to Alexander Ramsey in March, 1851, Sibley noted, "I do not know a single man, who is not anxious that the Government shall succeed in making these treaties . . . in which the traders . . . are particularly interested." Ibid., 269.

Chapitre treize

". . . I speak highly of him much more so than I think he deserves. His fingers you may be assured are buttered . . ."
- Madison Sweetser speaking of Alexander Ramsey in a letter to W.G. Ewing, October 26, 1851.

With the treaty negotiations passed, I returned to Fort Snelling and my temporary quarters in Mr. Prescott's loft. But, unfortunately, a sickness had come upon me. It was a combination of blueness and homesickness induced by months of travel and the tribulations I had encountered. Without comfort, without sympathy, without amusement, with fever, with cold, with dirt, with disgust and with comparisons with home—I thought long and hard of ending my stay in Minnesota. But I decided I could not. I decided that I had more to do in finding some form of resolution for the Dakota.

"He comes from Fort Wayne, Indiana, and is said to be a very respectable citizen and a capable merchant," I explained to Ashton as we sat on the bluffs below Fort Snelling awaiting my departure down river. "He has been brought here by the recent treaties and the very flattering accounts of the region."

"What did you say his name was?" asked Ashton with a curious look on his face.

"Madison Sweetser," I replied.

"I have not heard of this man," returned Ashton. "But being from Indiana he must certainly be connected to the Ewing brothers."

"Indeed," I answered positively. "I believe, in fact, he is a brother-in-law to the Ewings. Or so I was told."

"Brother-in-law," repeated Ashton still having a curious look on his face. "You must be rather careful when getting involved in such delicate matters. Are you sure you want to meet with this so-called merchant?"

"I feel as if I have to," I said truthfully. "The warnings of Mr. Sibley only intensified my curiosity, and as it may be, my misunderstanding of matters. I have been told this Sweetser character can help reveal the deceit that has been perpetrated here. I owe it to my own conscience to make an effort."

"There is more here than meets the eye, Frank," replied Ashton. "I want you to be careful."

"I will, I will," I persisted.

"We have become friends and I only wish to protect you. And besides, you appear to have grown ill, are you not too homesick?"

"I appreciate your concern, Ashton," I answered. "But I remain resilient and my home will always be waiting for me. I will return when I feel that I am finally ready to do so."

"You are a good man, Frank Mayer," said Ashton with a smile as he shook my hand. "I have been pleased to make your acquaintance and to be a part of your journey."

"What about you, Ashton. What is next for you?"

"I will return to Washington," answered Ashton looking somewhat forlorn. "Having been away so long there is much work to do. Mostly papers to push."

We laughed.

"I will be sure to visit you upon my return to Baltimore," I promised.

"I will look forward to that," Ashton said with a wink.

"Gentlemen!" came a voice from the prairie above. We turned to see Gubbo, an affable and energetic half-breed with whom we had shared company over the preceding days.

"I must bid you adieu," he shouted as he sat mounted upon his horse with a rifle across his lap and a buffalo robe over his shoulder.

"Farewell, Gubbo," I said with a smile and a wave. "Are you off to Pembina?"

"To the Red River Valley of the north," he said with a grin and a wave.

As he turned and scampered along the prairie I envied the young frontiersman. His life was one of freedom and adventure. Though I could envy him but little, for I had other things on my mind.

I said good bye to Ashton and headed south once more for the Traverse des Sioux. It was here I was told that Madison Sweetser had established a claim. As I traveled I noticed that the unmistakable quality of autumn had entered the air. The breezes became cooler and the skies grayer. At night too, the temperature dipped below freezing. It seemed far too early in the season for such biting temperatures, but such were the characteristics of this northern latitude.

I arrived to Traverse des Sioux seeing that it appeared much different than it had before. Almost all of the Indian tepees had been removed with the exception of ten or fifteen which likely represented Red Iron's band. The subtraction of the Indian presence brought about a noticeable addition of a trading presence. Several wood frame homes had been constructed where none had been before. This, I assumed, was in anticipation of a great town that was expected to spring up on the site.

I departed from my ship and began immediately searching for Mr. Sweetser. For the time being I was truly on my own without any real idea how I might take care of myself, and for this reason I knew I must immediately pursue my purpose. I asked several residents if any had seen or been acquainted with Mr. Sweetser, but none could answer in the positive. This was of little consequence. The town was still quite small and I needed only search a little while.

"You cannot build there," I heard one man say to another as I approached the two of them during an apparent disagreement. "You cannot build there," he repeated. "It is too close to my claim. Yours must be at least a half-mile distant."

"I beg to differ," returned the man who stood near a pile of lumber and building supplies. "I have obtained this claim under proper license and I intend to build on this very spot."

"You shall do no such thing!" exclaimed the first man. "Be assured that if you build here I will file protest with the agent Mr. McLean."

"I have been to see Mr. McLean," replied the second man. "He made no demands as to the location of my claim. He supported my claim and I am sure he will deny your protest."

"We will see," responded the first man, still fuming from the disagreement.

At this point the men became aware of my presence and therefore did not wish to prolong their argument.

"If you build here," warned the first man, "no license will protect you. We will tear down your post piece by piece."

He turned and quickly walked away, taking one glance toward me, but saying nothing. I recognized him as Mr. Alexander Graham, a trader who had been present at the treaty negotiations.[52]

"The audacity of these traders," exclaimed the man who intended to build and whom I was now near enough to speak with.

"Disagreements in business are bound to occur," I said trying to relieve the situation.

"I have met only with trouble since arriving here," he said with his eyes to the ground and a shake of his head. "They have done all they can to keep me out of this country and now they seek to deny my proper claim."

"They?" I inquired.

"The Company," he replied as if the answer were obvious.

"Who represents The Company?" I asked, though I had an inclination.

"Nearly everyone it appears," he answered despondently. "Those working for Pierre Chouteau, formerly the American Fur Company. Most

---

[52] In a letter addressed to Nathaniel McLean, Alexander Graham complained that, "he (Sweetser) is now hauling materials and preparing to erect buildings on the first rise of ground, directly in rear of my post and not one fourth of a mile removed from it. This he does in disregard of my remonstrances to him against his building in that place, and within the marks which have been made designating the claim belonging to the post." Much of what follows throughout this novel was derived from correspondence like this between the various traders of this region at the time. The letters were compiled and published by Rebecca Snyder. Rebecca Snyder, Ed., *The 1851 Treaty of Mendota: A Collection of Primary Documents Pertaining to the Treaty*, (South St. Paul, Minnesota: Dakota County Historical Society, 2002).

notably, of course, is Mr. Henry Sibley. All others, such as this man who seeks to deny my claim, are subordinates of Mr. Sibley."[53]

This was exactly as I had presumed based on my experiences with the treaty negotiations.

"Is that so," I replied in acknowledgement, but not giving away any of my own suspicions.

"The object of these men," continued the stranger, "is almost certainly to be to keep everyone out of the country that they may secure all the valuable permits. To make matters worse, I believe Governor Ramsey is colluding with Mr. Sibley and therefore all Ramsey men are without an exception Sibley men. Together they have a community of interest in this claim arrangement. I can't explain my reasons for this opinion, but it is so!"

He sat, clutching his head, unawares of everything he had just revealed to a perfect stranger.

"I beg your pardon," I said interrupting his moment of pity, "but are you Mr. Madison Sweetser?"

His head immediately lifted. "I am he."

We now looked at each other, face to face. Mr. Sweetser was a diminutive looking man of probably forty or so years. He had a long, narrow face with somewhat delicate features and a head of thick, curly black hair. He sat upon his lumber, leaning forward with his elbows on his knees and his hands crossed. He was peering at me with curiosity.

"I am Frank Mayer, an artist from Baltimore who recently attended the negotiations for the treaties of Traverse des Sioux and Mendota."

Mr. Sweetser sat straight up, giving me his attention.

"I have been referred to you by a Mr. Richard Chute," I informed him.

"Yes, I know Mr. Chute," he said, still looking intrigued. "For what reason did he refer you to me?"

"Well, that part is difficult to explain," I said delicately. "While observing the negotiations I witnessed the signing of a document—a

---

[53] Because the fur-bearing animals were no longer so plentiful and the Indians, spoiled by cash annuities, no longer hunted with diligence, the fur business had much declined. In 1842 the American Fur Company was forced to assign, and in the following year Pierre Chouteau Jr. and Company of St. Louis took over the business. Folwell, *A History of Minnesota*, 163.

separate document from the treaty. It was neither read nor explained to the Dakota Indians."

"The Traders' Paper," he said interrupting me.

"You know of it," I replied with astonishment.

"Yes, I know very well," he said in a sort of guarded manner. "But of what interest is that to you? I thought you said you were an artist?"

"A reasonable question," I acknowledged. "I did not expect to take such an interest in the proceedings, but after having traveled here; after learning what makes this region so unique and different, I have sort of become absorbed. And more significantly, I learned about the Dakota people, culture, and way of life. It has become a fleeting culture, mostly, I think, because of treaties like this and the men behind those treaties."

"I won't argue with you on any one of those points," responded Mr. Sweetser, now hunched over once more but still very much engaged. "I have been here just a few days and I can already say that this is destined to be the garden spot of America. The wealth of the country, its soil, and in every other light you may view it, places it decidedly ahead of any other portion of the Western country."

"Certainly," I agreed.

"And I know all too well about the treaty system and the men behind it," he continued. "But what precisely do you wish to accomplish?"

Mr. Sweetser looked at me keenly as if this question were of utmost importance.

"To be perfectly honest," I said, "I find it appalling that the traders would manipulate the treaty and circumvent the law in order to collect their debts. Whether those debts are valid or not, it was done in an underhanded manner that further accommodates the exploitation of the Dakota of Minnesota who, with the exception of but few, have no one to defend their interests."

"So you wish to help the Indians?" Mr. Sweetser asked.

"Not necessarily," I answered. "Rather, I oppose iniquity."

"Certainly you cannot battle with all iniquity," Mr. Sweetser pointed out.

"No," I agreed. "But this has struck me deeply and having traveled this far and having become so involved with the people and places, I have decided that I ought to do something where it seems no one else would."

"Then you wish to expose the fraud committed by the Company?" again prodded Mr. Sweetser.

"If you must articulate my purpose, then I suppose, yes," I replied. "I wish to expose the Traders' Paper for what it is; a method of fraud and deceit. And further, to ensure that the monies owed the Dakota are paid into their hands and not into the hands of Sibley and his men."

"That is a rather tall task," cautioned Mr. Sweetser.

"I believe you are right," I admitted.

"Well," replied Mr. Sweetser with a groan as he stood from his lumber perch, "You have come to the right man."

I did not reply, but looked at Mr. Sweetser inquisitively as a slight smile came across his face.

"There is something I must admit to you," he said in a whisper as he turned his shoulder and leaned close to me. "I believe I can trust you. You seem genuine enough. And besides, I need your help."

Mr. Sweetser paused and looked at me. I was curious and ready to listen.

"I have been sent here as a spy for the Ewing trading firm," he said shockingly. "I know about the Traders' Paper. I know about Sibley and his partners and the manner in which they manipulated treaty negotiations for their own purposes. I have been sent here to expose the Traders' Paper and prevent payment to those working for the Company. Furthermore, I am very much at odds with that fiend Mr. Sibley and it would please me greatly to ruin his plans."[54]

I was taken aback by Mr. Sweetser's admission. But I was also enlivened. I was told nothing could be done, but here was a man whose sole purpose was to prevent the wrongdoing that I had witnessed, and which had so provoked me.

"And you think I might be of assistance?" I asked as if to nudge Mr. Sweetser to continue.

---

[54] Along with Sweetser, Richard Chute was also a spy working for the Ewings. In a letter written to his employers, Chute noted, "Knowing how important it was to be friendly with the Commission I acted very circumspectly and laid low, giving them no clue on me or my claim. He later complained that all except Kenneth McKenzie and Louis Robert were "pinned on Sibley." Kane, *The Sioux Treaties*, 76.

"Yes," he answered with enthusiasm, but in a reserved manner as he looked around to ensure no one was observing our conversation. "Yes, I do. First of all, you witnessed the negotiations and you are familiar with many of those involved, both Indian and white. Also, I need a strong pair of hands and another set of legs. I am a newcomer to this region and I have few contacts and even fewer friends. A young man like you could get a lot of useful work done."

"Would I be paid?" I asked apprehensively, not wanting to belittle my motivations. "I have nearly exhausted my travel funds and if I am to remain in the region, I will need paid work."

"Yes, of course," replied Mr. Sweetser. "I believe several hundred dollars is not out of the question."[55]

I paused for a moment, though there was no doubt in my mind what I would do. I had come this far, and this unexpected opportunity was much too captivating to turn down.

"Very well," I responded as if accepting some egregious chore.

"Excellent, excellent!" proclaimed Mr. Sweetser with a nod of his head.

"What exactly is your plan?" I asked. "How do you intend on preventing payment to the traders?"

"A suitable question indeed," said Mr. Sweetser as he began pacing in front of me. "I have put a lot of thought toward the subject, it being the reason I have traveled here. First and foremost, I need to complete the construction of my trading post. Then we will need a boat."

"A boat?"

"Yes," quickly answered Mr. Sweetser. "The Company has every boat on the river employed. But I need one to get up to St. Paul and collect my goods. This is of utmost importance because I need those goods to establish influence with the Dakota Indians."

"Influence?" I was skeptical.

"If the Dakota are going to accept our help, we must first gain their trust," explained Mr. Sweetser as he continued pacing. "You see, I must earn from them power-of attorney in order to act on their behalf in regard to political and legal matters. Once I have earned their trust and been

---

[55] According to Fred Sibley, Sweetser obtained the services of Antoine Joseph Campbell and Henry Auger. Sweetser also admitted to hiring a half-breed named Pellon whom he paid $200. Ibid., 54, 44.

granted power-of-attorney, then I can listen to their grievances and submit their protest to Congress."

I was unaware of the entire process. Like the treaty before, it was becoming more complicated than I imagined.

"Without trust, we cannot be granted power-of-attorney, and without power-of-attorney, we cannot place anything before Congress," explained Mr. Sweetser noticing my hesitation. "Do you understand?"

"Yes, I believe I do," I answered.

"Good," said Mr. Sweetser with a smile.

"We will need an interpreter," I indicated.

"Ah," spurted Mr. Sweetser, "I have already been in contact with a Mr. Pellan, a young half-breed who says Mr. Sibley prevented the Indians from giving him $17,000 which he says they desired to do. He has connections among the upper chiefs and he will be of good service I am sure. As for the lower chiefs, I believe we can get Little Crow on our side. He is an influential chief and opposed to the whole arrangement."

"That is quite true," I added. "His presence alone is remarkable."

"Then you have met Chief Little Crow?" asserted Mr. Sweester enthusiastically.

"Yes," I replied. "He allowed me to draw his portrait."

"Very good," responded Mr. Sweetser. "With your help, the assistance of Mr. Pellan, the influence of Little Crow, and, as I am led to believe, the support of the agent Mr. McLean, I don't see how we could fail in exposing the deceit perpetrated by Sibley, Ramsey, and the traders. Congress will be forced to recognize the rightful protest of the Indians and then prevent payment to the traders."

Mr. Sweetser paused and sat back down. His expression changed to one of childlike delight.

"Oh, how exceptional," he said almost as if speaking only to himself. "If I can establish myself in this region, be assured I will knock Mr. Sibley's two hundred thousand dollar arrangement so high he will not get a glimpse of it until his congressional term expires."

And so the stage was set. Madison Sweetser sought to ruin Henry Sibley and his band of subjects while I sought some form of justice for the Dakota Indians and hope for the young boy Takoda. While we had separate motives, it appeared those motives would accomplish the same outcome.

However, I could not help but feel disturbed at my new found situation. Yes, it was true that Madison Sweetser could help the Dakota recover from the deception they happened upon, but there was something unnerving about the manner in which he carried himself. He seemed shameless. And his apparent thirst for retribution only amplified my uncertainty. But I was too caught up in my own cause to heed any ambivalence I may have felt about Mr. Sweetser or the plans he had in mind. Instead, I was ready to carry out those plans, perhaps losing sight of some of the wisdom I had gained throughout my long journey. Just as my new compatriot, Mr. Sweetser, I was ambitious and determined.

Old Trading House, Traverse des Sioux

Chapitre quatorze

"The government, being the guardian of the Indians, and the point to which they naturally turn for protection, should, it seems, interpose and prevent the carrying into effect so stupendous a fraud as the one attempted against the Sioux, and this done in a manner so subtle as to seemingly involve the government with them."
- Madison Sweetser to Luke Lea, January 19, 1852.

True to his commitment, Madison Sweetser showed himself to be diligent and hard-working. In the weeks following our initial meeting, Mr. Sweetser set out whole-heartedly to accomplish his goals. In just a matter of days we managed to complete his trading post and home. A few days later, with the addition of some hired help, we constructed a keel-boat and used it to collect and transport Mr. Sweetser's goods from St. Paul to the Traverse des Sioux. With these things done, Mr. Sweetser then set about establishing good relations with the separate bands of Dakota Indians. In order to accomplish this, he gave them many gifts such as blankets, leggings, and flour. The Dakota immediately saw him as a friend despite the fact that he was a stranger to the region. As Mr. Sweetser said to me, "These Indians are poor and hard run for provisions and will go anywhere to be fed." This, perhaps, was true and Mr. Sweetser used it to his advantage.

In addition to the Indians at the Traverse des Sioux, Mr. Sweetser walked many miles without a horse to meet with the surrounding bands, camping out and sleeping in Indian tepees. For those bands he could not reach by foot, he sent out runners to meet with those scattered over a two hundred mile wide region.

When Mr. Sweetser was not consulting with the Dakota or making some new deal, he sat silently for hours while writing correspondence. Late into the night he would write, sending news to his employer and business partners about their schemes and the progress he had made. He never shared with me the information in these letters, only that they were necessary in completing our mission.

All this I watched with patience and uncertainty. Immediately I came to respect Mr. Sweetser for his hard-work and dedication. It became easy to do as he asked because I did not see him with a single idle moment.[56] I sought, therefore, to assist him as much as I could, despite the menial nature of some of the tasks. I was indeed missing my home, and rather anxious to return to my endeavors as an artist. Whatever weariness I experienced, was set aside by Mr. Sweetser's clear and present purpose. Yet I had to remain skeptical. Could a man be so indefatigable for a cause that was less than noble? In this case, to ruin the plans of Henry Sibley and Minnesota's trading interests. Mr. Sweetser spoke of other traders, poor and destitute, whose rightful claims were ignored in favor of the American Fur Company's wrongful and inflated claims. Could this explain his motivation for working so tirelessly? Or was it he who stood to gain financially by his current ambitions? It was this notion that I suspected but which I fought to reject.

The day for which we had worked for finally came when the chiefs, headmen, and braves from wide and distant locations gathered. The meeting place was the officers' quarters at Fort Snelling. Here, in a long and narrow room and along a long and narrow table congregated twenty-one

---

[56] In his own words Sweetser writes, "I have not been idle here, in less than three weeks after I got into the Indian Country I had collected these people scattered over a country two hundred miles apart, with all the opposition the Company could give me to turn them back, without a horse or any other means than my legs . . ." Snyder, *The Treaty of Mendota*, 58.

Dakota chiefs, headmen, and braves. Some were familiar to me, some were not. All were dressed in layers, wearing calico shirts, deer skin leggings, and covered with thick buffalo robes. They adorned themselves with neat, but less than elaborate headdresses. Many of them had traveled a long distance at a key time in their hunting season thereby risking much merely by their participation in this meeting. But, the matters-at-hand were important for the well-being of their people.

Those non-Indians present included Mr. Sweetser, Agent Nathaniel McLean, and me. Agent McLean was of much assistance in establishing and organizing this meeting, as he seemed as much concerned as Mr. Sweetser regarding the actions of Sibley, Ramsey, and the traders. Also present at the meeting was Joseph Campbell, our capable interpreter, and Eli Pettijohn, the son-in-law to Mr. Prescott who I had met prior to the treaty negotiations. Finally, there was Alexander Wilkin, Minnesota's Territorial Secretary and a former officer in the United States army.[57] Little Crow, to my surprise, was not present.

Seated at the head of the table was Madison Sweetser who was to conduct the meeting. To his left was Agent McLean and to his right was Secretary Wilkin. The Dakota were seated alongside the table all the way to the end. Along the perimeter was Mr. Pettijohn and me. Standing near the head of the table was Joseph Campbell, ready to translate all necessary information.[58]

"Chiefs and Headmen of the Sisseton, Wahpeton, Mdewakanton, and Wahpekute bands," began Mr. Sweetser in his somewhat high and nasal voice, "I wish to extend my gratitude for your coming here today. We know . . ."

Mr. Sweetser paused and looked to the interpreter. Mr Sweetser appeared a little unsure of himself. Although he had spent weeks conducting business with the Dakota, it was still obvious that he was a newcomer to the region.

---

[57] This meeting took place on December 6, 1851. It did not include Frank Blackwell Mayer who had departed St. Paul on August 23, 1851. He is inserted here for the purposes of this novel.

[58] There is no documentation of exactly what took place at this meeting, only the papers that were signed as a result. What follows then, is fictionalized to my best understanding of what might have happened.

He continued, "We know you have traveled a great distance to be here and at great risk to your bands' prosperity over the coming winter season."

Mr. Sweetser paused again. The Dakota, as was usually the case, sat silently and at full attention.

"But we have discovered a matter of utmost importance and we wish to make the matter known. Doubtless by now you have been made aware of the deceit conducted against you by traders at the signing of the treaty. You have learned that one of the documents that was signed by you, one which was never read nor explained, but which was a solemn oath arranging that you would pay your creditors directly from the hand money stipulated in the treaty. At the time of signing, this document did not include a list of creditors or their claim amounts. It was a deceitful act perpetrated in an underhanded fashion in an attempt to defraud you of the monies promised you in the terms of the treaty."

Mr. Sweetser paused, apparently feeling proud of himself as he held his chin up and peered across the room.

"Though I have not been in this country for long," continued Mr. Sweetser, "you have come to know me, and you know that I am a good man. I have seen your unfortunate condition and I have provided for you beef, corn, blankets, powder, and other provisions. I am a friend to the Dakota. Your land is beautiful and I do not wish to see it taken from you without proper compensation. Your people are kind and welcoming and I want to see you in prosperity. That is also why we have gathered here. Evil men have seen what is yours and have sought to take it. We here," as he held his hands out at the non-Indians present, "wish to prevent such wrongs. We wish to notify your Great Father what his children have done so that your Great Father can stop it from happening and punish those involved. But just knowing these things will not stop the wrong from taking place. We have gathered so that we can put your objections in writing. Your written protest will expose the deceit that has occurred and ensure your money is paid into your hands. Be assured that your Great Father would not desire his red children to be wronged."

Mr. Sweetser stopped here. Again, he looked pleased with himself as he looked over the contemplative Dakota. A few moments passed when a Sisseton named Mazekutemani, called Little Paul by the whites, decided to speak.

"When we signed paper giving our lands," began Mazekutemani, who was one of the few Dakota who spoke English. "We not know what we were doing. We were hungry, like wolves crying at the moon. We know only that if we sign paper we be given food. Our white Fathers they say to us that we be given food to fill our bellies and blankets to warm our skin. That our Great Father would protect our people for many seasons to come. That is why we signed his paper. Why would we sign a paper that gives us things and at same time sign a paper that takes things away? We did not know what we were signing. We did not know we gave our money away, back to the white men who we consider friends. We only sign treaty twice. This is what we believed. That is all that I have to say."

"Thank you, Mazekutemani," said Agent McLean. "We understand that you believe you were only signing a second copy of the treaty. We are glad you have told us this so that we might tell your Great Father."

"I desire to be heard," said Red Iron, the chief at the Traverse des Sioux and a man I had come to know and like. "When we made the treaty with our white friend Luke Lea, we were told that he represented our Great Father. Mr. Lea said that he speaks directly to our Great Father and that he knows his wishes. If this is true, what good is it to send our objections to our Great Father who knew all along what we were signing? That is what I desire to know."

"I have heard you, Red Iron," replied Mr. Sweetser, "and I understand your confusion. You are right that the Honorable Luke Lea is a representative of your Great Father. But he did not play a role in the signing of the second document. This was done separately from the treaty and done against the wishes of your Great Father. Your credits and debts are done in private where your Great Father cannot see them. He trusts that his white children are fair and just when dealing with his red children, but when they are not he wishes to know. Though it was done at the same time and in the same meeting place, it was done in private apart from your Great Father. This was a part of the deception committed against you. They wished for you to believe that you were signing a paper created by your Great Father who you know wants you to prosper. That is why we must tell your Great Father so that he can prevent this from happening."

There was a long silence as apparently no one wished to speak. Finally, Mazekutemani took his turn, this time standing from his spot at the table.

"I speak for all chiefs and braves here," he said, directing his words to Mr. Sweetser. "We thank you for good things you give us. Our people are much in want. We wait for promises of the Great Father. He has much and we have little. But every time the sun rises and falls again we still wait. Nothing comes. The Great Spirit told us that a strange friend was to come among us soon to take care of us.[59] We believe this is you. You have seen our poor condition and give us food and cloth. You are kind to us. We are ready to call you friend."

Mr. Sweetser sat silently at the head of the table absorbing the praise and adoration he was receiving. He must have been glad to have so quickly earned the Dakotas' trust.

"Because we call you friend," continued Mazekutemani, "we desire that you help us. We are like children when they fight with wooden sticks. We talk to whites but our words have no result. We do not understand the wisdom of the Great Father or his many children. But you know better. You will show the Great Father we have been wronged and he will listen. You will show the Great Father we are hungry and he will feed us. I speak for all."

Mazekutemani sat and looked to the three white men at the head of the table awaiting their response. There was a brief hesitation as the men conferred with each other. Then, Secretary Wilkin turned, facing the Dakota and began to speak.

"We thank you for your kind words and we understand your request," began Secretary Wilkin who was a small but serious looking gentlemen. "I believe it is right for Mr. Sweetser to accept your call for help and assist you in recovering your monies. To do so, we have prepared for you two documents that must be signed by all here present," explained Secretary Wilkin. "The first such document gives Mr. Sweetser power-of-attorney which is written authorization to act on your behalf as you have requested him to do. This will allow Mr. Sweetser the legal right to make your objections known before your Great Father and his lawmakers. The second document is a written protest expressing to your Great Father that you were wronged. The protest will resolve that when you signed the traders' document, you believed that you were signing a second copy of the treaty

---

[59] This was reported by Sweetser himself in a letter dated November 17, 1851. Snyder, *The Treaty of Mendota*, 53.

and that this Traders' Paper, as it has become known, was never read nor explained to you in open council. Do you now understand and will you sign these documents?"

It seemed evident that the Dakota would agree and sign the documents, but we waited quietly as the interpreter tried to adequately relay the information. The Dakota appeared stoic and emotionless, as was often the case. They looked at each other, nodding in agreement. Red Iron was the last to nod as he waved his hand forward indicating that they ought to accept and sign the papers.

"Yes," answered Mazekutemani. "We wish this to be done."

"Very well," replied Secretary Wilkin, "let the documents now be read aloud for you to hear."

The first document read was the power-of-attorney. It was a brief but complicated document filled with legal jargon. It must have been difficult for the Dakota to understand, but in general terms it was an agreement authorizing Madison Sweetser to act on behalf of the Dakota nation in all legal matters. The second document read was the Dakota Protest.

"We, the undersigned, chiefs, headmen, and braves of the Sisseton, Wahpeton, Mdewakanton, and Wahpekute bands of the Dakota nation," began the interpreter in a slow and deliberate manner. "Being a majority of said chiefs, headmen, and braves, and as such fully competent to transact national business."

Mr. Campbell, the interpreter, went on like this, slowly reading the political language of the document. Essentially, the Dakota protest was an acknowledgement that the Indians had signed an obligation to pay their traders, but that they had not intended to sign such an obligation. The Dakota, through their protest, argued that their signatures were obtained through fraud and deceit. In other words, they were tricked. The protest, which was directed toward the President of the United States, went on to ensure that the Dakota wished to pay their debts, but to do so in their own time and in their own manner. They ended their protest by appealing to the good nature of the President for his timely aid and protection. The entire document seemed to me a suitable request that the United States Government would be hard pressed to deny.[60]

---

[60] See Appendix A

The protest and power-of-attorney were read and understood and having been satisfactory to all Dakota present, were signed with the mark of an "X" by twenty-one chiefs, headmen, and braves. It was also signed in witness by, Joseph Campbell, Eli Pettijohn, Alexander Wilkin and me.[61] The Dakota shook hands with Mr. Sweetser, Agent McLean, and Secretary Wilkin and then peacefully exited, returning to their distant homes.

"A successful day," I remarked to Mr. Sweetser once his business had been concluded.

"Quite," he replied with a smile. "We have done much work to realize this day and our work has rewarded us. I must wholeheartedly thank you for your assistance."

"It has been my pleasure," I said humbly, "but I must ask, why was Commissioner Lea never indicted as a part of the protest? He seems to me nearly as responsible as the traders through his manners of persuasion."

"That may be, but he represented the interests of the government," explained Mr. Sweetser. "We wished to thoroughly separate his conduct from the conduct of the traders as a method of more deeply implicating the private interests involved."

"I see," I said, not at all surprised by the use of such a method. "What happens next?"

"We wait," answered Mr. Sweetser succinctly. "The protest will be sent to Washington where it will be presented before Congress during the ratification debates. If the treaty is not ratified the point is moot and there is no money to be had one way or another. If the treaty is ratified, as I expect it to be, Congress will have to consider the Indian protest and determine whether the claims should be paid directly to the traders or directly to the chiefs. Our hope, of course, is that the treaty is ratified and that the money is paid into the hands of the chiefs."

"Our hope, indeed," I said softly, and for a moment realized the delicate balance of all people and things involved. Everyone wanted something out of this treaty deal, some rightful, some not, but all believing themselves

---

[61] The paper was not signed by Frank Mayer, but was instead signed by a man named W.F. Masterson. He appears to have been a notary republic for Ramsey County.

entitled. The results would not be left to chance, they were left to interest. Where the interests lay the money would follow.

"We wait."[62]

---

[62] During this time Sweetser did not remain in Minnesota, but went down the Mississippi to Galena, Illinois. In a letter to his employer he wrote, "My reasons for leaving St. Pauls at this time, I had established my posts, done all I could with the Indians for the present, the Wahpekutes being entirely out of reach on a buffalo hunt nothing could be done with them this winter. My stay in Minnesota this winter could not advance our interests at Washington or here where I could communicate with you much may be accomplished." Snyder, *The Treaty of Mendota*, 62.

Chapitre quinze

"It is my opinion that he came here to do all the evil in his power."
  - Duncan Kennedy to Fred Sibley speaking about Madison Sweetser, November 30, 1851

"You wish us to pay how much!" said Hercules Dousman, who sounded shocked.

"Certainly thirty thousand is not too much to ask in the face of your two hundred ten thousand," replied Madison Sweetser in a vile manner. "With this payment I will pull back all opposition to your traders' agreement."

All of the sudden my heart sank. Heavy as a rock, down to the pit of my stomach and I felt sick.

"You detestable and vile fiend," accused Dousman callously. "You are making powerful enemies for yourself."

"How dare you," retorted Sweetser. "I have done no more wrong than you and your Company. You are anxious to get your money and I am only asking for a piece."

The two were unaware of my presence. Sweetser and I had remained in St. Paul several weeks following the signing of the protest. On this particular evening I had returned to find Mr. Sweetser in an attempt to bribe Hercules Dousman, a trader from the Company and one of Sibley's main men. This was not a stunning revelation, but one which I found to be extremely disappointing. Were there no decent men in this treaty deal?

"A piece!" replied Dousman indignantly. "The traders of my company will never agree to pay for their own money, or certainly not to the amount of thirty thousand."

"Of course they will," countered Sweetser. "I know you are anxious to discourage and prevent opposition to your claims being paid. I have already gained power-of-attorney and I have sent a written protest to Congress. If I don't pull back my opposition, I can assure you that you and the Company will not see a dime of your claims. And besides," continued Sweetser, "I know Sibley has authorized you to conciliate me and my faction. Franklin Steele has come to me recently looking for a compromise."[63]

"That may be so," responded Dousman, "but we are more confident than ever that your opposition will fail. That old dotard of an agent fears Sibley and Ramsey and has already refused to certify your words. Also, we have bribed several of your former cohorts and led them onto our side. They are poor and it did not take much. Finally, we have nabbed, through bribery, your key Indian, Little Crow. Our influence is much greater than yours and we no longer fear your opposition."[64]

"Villains!" admonished Sweetser. "You are all villains. You will regret not making this deal."

"And you will regret coming to this region and tampering with our claims," replied Dousman in a relaxed manner seeing that he had the upper hand. "You may have gained temporary influence, but ours is deeper and more lasting."

---

[63] In a letter written to Pierre Chouteau Jr. and Company, Henry Sibley wrote, "I have from a confidential source that the Ewings who make it a point to intermeddle with other people' affairs, are now engaged with others in this Territory, in a scheme to have the papers signed by the Indians declared null and void." He went on to write, "We have opposition of a formidable character to encounter, as I have had from the commencement, and to overcome it at this crisis by all proper means, must be the endeavor of us all . . . I have authorized Mr. Dousman to conciliate this faction, even at a small sacrifice to ourselves, as I feel that any strong demonstration from the Territory against the Treaties would do more to defeat them, than if coming from any other quarter." Ibid., 47.

[64] In a letter to Fred Sibley, Joseph Lue reported that Louis Robert "says that $500 will bring Scott on our side." It appears that among the traders there was much bribery going on in order to gain support for one faction or another. Ibid., 54.

"Be gone, you scamp," demanded a distraught and frustrated Madison Sweetser.

Hercules Dousman coolly exited the quarters. I could not avoid him as he passed in the hallway, chuckling to himself.

I was frightened. Having learned of the diabolical intentions of Mr. Sweetser, I felt like a fool. I hated to think that I had assisted this man when he was merely a profiteer just like the majority I had met in the treaty business. And now I had no choice but to confront him.

I walked into the room to see Mr. Sweetser with his head in his hands, much like the first day I had met him at the Traverse. There were candles lit on both sides of the room, giving him dual shadows that moved with the flickering of the light. He looked tired and worn out.

"Upon my return to the Traverse des Sioux," I said calmly, "I will gather my things and return to Baltimore."

"Are you so naive?" said Mr. Sweetser still seething from his prior encounter.

"I suppose that I am," I said discontentedly. "Although I knew you wished to foil the Company, I thought somehow this was your method of helping the Dakota."

"Listen to me," clarified Mr. Sweetser. "That money will find its way into the hands of white men one way or another. I am merely doing business here. You just do not understand how frontier business works. It is unprincipled—only the keen survive. And in any case, you must have known what you were getting into when I told you I was a spy."

"My judgement was clouded by my fixation for justice," I replied, realizing the sad truth of the matter.

"Then you have no idea, do you?" Mr. Sweetser said plainly.

"No idea? Regarding what?," I returned, apprehensive of what I might learn.

"This goes far deeper than a few bribes," answered Mr. Sweetser, who, having been found out, had nothing to lose by confessing. "The real reason I sought to deny those claims was so that the Company money would become my money. I have already racked up my own claims amounting to fifteen thousand dollars which I intend to mark up at forty-five thousand dollars," expounded Sweetser, looking shameless from his seat before me. "Once the money is denied the traders and paid into the hands of the

Indians, it will very quickly find its way into my hands. Because the Dakota owe me and they trust me, they will not hesitate to acquire their needs through me."

"It was always about exploitation then."

"Of course," replied Sweetser. "Not just exploitation of the Indian money, but a complete takeover of the Company. First I will buy all the land at Traverse des Sioux. When the treaty is ratified and the settlers come pouring in I will become rich through real estate profits. Then I will depose that old fool McLean and replace him with my own man, Captain Murray who is now agent at Lake Superior. He will be more favorable to my interests and the Ewing firm. With this I will have enough influence to begin appointing all officers in the territory, and then who knows—I may even be able to remove the Governor and get myself appointed in his place," he said fiendishly.[65]

"You are no better, you are no different," I replied calmly, now feeling numb inside. "You have sought to take the Indian money and exploit the system in the same manner as the men before you. You are merely replacing them with yourself. In either case, the result for the Dakota is the same, and I find that heartbreaking."

"The result for the Dakota is inevitable," asserted Sweetser. "It is time you learned that and got out of the way."

"You are right," I affirmed, feeling more dejected than at any point in my life. "You are absolutely right."

I departed Mr. Sweetser in no mood to argue or fight. Nothing I said, I decided, would matter now. I would return to the Traverse, collect my meager belongings and continue my life in Baltimore—something I ought to have done months ago.

---

[65] Trader Duncan Kennedy complained, "He (Sweetser) not only intends to manage the money given to the Indians to pay their lawful debts but to appoint officers in the Territory, the next thing he will try will be to remove the Governor and get himself appointed in his place." Ibid., 57.

I arrived at the Traverse des Sioux a few days later to find a bit of a commotion. About two hundred Dakota had gathered and they were preparing for a confrontation.

"What is happening?" I asked one of the half-breeds?

"The treaty has been ratified," he answered, "and soon Ramsey will be here to obtain receipt for the money owed the traders."

But the protest, I thought to myself. Perhaps it had not yet been received. Perhaps it had been ignored. In either case, with the ratification of the treaty the Dakota were to receive their first payment which was meant to assist with removal and one year subsistence. But a majority of that money was expected to go straight into the hands of the traders in accordance with the Traders' Paper. This, it appeared, the Upper Bands of Dakota were unwilling to accept.[66]

A few days later a boat arrived with Governor Ramsey, Agent McLean, and Hugh Tyler. Also on board was Madison Sweetser. Rather than take the boat back to St. Paul and then down to St. Louis, I decided to remain at Traverse des Sioux in order to see the outcome. I had come this far and I had truly wanted to know if the Dakota would be paid their money. Takoda's words also echoed in my head—*Don't give up.*

What Governor Ramsey and the others found when they arrived was a wild and turbulent setting. Some of the Dakota, led by Chief Red Iron, had formed a "soldiers' lodge" thereby invoking martial law among them. Traditionally, a soldiers' lodge regulated hunting efforts within a village, but they could also be formed to preserve Dakota tribal traditions. The soldiers' lodge harassed Governor Ramsey, hooting and hollering, demanding their hand money be paid to them in open council.

But not all of the Dakota acted in this manner. Some were peaceful and calm, showing no signs of dissatisfaction. Apparently, they had it in their minds to accept and pay the claims as they were.

Whether or not that was the case, it did not seem to matter. Over the days following Governor Ramey's arrival, the soldiers' lodge moved

---

[66] In reality, ratification was not secured until June 23, 1851. And even at that time it was not confirmed due to amendments made to the treaties. The confrontation at the Traverse des Sioux did occur, but not until November of 1852. For more on the ratification of the treaties and the debt repayment that followed see Folwell's, *A History of Minnesota*, Volume 1, pages 290 – 304.

between camps yelling, flourishing their weapons and discharging their guns. They created an atmosphere of excitement and in doing so, suspended the transaction of any and all business whatsoever.

I could not help but notice that the soldiers held their meetings at the house of Mr. Sweetser who was apparently the organizer of the Dakota resistance. I believed it was Sweetser who was compelling the soldiers to act in such a manner. Governor Ramsey himself, who so graciously allowed me to stay with him and his faction, said, "The Indians are being duped by the bad advice of a sinister man." Truthfully, I no longer knew who to believe. But, it was true that Red Iron changed his tone since we first met, when he spoke of accepting the winds of change. Knowing what I knew now of Mr. Sweetser, perhaps Governor Ramsey was right.

Because of the excited atmosphere that was not conducive to business, Governor Ramsey called upon Captain James Monroe, Jr., and a detachment of sixty soldiers from Fort Snelling to relieve the situation. Upon arriving, the soldiers posted themselves along the road leading to Governor Ramsey's station. The troops were instructed to allow only one visitor at a time and any visitor was to be accompanied by four guards.

Before long, Red Iron, accompanied by Madison Sweetser and about forty armed Dakota soldiers, came down toward Ramsey's station and attempted to pass the troops outside. Red Iron was told he could go through along with one to four of his men, but no more. The soldiers' lodge loudly refused to permit this. They insisted on passing the troops but were denied on every attempt. Then they began raising their weapons and shouting their defiant war-whoop. A violent collision, it seemed, was imminent.

"We will not speak with you now," shouted Captain Monroe. "You may return when you are more fit to negotiate. Until then we have nothing to discuss."

The Dakota, although thoroughly excited, accepted Captain Monroe's words and dispersed. However, they maintained their wild and violent atmosphere by riding quickly through camp and firing their guns in the air. For now, violence was avoided. But even so, I was anxious and afraid. I never expected to be a part of any war or outbreak.

"We must take decisive action to break up the soldier's lodge," demanded Governor Ramsey to his advisors. "This is the only way for peaceful council to be opened."

"How can we do that?" asked one of the advisors.

"We will withhold the funds we came to deliver," explained Governor Ramsey confidently. "Then we will call upon Red Iron to discuss permanently abandoning the soldier's lodge."

All the men were in agreement.

An officer was sent to Red Iron requesting his presence before the Governor, but he did not come. Then an interpreter was sent, making the same request, but again he did not come. Rather, Red Iron was seen enjoying a feast with his warriors, apparently unwilling or uninterested in meeting with the Governor. At this point Governor Ramsey decided to send a large group of soldiers to detain and arrest Red Iron. Furthermore, he deposed Red Iron of his position as chief.

I was sad to see all that had taken place, but nonetheless these actions had their desired effect. It caused the immediate dissolution of the soldiers' lodge and a request by the Dakota chiefs and braves for the immediate release of Red Iron and the opening of peaceful discussions.

It was about noon the day following the arrest of Red Iron when a council was organized. The council was held out in the open for all to attend. There must have been more than two hundred Dakota, standing anxiously around the center of the council. Mixed throughout the crowd were also twenty or so white men, all traders and officials. At the center was Governor Ramsey appearing undaunted in his suit, vest, and necktie. Seated opposite him was Red Iron, the normally submissive chief who, along with Madison Sweetser, had incited the previous few days of commotion.

Governor Ramsey raised his hand in the air to indicate that all was ready. The crowd became silent awaiting the opening of this important council—this council that would determine once in for all what would happen with a large portion of the treaty money.[67]

---

[67] This council was reported by historian Isaac V.D. Heard who states that it was obtained from an educated half-breed, who was present during the scene described. Isaac V.D. Heard, *History of the Sioux War and Massacres of 1862 and 1863*, (New York: Harper and Brothers, 1865). 35-40.

"Red Iron, what excuse have you for not coming to the council when I sent for you?" asked Governor Ramsey with the aid of an interpreter.

Red Iron rose to his feet, his blanket draped across his shoulders and wrapped around his chest, appearing stern and defiant.

"I started to come, but your braves drove me back," he answered coolly.

"What excuse have you for not coming the second time I sent for you?"

"No other excuse than I have given you," Red Iron said standing firm in his defense.

"At the treaty I thought you a good man," said Governor Ramsey recognizing Red Iron's defiance. "But since, you have acted badly, and I am disposed to break you—*I do break you*."

"You break me!" replied Red Iron angrily. "My people made me a chief. My people love me. I will still be their chief. I have done nothing wrong."

"Why then did you get your braves together, and march around here for the purpose of intimidating other chiefs and prevent their coming to council?"

"I did not get my braves together," Red Iron answered quickly. "They got together themselves to prevent boys going to council to be made chiefs to sign papers, and to prevent single chiefs going to council at night to be bribed to sign papers for money we never got. We want all our people to go to council together, so that we can all know what is done."

"Why did you attempt to come to council with your braves when I had forbidden your braves coming to council?" asked Governor Ramsey.

"You invited the chiefs only, and would not let the braves come too," answered Red Iron, still appearing cool and defiant. "This is not the way we have been treated before; this is not according to our customs, for, among Dakotas, chiefs and braves go to council together, and know what was done, and so we might all understand the papers, and know what we were signing. When we signed the treaty the traders threw a blanket over our faces, and darkened our eyes, and made us sign papers which we did not understand, and which were not explained or read to us. We want our Great Father at Washington to know what has been done."

"Your Great Father has sent me to represent him, and what I say is what he says," responded Governor Ramsey sounding rather displeased. "He wants you to pay your old debts in accordance with the paper you signed when the treaty was made, and to leave that money in my hands to pay these debts. If you refuse to do that I will take the money back."

Red Iron laughed. "You can take the money back. We sold our land to you, and you promised to pay us. If you don't give us the money I will be glad, for we will have our land back. That paper was not interpreted or explained to us. We are told it gives about three hundred boxes of our money to some of the traders. We don't think we owe them so much. We want to pay all our debts. We want our Great Father to send three good men here to tell us how much we do owe, and whatever they say we will pay, and," he said pointing to the surrounding Dakota, "that is what all these braves say. Our chiefs and all our people say this."

"Ho, ho!" responded the crowd of Dakota Indians.

"That cannot be done," said Governor Ramsey who was clearly losing patience with the way the council was going. "You owe more than your money will pay, and I am ready now to pay your annuity and no more. When you are ready to receive it the agent will pay you."

"We will receive our annuity, but we will sign no paper for anything else," said Red Iron disregarding all the Governor had just said. "The snow is on the ground and we have been waiting a long time to get our money. We are poor, you have plenty. Your fires are warm, your tepees keep out the cold. We have nothing to eat. Our hunting season has passed. A great many of our people are sick for being hungry. We may die because you won't pay us. We may die, but if we do, we will leave our bones on the ground, that our Great Father may see where his Dakota children died. We are very poor. We have sold our hunting grounds and the graves of our fathers. We have sold our own graves. We have no place to bury our own dead, and you will not pay us the money for our lands."

Governor Ramsey did not reply. He sat silently, while everyone around him was awaiting his response. It was clear that as long as Red Iron stood in the way, the Dakota would not sign the receipt for their debts. Further discussion would be fruitless.

"Take him into custody," Governor Ramsey demanded, and then quickly exited the council grounds.

The troops from Fort Snelling moved quickly through the crowd, protecting Governor Ramsey and detaining Red Iron. The chief did not resist, but went willingly as a soldier clung to each side of him.

I was surprised and saddened. I knew Red Iron had a calm and patient spirit, but that he now fought for what was right. I watched him go, surrounded by soldiers, and I wished it hadn't turned out this way.

The crowd of Dakota reacted with indignation, shrieking and yelling and beating their chests. They did not attempt to interfere with the arrest of Red Iron, but instead gathered as one immense unit, raising their weapons and showing their discontent. Suddenly they turned from the council grounds and ran toward their various camps. All the while they continued to call out their war cry. Soon they would return and when they did, they would be ready for war.

Chapitre seize

> *"In completing the memoranda of a journey which, I trust, has added to my experience of life, fostered a taste for the beautiful, and developed a stronger feeling of nationality, I have endeavored to give an unexaggerated statement of the scenes I have witnessed and I hope I shall not be accused of having told 'A Traveler's Tale.'"*
> — Frank Blackwell Mayer

Seeing that their hereditary chief had been imprisoned once more, and that their payment had been withheld, the Dakota collected their weapons and applied their war paint. Like bees to a hive they swarmed their camps and tepees getting themselves ready for a fight. It would only be minutes, I feared, before certain catastrophe.

I ran to Governor Ramsey's station to try and stop this seemingly inevitable conflict.

"Governor Ramsey, sir," I beckoned as I reached the station. "Can't you see that imprisoning Red Iron will lead to violence? The Dakota are preparing themselves for war as we speak."

"Let them come," said Governor Ramsey impassively.

"Should we not try and spare our own soldiers from a deadly fight," I pleaded. "Simply release the prisoner and they will cease violent resistance."

"I cannot bow to the insolence of a few misguided Indians," argued Governor Ramsey. "If I release Red Iron, I leave Mr. Sweetser and his fellow conspirators masters of the field, at full liberty to pursue their machinations to obtain possession of the fund plainly set apart to pay the Indian debts contracted prior to the treaty. I am determined otherwise, to make the annuity payment, with the receipt for debts owed, at all hazards, as well as maintain, at every risk, the authority of the government. Therefore I say let them come."[68]

I had no response. Whether Governor Ramsey was right or wrong, he was firm in his conviction.

Suddenly the shrieks and war-whoops of the Dakota warriors could be heard coming near the station. So too could the commands of Captain Monroe shouting to his men, "Steady!" "Hold your line!"

I stepped outside to see forty to fifty warriors, firmly resolved to do battle or force the release of their cherished leader. A sudden tinge of fear enveloped me like a wave splashing against my body. Out in front was Lean Bear, the principal brave of Red Iron's band. The Dakota warriors halted their march about one hundred feet from the U.S. soldiers. Lean Bear, a large man with broad shoulders, thick arms, and powerful legs, removed his blanket and brandished his knife. He turned to his Dakota brethren and began recounting to them the war-like deeds of their imprisoned chief.

"Ho, ho!" they shouted with each statement Lean Bear made on account of Red Iron's brave exploits.

Then he turned, and for all to hear he began an impassioned call to war.

"Dakotas," he shouted with his knife raised high in his hand. "The big men are here. They have got Mazasha in a pen like a dog. They mean to kill him for not letting the white men cheat us out of our lands and the money our Great Father sent us."

"Ho, ho!" shouted the warriors with ferocity.

"Dakotas, must we starve like buffalo in the snow? Shall we let our blood freeze like the little streams? Or shall we make the snow red with the blood of the white braves."

"Ho, ho!" they answered with even more ferocity than before.

"Dakotas, the blood of your fathers talk to you from the graves where we stand. Their spirits come up into your arms and make you strong. I am

---

[68] Governor Ramsey shared his actions and expressed his opinions while on trial during the Ramsey Investigation. 33 Congress, 1 Session, *Senate Executive Documents,* no. 61, 328-331.

glad of it. Tonight the blood of the white man shall run like water in the rain, and Mazasha shall be with his people"

"Ho, ho!"

"Dakotas, be ready and I will lead you against the Long Knives and the big men who have come to cheat us, and take away our lands, and put us in a pen for not helping them rob our women and children. Be not afraid, Dakotas. We are stronger than the whites. We fight for what is right. We fight for what is ours. Be ready and I will lead you to victory!"

The warriors shrieked and yelled in an uproar of excitement and pandemonium which literally shook the earth below my feet.

"Take aim!" commanded Captain Monroe as the troops lowered their bayonets from their shoulders and pointed them straight ahead.

I looked to Governor Ramsey who seemed unmoved and unwilling to step in and mediate the situation. But something had to be done. Somehow I had to prevent such futile and meaningless disaster.

I was scared and so I waited, hoping for someone to step forth and stop this. No one came. Suddenly I remembered young Takoda. I remembered his grief and sadness. I remembered him telling me not to give up. And I remembered the words his father gave him—*Be strong but gentle, brave but cautious, firm and true.* I had to do something. I owed it to Takoda.

"Stop!" I shouted. "Stop!" I shouted again as I raised my hands and ran to the open space between the Dakota warriors and the U.S. soldiers.

Everyone became silent. With their weapons still raised, they looked to me.

I turned my head from side to side, ensuring that I had the attention of everyone present. In that moment, surrounded by armed and angry combatants, I did not feel afraid. I felt a complete absence of fear. I was tired of everything and was no longer apprehensive about what I did or didn't know—about what I did or didn't understand. I sought once and for all an end to the treachery, dishonesty, and miscommunication.

"Nothing can be gained from fighting," I said, not pleading but declaring.

One of the mixed-breeds, seeing my noble purpose, came out and assisted in translating my words.

"Are your people not enough in want," I said directing my words toward Lean Bear. "If you fight now, you will receive nothing, and there

Ceding Contempt

will be no one to spare your people's suffering over the long winter months. But if you lay down your weapons you will receive payment, and though not in its entirety, it will save your people much hardship."

"If we accept this thievery today," replied Lean Bear, "there will be nothing to stop the thievery tomorrow."

"Ho, ho!" called the warriors showing their support once again.

I knew Lean Bear was right, but I also knew it would not matter. No good could come from fighting now. I paused, collecting my thoughts. Then, with a long and deep breath, I began to speak.

"I have learned much since arriving to this region in June," I said, speaking spontaneously and from the heart. "I have learned that this is indeed a majestic land overflowing with beauty, from its dazzling sunsets, to its ferocious thunderstorms, it is magnificent in all ways. I've learned also of its abundance in resources such as the indomitable forests, the mighty and useful rivers, the unending prairies, and the rich and fertile soil. For in this land there is much to be desired and much to be sought after. Whether it is the French fur trader who travels thousands of miles to share in its bounty, or the Eastern pioneer who wishes to start a new life and raise a family, or the caring missionary who desires only to spread his faith, his wisdom and his moral prudence, or the Dakota Indians who merely seek to protect their cherished homeland and their beloved culture, all have come here seeking something. But this will always be the case. Not just today, but forever. People will always seek the bounty and beauty of Minnesota—Mni Sota Makoce—the land where the waters reflect the clouds. Try as you might, but you will never keep them out. And no matter what happens here today, this place is bound to be a prosperous, flourishing country with many varieties of peoples and cultures all seeking their own goals while all contributing to a brilliant and flourishing collective."

I paused and took a breath.

"I mean no disrespect to the Dakota nation and I sympathize with you over the manner and methods in which your homeland has been taken from you without fair and just compensation. I have learned more from the Dakota people about beauty, patience, simplicity, and connectedness than my entire life beforehand. I stand here now with the utmost respect and admiration for a people and culture I once thought to be only a thing of stories, poems, and legends—a relic. I have seen your suffering but more importantly I have discovered your gracefulness. When the Great Father asked you to cede your land it meant more to you. You were ceding not just your land, but your lifeblood. The Earth and everything in it is sacred to you, it is your own family. But as we stand here today, you are ceding contempt. I ask you, do not let it come to this. No matter what they've taken from you, they will always take more. Guard your people, not through violence, but through your willingness to endure. Make certain that when all of this is over, and when all of us have passed from this land, that your people are still here and that your stories are still told. Here, where the Dakota have always been, and where the Dakota shall always remain."

The grounds were silent. Both parties and all observers were still. It was so quiet that the gentle flowing water of the Minnesota River could be heard a half mile away. Then, breaking the absolute silence, the troops from Fort Snelling began lowering their weapons. In the same manner, Lean Bear sheathed his knife and his soldiers put away their tomahawks, arrows, and rifles. Without a word, the Dakota, both soldiers and bystanders turned and walked away. The troops breathed a sigh of relief and stood at ease. I lowered my head and closed my eyes, exhausted from emotion. War had been averted. The pain and the suffering was real. The confusion, deceit and wrongdoing—it was all real. But honesty prevailed, if only for this moment. I had been strong but gentle, brave but cautious, firm and true. I did not give up. I had made a difference and I had earned a spot in this history. I had earned a spot in Minnesota's most significant historical event.

Epilogue

I don't have a happy ending for you. After the near outbreak of violence things remained the same at the Traverse des Sioux. Governor Ramsey continued to deny payment while the Dakota refused to sign the receipt for their debts. It should be known that this receipt represented no small sum. It relinquished $210,000 to the traders out of a total of $275,000 that was to be paid to the Upper Bands. In the days following the near outbreak, the only attempt at negotiation was a revised document written by a half-breed employed by Madison Sweetser. This document was intended to be a compromise which cut the amount to be paid the traders down to $70,000. In order to do this, Sweetser eliminated many of the claimants while significantly reducing the claim amounts. At the same time Mr. Sweetser included his own claim of $10,000. Needless to say, Governor Ramsey rejected this document which he called a "manifest concoction of fraud and roguery."

Eventually the Dakota withdrew their resistance. Many of them had come hundreds of miles and winter had nearly set in. By striking a deal of sorts, Governor Ramsey agreed to release several Dakota who had been previously imprisoned as well as promising the Upper Bands large presents. With this, eleven chiefs and braves were found willing to cease opposition and sign the receipt thereby paying the traders directly out of the annuity funds. Of the eleven signees, only one had actually been present at and signed the treaty of July 23, 1851. The money that remained was distributed among the bands, and so all departed, leaving the Traverse des Sioux quiet once more.

As for Madison Sweetser, things did not end well. When the Dakota signed the receipt for their payments, they also effectively annulled all previous power-of-attorney, awarding it thereafter to Governor Ramsey. Sweetser was left with no leverage and no way to recoup his losses. With the money paid to the traders, there wasn't much else to go around. Furthermore, he had lost much of the trust he had once earned. Red Iron even admitted that he had been badly advised by a white man. The trader Hercules Dousman summed up Mr. Sweetser's condition in a letter he wrote to Henry Sibley in which Dousman stated, "He (Sweetser) looks and feels used up so much so that I did not have the heart to put my thumb to my nose as I had promised when I met him. He is bound for Washington and says that he will never cease 'til he exposes the villainous misapplications of the Sioux money."[69]

True to that statement, Madison Sweetser did not give up after the payment was made to the traders. Despite receiving no pecuniary awards for his efforts, he felt compelled to prosecute, on a national level, those responsible for the Traders' Paper. Shortly after the receipts had been signed, Sweetser drew up a new protest. Like the first protest already submitted, this one repudiated the traders' claims and demanded scrutiny of those claims. This time, Sweetser himself traveled to Washington to lay the protest before Congress and file formal charges against Governor Alexander Ramsey. The charges made against Governor Ramsey were as follows:

1. Having refused to pay the Indians their monies directly but having paid them to claimants, traders, and half-breeds; 2. With confederating with Henry H. Sibley, Hercules L. Dousman, Hugh Tyler, Franklin Steele, and others, to absorb the whole fund named the hand money, to the exclusion of meritorious creditors; 3. With having used improper means and cruel measures to compel the Indians to sign receipts and assignments; 4. With holding councils and making payments in a private trading house rather than at the agency; 5. With not reserving sufficient funds for removal and subsistence, thus increasing funds to be distributed among traders and half-breeds; 6. With depositing the gold received from

---

[69] Snyder, *The Treaty of Mendota*, 88.

the treasury in banks and paying by means of drafts and bank notes—all these in violation of the law and treaties.[70]

In March of 1853, the Senate committee on Indian affairs launched an investigation surrounding Governor Ramsey's conduct regarding the Sioux payment. The committee determined that it could not adequately consider the case in Washington being so far away from the actual events. Therefore, President Pierce authorized the case to be tried in Minnesota and requested that the findings be reported back to the Senate. The investigation began at St. Paul on July 6, 1853.

Known as the "Report of the Commissioners . . . to Investigate the Official Conduct of Alexander H. Ramsey . . .," the investigation lasted three months and included forty-seven witnesses, sixteen of whom were Dakota Indians. It was by all means a thorough investigation as every possible opening for evidence was implored. The witnesses all seemed to corroborate the evidence leaving little dispute about the facts of the case. But, for reasons unknown, the prosecution never saw fit for the examination of Madison Sweetser. When Governor Ramsey was called upon, he showed support for the traders arguing that, "Without the assistance of the traders no treaty could have been effected at all." Ramsey also defended his own actions by concluding that, "I cannot observe that in any particular I would change my action, if the whole affair was to be gone over again."

In January, 1854, the Investigation Report was received by the Senate Committee on Indian Affairs. After examining the report, the Senate Committee believed that the Dakota were aware of their debts, which equaled an amount greater than the claims, before the treaty negotiations took place. However, the committee also acknowledged that "oppressive measures had been used to compel acquiescence in such payment." The final decision, submitted February 24, 1854, concluded "that the conduct of Governor Ramsey was not only free from blame, but highly commendable and meritorious." None of the six charges had been sustained and the committee was discharged from any further consideration on the subject. For his part, the Senate apparently believed that Governor Ramsey acted

---

[70] Information about the Ramsey Investigation can be found in the appendix of Folwell's, *A History of Minnesota*. All quotes following can be found there. Folwell, *A History of Minnesota*, 462-470.

as a statesman doing his civic duty to carry out a great national measure, regardless of technicalities, errors, or the interests of individuals who sought to deceive or disrupt the proceedings.

As for Henry Sibley, before the investigation was submitted to the Senate, a friend of Sibley's was allowed to read the report in order to ensure it contained nothing injurious to Sibley's fair standing, a promise made by the judge in the case. Whether or not Sibley's conduct during the negotiations and thereafter were ethical or not is left for conjecture. As a result of the Treaty of the Traverse des Sioux, Henry Sibley received $66,459 for his claims. It is true that Sibley sought to end the opposition of Madison Sweetser as indicated in several correspondence of the time. In one such correspondence, while writing to the Chouteau's, Sibley suggested that the Ewing's be allowed one-fourth of the town plat of Traverse des Sioux if they would not interfere with the treaty before it was ratified. It is unclear, however, how Sibley was motivated. Although he stood to gain monetarily from ratification of the treaty, he may also have been considering the best interests of the territory as he saw them. In a letter written to Wisconsin Senator Henry Dodge in May of 1852, Sibley wrote regarding his personal claims, "But if this contemplated arrangement, or any feature of the treaties stands in the way of their ratification private considerations however important must give place to the general good. The treaties must be ratified, and we who are interested must submit to the sacrifice however ruinous to us."[71] In this Sibley exhibited a great deal of unselfishness and magnanimity.

That fact is that what happened to the Dakota during and as a result of the treaty negotiations was by no means an aberration. The treaties of the Traverse des Sioux and Mendota were just two of the hundreds of treaties signed between the United States Government and Native Americans nations. When asked about the treaties of Traverse des Sioux and Mendota, Interpreter William Quinn said, "They were as fair as any Indian treaties."[72]

The Dakota did not fare well following the treaties of 1851. They had difficulty adapting to reservation life. Some were reluctant while others accepted their new way of living which included farming, Christianity,

---

[71] Ibid., 291.
[72] Ibid., 304.

European style clothing, immovable wood frame homes, and the English language. But whether they held on to their traditional lifestyle or adopted farming, all the Dakota remained starving and much in need. And the Indian System under which they lived was in most cases corrupt and unjust. Annuity payments were often late and the treaty terms were rarely met. Many traders, contractors, merchants, and government officials used the system for their own personal and financial gain while exploiting and neglecting the Dakota Indians.

Having become further impoverished, the Dakota signed another treaty in 1858 giving up half of their reservation lands. Four years later, the Dakota, starving and sick and without their promised annuity payment, decided to rise up and fight for their survival. This was the U.S. – Dakota War of 1862 and it resulted in the permanent exile of the Dakota Indians from beyond the borders of Minnesota. It was a tragic end, but based on everything that had happened for years and years prior, it was a foreseeable and inevitable end.

So what is the ending if not a happy one? I would submit to you, dear reader, that perhaps the ending has yet been written. When I met with Chief Red Iron, he told me that my presence was enough. He asked me to continue my work as an artist, recording the Dakota people with my crayon. I have done that. I have taken part in this historic event and I have recorded it for you to see and you to know. Yes, my time has come and gone. But here, my art and my words live on and they are made new again. How was I to know that my work would be found, and presented for you to see—to know. So, no, there is no ending. Because you've only just learned about the Dakota Indians and the abundant and beautiful homeland you share with them. Now it is your turn. Learn more. Discover more. Appreciate more. We cannot right the wrongs of our past, but we can understand them. More importantly, we can resolve who we were, and become who we ought to be.

Appendix A

WRITTEN PROTEST OF THE DAKOTA INDIANS TO THE PRESIDENT OF THE UNITED STATES, DECEMBER 6, 1851.

To our Great Father the President of the United States,

We, the undersigned, chiefs, headmen, and braves of the Sisseton, Wahpeton, Mdewakanton, and Wahpekute bands of the Sioux or Dakota nation of Indians, being a majority of said chiefs, headmen, and braves, and as such fully competent to transact national business, would most respectfully represent to you, that soon after or about the time and date (the twenty-third day of July, and the fifth day of August, 1851) of our treaties with the government of the United States, wherein the Hon. Luke Lea, and Governor A. Ramsey acted as commissioners on behalf of the United States, we did sign an obligation to our creditors, or those assuming to be such, which obligation, we are informed and believe, binds us and our people to pay large and extravagant sums in money to our said creditors—seems we do not owe, and never intended to obligate ourselves or people to pay.

And whereas said agreements were obtained from us through fraud, misrepresentation, and deceit—they never having been fully explained and interpreted to us by said traders, or those acting for them—we never having understood by any interpretation made by our said traders, or any one acting for them, that we were binding ourselves and people to the payment of a sum equal to from one-fourth to half a million of dollars, or any other amount. At the time of signing said papers we believed them duplicates of the treaties made with our Father the President, and necessary to carrying into full effect the treaties aforesaid—an object much desired by us; the result of which, we believed, would be to the benefit of our people, to the interest of the United States, and gratifying to the feelings of our Great Father the President and our friend the Hon. Luke Lea, Commissioner, towards whom we formed strong attachments for his honorable and just conduct to us in all the relations which we have sustained to him, and towards whom we entertain feelings of the strongest regard, and would with reluctance do any act which would receive his disapprobation, however much our interests would be exposed. In this act, we feel assured, from our knowledge of him, that we will not incur his displeasure by attempting to correct an error which we have been, by fraud and misrepresentation, led into, but will meet and receive his cordial approbation and cooperation in our behalf.

Had we hearkened to the council and advice of our friend, the Hon. Luke Lea, and disregarded the advice of our traders aforesaid, we would have been saved this trouble, and our people relieved from the painful anxiety of the payment of the fraudulent demands aforesaid. And, in view of the considerations aforesaid, we most solemnly protest against the payment (by our Great Father the President of the United States, or any other persons having charge of our money and disbursing officer of the government, or in any other capacity) of any money belonging to our said nation or bands to our traders aforesaid, or to any other person having claims against us.

We ask and expect to receive the aid of our Great Father, the President of the United States, to protect us against the payment of any and all unjust demands, and particularly against the fraudulent contracts aforesaid.

Believing that our interest will be fully cared for and protected by and through the aid of our Great Father, the President, we have with confidence made this appeal for his timely aid and protection, to save our women and children from the starvation and distress which the payment of the aforesaid fraudulent contracts would most certain produce.

Signed in open council, at St. Peter's agency, this the 6th day of December, A.D. eighteen hundred and fifty-one.

32 Congress, 2 session, *Senate Executive Documents,* no. 29, part 1, 25-26.

Appendix B

Traders' Paper: An Agreement Made with the Sisseton and Wahpeton Bands of Dakota Indians, July 23, 1851

We, the undersigned, chiefs, soldiers, and braves of the Wahpatoan and Seesetoan bands of Sioux Indians, having this day concluded a treaty with Luke Lea and Alexander Ramsey, commissioners on the part of the United States, whereby we have ceded to the United States certain lands for a valuable consideration, and being desirous to pay to our traders and half-breeds the sum of money which we acknowledge to be justly due to them, do hereby obligate and bind ourselves, as the authorized representatives of the aforesaid bands, to pay to the individuals hereafter designated the sum to us as soon as practicable after their removal, and the necessary appropriation shall be made by congress for arranging our affairs preparatory to our removal to the country designated in said treaty for our future abode, and for other purposes; and as it is specified that said sum shall be paid in such manner as requested by the chiefs in open council thereafter, we do hereby in open council request and desire that the said sums below specified shall be paid to the quest and desire that the said sums below specified shall be paid to the persons designated as soon as practicable after the necessary appropriation shall be made by congress for the purpose; and for this payment the faith of our nation. And we do hereby release and acquit the United States, upon the payment of sum aforesaid as herein specified, from any further liability to us or to our nation, for so much of the amount so to be paid as is provided for in the 4th article of the treaty aforesaid.

Dated at Traverse des Sioux, in the Territory of Minnesota, this twenty-third day of July, A.D. eighteen hundred and fifty-one.

NAMES AND SCHEDULE ARE HERE OMITTED

32 Congress, 2 session, *Senate Executive Documents*, no. 29, part 2, 22.

Appendix C

Traders' Paper: An agreement made with the Wahpeton Band of Dakota Indians, August 5, 1851

We, the undersigned, chiefs, soldiers, and braves of the Wah-pa-coota band of Sioux Indians, having this day concluded a treaty with Luke Lea and Alexander Ramsey, commissioners on the part of the United States, whereby we have ceded to the United States certain lands for a valuable consideration, and being desirous to pay our traders the sum of money which we acknowledge to be justly due to them, do hereby bind and obligate ourselves, as the authorized representatives of the aforesaid band, to pay to the individuals hereinafter designated the sum of money set opposite to their respective names, so soon as the same shall be paid to us, in accordance with the 4th article of the treaty aforesaid, which provides for the payment of a certain sum to us as soon as practicable after our removal, and the necessary appropriation shall be made by Congress for arranging our affairs preparatory to our removal to the country designated in said treaty for our future abode, and for other purposes; and as it is specified that said sum shall be paid in such manner as requested by the chiefs in open council, therefore we do hereby, in open council, request and desire that the said sums below specified shall be paid to the persons designated, as soon as practicable after the necessary appropriations shall be made by Congress for this purpose; and for this payment well and truly to be made, we hereby solemnly pledge ourselves and the faith of our nation, and we do hereby release and acquit the United States, upon the payment of the sums aforesaid as herein specified, from any further liability to us or to our nation for so much of the amount so to be paid, as is provided for in the 4th article of the treaty aforesaid.

Dated at Mendota, in the Territory of Minnesota, on this 5th day of August, A.D. eighteen hundred and fifty-one.

NAMES AND SCHEDULE ARE HERE OMITTED

32 Congress, 2 session, *Senate Executive Documents,* no. 29, part 2, 32.

Appendix D

Commissioner's Report: Luke Lea and Alexander Ramsey to A.H.H. Stuart, August 6, 1851

We have the honor to submit the following Report of our proceedings, as Commissioners on the part of the United States to negotiate with the Dakota or Sioux Indians of the St. Peters and Mississippi Rivers for the purchase of a large tract of their country in the Territory of Minnesota and also of a considerable area in the State of Iowa to which the Indian title has not been extinguished.

After making the necessary preliminary arrangements the undersigned left the Capital of Minnesota Territory on the 28th day June, 1851, and proceeded to Traverse des Sioux on the St. Peters or Minnesota river in the country of the Seeseetoan and Wahpaytoans Sioux; that place having been fixed upon as the most eligible point for holding negotiations with those bands. It was our intention and desire in the first instance to meet all the bands in Council at some spot near the mouth of the Minnesota river and to make but one treaty with them all; but upon inquiry we found that the feelings of the upper and lower Dakotas were so diverse and their interests, as they imagined so opposite that we were constrained to abandon the project of uniting them in one general negotiation.

The upper bands having received some weeks previous notice that they would be called together by the first of July, it was expected that they would convene at Traverse dies Sioux within a short time after our arrival; but as these people were under the necessity of furnishing themselves with subsistence by hunting at a distance from the Villages and as there was great difficulty in traversing the country in consequence of an unprecedented flood in the Minnesota and its tributaries, the Indians inhabiting the region about the head waters of the river did not reach the Council ground for many days after we were ready to receive them. Messages were dispatched to hasten their movements and provisions were transported to meet them on their way; but they were not disposed to be hurried and considerable delay was unavoidable.

Meanwhile, it was imperative upon us to supply the large number already on the ground with daily rations of food, which was rapidly curtailing our stock of provisions, a matter of serious concern in view of the fact that our remoteness from the settle portions of the Territory precluded the possibility of procuring additional supplies without great difficulty and expense. By extraordinary exertions the Chief and a few of the principal men of the Upper Seeseetoans were induced to leave the large body of their delegation and to hasten forward on horseback to the place of rendezvous. On their appearance it was decided at once to go into Council as the Chiefs and Headmen of the bands interested were all present.

It was on the 18th of July, full three weeks after our arrival at Traverse des Sioux that the first council was held. The Indians were told in very distinct terms what their Great Father's object was in sending commissioners into their country and a formal proposition was made them for their lands east of a certain line and estimated to contain upwards of 20 million acres. It was explained to them, that the pressure of immigration rendered it necessary that the whites should be furnished with a larger area while the comparatively small number of Dakotas might very advantageously be restricted within more confined limits; and that the President was disposed to place them in a permanent home where they might be concentrated, and apply themselves, under the protection of the Government to learning the arts of Civilized life, and particularly that of a proper cultivation of the soil, upon which they must in future depend for subsistence, rather than upon the precarious and uncertain fruits of the chase. They were further told that the President was willing and desirous, indeed, to give them a liberal sum in exchange for the lands which it was the intention to purchase and which to them could not be considered of much value; and that the purchase money should be so applied as to minister not only to present wants but to their future advancement.

It was soon perceived that although there was a vague and indefinite idea on the part of these people, that it was necessary for them to sell at least a portion of their Country, in order to secure them against the misery and almost starvation which the diminution in number of Buffalo and other game for the last few years had inflicted upon them yet when they were brought to meet the proposition in a distinct and intelligible form, they appeared to shrink with undisguised reluctance from taking a step too important in its results. Several days elapsed before they would consent to any but terms of the most extravagant character; some few of their own number having been taught to read, had impressed them with an idea that their country was of immense value and they at first refused to treat unless the sum of six millions was paid them. Finally, on the 23d of July they were induced to sign a Treaty which while it secures to the Government a large Territory, second in value to none in the North west, embodies provisions of a simple but most beneficial character for the poor savages themselves, and well calculated we think, if judiciously carried out, to save and elevate them from their present degraded condition.

Having distributed medals and presents and concluded our business with the upper Bands, we left Traverse des Sioux on the 24th of July and descended the Minnesota river to Mendota, the trading post at its mouth, at which point the Medaywakantoan, and Wahpaykootay band were already in part assembled. On the 29th of July we were enabled to get into council with these Indians, but found the obstacles to negotiating with them successfully, much greater then with the Upper Sioux, difficult as it was to bring them to reasonable terms. Several causes conspired to render a treaty with the lower Dakotas exceedingly difficult of attainment. Among them we may mention, first their proximity to the flourishing settlements on the east side of the Mississippi producing necessarily frequent contact with the whites, whose ideas of the great value of the country had been imparted to these Indians; secondly their greater experience in Indian diplomacy, being in the enjoyment already of liberal annuities; rendering them as indifferent to the making of another treaty at present as the whites on their borders were anxious that their lands especially should be immediately acquired. Several public councils were unavailingly held before an approach to agreement was had between us. But finally on the 5th day of August, after a tedious session of the Grand Council, we were enabled to obtain their assent and signatures to a Treaty similar in general features to the one negotiated with the upper bands; extinguishing on moderate but just terms, the Indian title to the splendid region of country Nicolett and others long ago described as the garden spot of the Mississippi valley.

Thus, the undersigned, contending with many difficulties, have been enabled to effect two treaties which may be considered among the most important ever negotiated with our Indian Tribes. They are important on account of the extent of valuable country purchased for a moderate price and the provisions they embody for the future happiness, prosperity and civilization of the Indians who are parties to them.

The amount of land acquired by these treaties is computed at over 35,000,000 of acres, and this amount, though large seemingly is not greater than is consistent with the past policy of the government on this subject; having in 1841, and 1849, as well as now in 1851, instructed its Commissioners to embrace in their negotiations with the eastern bands of Sioux, even a larger tract of country than we have just obtained. To have purchased a less number of acres would not have lessened proportionably the price for it because it was evident to us in the progress of the negotiations, that the influencing motive to sell at all was to obtain a large and certain amount of money, and that the number of acres in the country relinquished entered but little into the calculations of the Indians. If we had purchased less, we must necessarily have stipulated to pay less to keep within the limit of our instructions; and this would have defeated the humane policy, now universally regarded as incumbent upon government, of concentrating the Indians within fixed and narrow limits and of making, at any rate, suitable and adequate, provisions for their civilization, and early abandonment of the Hunter state, for the steady, settled and more profitable labours of an agricultural life. Still as all changed in the habits of a people, however rapidly pushed on, must be gradual to some extent it is gratifying to know that the Indians in this instance will suffer no serious inconvenience by the sudden transfer of their entire country, as they will continue to hunt and fish as at present over a large portion of it for a number of years and until needed for the white settlements. In making a large purchase, another consideration had weight. As a general policy, the government should own the lands on which Indians live or at least the lands to some extent around them. It is thus enabled the better to control the Indians and prevent wars and outrages among them. In this case, and for this reason, there was strong necessity that a wide expanse of country owned by the United States, should be interposed between the boundaries, respectively, of the Sioux and Chippewas. They are old hereditary enemies, who from time immemorial have carried on a war against each other. Their hunting grounds adjoin and war parties of either tribe roaming into the Territories claimed by the other. Frequent collisions and loss of life are the consequences, and when the agents of government call on a tribe to account for lives they have taken, the excuse is offered that the slain were intruding upon their lands, a sufficient justification according to Indian ethics for the most atrocious massacres. The insulation of the Sioux with the allowance to them of annuities, will be more effectual in putting a stop to the war between the two tribes than an army would be if kept constantly in the field for the purpose of holding them in check.

The extent of the purchase was augmented, also, by the necessity which for extinguishing the title of the four bands of Sioux negotiated within the two treaties to a large body of land, five or six millions of acres in amount, lying in the state of Iowa between the line of the old "Neutral Ground" and the northern and western boundaries of the State. This tract of country and generally all lands whatever in the state of Iowa claimed by the Sioux, were therefore embraced in the articles of Cession of both Treaties.

The terms upon which the cession of so large a Territory was made are undoubtedly most favorable to the United States while at the same time they are just and liberal to the Indians. From all the information that could be obtained from reliable sources and judging from what we ourselves saw of a considerable portion of the region purchased, we are satisfied that only a very insignificant portion of it is unfit for tillage and settlement. The greater part is of unsurpassed fertility, capable of producing all the cereal grains and vegetable common to the middle and northern states, and also admirable adapted to the raising of stock. The whole cost to the government of the cessions made by both upper and lower Sioux is nominally $3,075,000. Of this sum $575,000 do not bear interest, but are to be paid in hand for various purposes specified in the Treaties. The balance of $2,500,000 is held in trust by the Government, and five per cent interest theron is to be paid under different heads of Expenditures, for fifty years, when the Interest ceases and the principal reverts to the Government. So that in one sense, estimating the lands ceded to be worth and to yield the interest on their price, the actual cost to the Government for this magnificent purchase is only the sum paid in hand. Nor is any injustice done to the Indians by this arrangement. They received a liberal provision for fifty years, in which period their civilization will have been effected, if it ever can be at all, and their ability to take care of themselves manifested; when a continuation of the payments of large sums annually would do them no further real Good and be inconsistent with sound Government Policy. The Medaywakantoan bands of Sioux are already in the receipt of a permanent annuity of $15,000, and with this precedent before them, it was only by taking a determined stand from the first, that the undersigned were able to effect the Treaties without yielding to the strenuous efforts of the Indians to have their annuities made perpetual. In pursuing this course it was by no means our purpose to act otherwise than justly and generously towards the Indians. While we wished to make a good bargain for the Government we were also anxious to secure to the poor Savages a proper provision in proportion to numbers for their present wants and for their future support, comfort and improvements. The number of Indians who will probably participate in the benefits of the treaty of Traverse des Sioux is estimated at about 5,000 while about 3,000 will receive annuities under the treaty of Mendota. Upon the basis of this estimate the price for the bands was in a great measure graduated—keeping in view the principals, before stated, of providing for the adequate present support and prospective improvements of such a number of Indians. This much at least, irrespective of the amount of land sold by them, we conceive to be due from the government to a people who are its wards and who have peculiar claims to our sympathy, protection and assistance.

In the details of these treaties and in adjusting the interest payments to various purposes, it was our constant aim to do what we could to break up the community system among the Indians, and cause them to recognize the Individuality of property. While the payment of annuities in goods has its advantages, its evil effects are equally apparent. The annual receipt of large quantities of merchandise in bulk, to be divided arbitrarily by the bands themselves cannot but exercise a powerful influence in keeping up their present loose ideas of the rights of property. Cash annuities, under the per capita regulation which distributes to each recipient a just proportion of all monies so paid, are far better calculated to give the Indians a powerful impression of the importance of amassing property individually. Another objection, which experience has shown to this kind of annuities, is that apart from the inequality and partiality attendant upon their division, families and individuals generally receive articles which they do not need instead of others which they are most in want of. It thus happens that a Gun falls to the share of a man who wishes a Blanket and a woman receives a kettle who is already provided with that article. When cash payments are resorted to and each receives a just proportion all have the opportunity at least of procuring such things as they desire, while extortion is prevented by the competition among their numerous traders. Our own experience and observation in this regard have been confirmed by the testimony of worthy and enlightened missionaries and of other intelligent and disinterested men who have watched the workings of the annuity system. They all concurred in stating their convictions, that cash payments should entirely supersede those of goods, if the present and ultimate Benefit of the Indians is to be consulted. Still, in deference to other intelligent and sincere well wishers of the Indians, who honestly entertain a different opinion on this subject and for some reasons of present expediency we concluded to adapt a medium, and while allowing liberal cash payments set apart a moderate amount annually for goods and provisions.

    The leading object in both treaties has been to apply a large part of the purchase money to the improvements of the Indians, having a due regard as before intimated, to their number, character, and condition. In addition to the fund for the establishment of manual labor schools and annual payment of $5,000 for their support, the fund reserved to be expended annually for beneficial objects connected with the speedy civilization of this barbarous people will be found to be a much larger proportion than has usually been the case. The general character which the Dakota nation bears is that of being warlike but are the same time friendly to the whites, and not disposed to follow in their footsteps as rapidly as their peculiar superstitions and erroneous ideas imbibed by them from their childhood, will permit. By a judicious expenditure of the Civilization and Improvement Funds provided for in these Treaties, it may reasonably be expected that this powerful branch of the red race will soon take the lead among the north western savages, in agriculture and other industrial pursuits. By furnishing them the implements of husbandry; and by the employment of farmers, blacksmiths, and other artisans of good character among them, to teach them farming and the mechanic arts; by training their youth to habits of Industry through means of manual labor schools, for which munificent provision has been made; and by the total exclusion of the spirituous liquors from among them, there is reason to hope that not many years will elapse before the Dakotas will show conclusively the absurdity of the hypothesis that the aboriginal race on this continent are incapable of civilization and doomed to speedy and utter extinction.

A new and most desirable feature, in our opinion, has been embodied in these treaties. The President or Congress is empowered to prescribe such rules for the government of the Indians themselves, as may be deemed proper and expedient. The adoption of such a provision will go far to cure one of the most obstinate evils with which those who labor for the civilization of the Indians have to contend. At present there is no law but that of the strongest. There is, consequently, no inducement held out to any individual to be more industrious than his neighbor or to strive to amass property of any description. No redress can be obtained in case of depredation and outrage and so the injured party or his relatives naturally resort to retaliation in kind. The power conferred upon the government against aggressions from others of the same tribe, and to punish the wicked and depraved, will, if exercised judiciously, operate to encourage the industrious to increase his stores and make himself and family comfortable, and will very soon break the Community System which is now the bane and curse of these tribes.

It was considered proper to provide by treaty also, for the protection of the Indians, that the "trade and intercourse laws," so far as the introduction of liquors is concerned, should remain in force over the ceded lands until otherwise determined by the President or Congress. Although the Dakotas are reputed comparatively temperate Indians rarely indulging in the use of spirituous liquors, it was considered proper to throw this additional safeguard around them and several of the chiefs stated in open Council their earnest desire that some stringent measure should be taken by the Government to exclude all kinds of liquors from their new home.

The interest of steady and orderly white settlers who will immediately pour in upon the new purchase, likewise demand that the law should be retained, as the only efficient means of restraining that depraved and pestilent class always found on an Indian frontier, whose despicable occupation is to make demons of both Indians and whites by an indiscriminate traffic in Intoxicating drinks.

One great difficulty to be overcome in effecting these treaties, was the selection of a location for the future residence of the bands equally satisfactory to us and to them. The lower Bands of Indians now inhabit a country abounding in timber. They could not be brought to consent to a removal to the open prairies and it was with much trouble that they could be induced to agree to go to the upper part of the Minnesota Valley where the reservation has been made for the four bands together. This region is sufficiently remote to guarantee the Indians against any pressure on the part of the white population for many years to come—the country which they now inhabit and from which they are to remove being very extensive, and well calculated to sustain a dense population. In this new home, which is of comparatively small extent, they will be so concentrated as to be readily controlled and influenced for their real welfare. Farms will there be opened for them. Mills and schools established, and dwelling houses erected; and as gradually the white settlements close in around them, destroying the game and rendering a hunting life impossible, and as they will have within their own Territory the means of living with a very little labor on their part, the force of circumstances alone will compel their resorting to agriculture for subsistence; and this first great step gained, the rest is easy and their complete and speedy civilization must inevitably follow. To induce their early location on this reservation it was deemed expedient also to stipulate that no part of the hand money should be paid them until after their removal; and means were likewise provided to subsist them the first year, it being contemplated to rapidly push on the farms and other improvements so as always to produce from the soil there after enough for their support.

Much more might be said but we have endeavoured to make the provisions of these treaties so plain and simple that they would need but little explanation to show their propriety. And we are well assured they are the best both for the Indians and the Gov't that could under the circumstances have been effected.

The region of country acquired by them is larger than the state of New York and rich and beautiful and fertile beyond description. It is needed as an additional outlet to the overwhelming tide of migration which is both unceasing and irresistible in its westward progress. From the best information we could obtain, thousands are already eagerly awaiting to enter upon this new purchase, as soon as it is open for settlement. With extreme difficulty can the agents of the government now restrain them from rushing forward in advance and occupying the lands without respect to the rights of the Indians or the authority of law. We are constrained to say, therefore, that in our opinion the time has come when the extinguishment of the Indian title to this region should no longer be delayed, if government would not have the mortification on the one hand of confessing its inability to protect the Indians from encroachment, or be subjected to the painful necessity, upon the other, of ejecting by force thousands of its citizens from a land which they desire to make their homes and which without their occupancy and labor will be comparatively useless and waste.

Rebecca Snyder, ed. The 1851 Treaty of Mendota: A Collection of Primary Documents Pertaining to the Treaty. South St. Paul, Minnesota: Dakota County Historical Society, 2002, p. 25-34.

Appendix E

Treaty with the Sioux—Sisseton and Wahpeton Bands, 1851 – July 23, 1851

Articles of a treaty made and concluded at Traverse des Sioux, upon the Minnesota River, in the Territory of Minnesota, on the twenty-third day of July, eighteen hundred and fifty-one, between the United States of America, by Luke Lea, Commissioner of Indian Affairs, and Alexander Ramsey, governor and ex-officio superintendent of Indian affairs in said Territory, commissioners duly appointed for that purpose, and See-see-toan and Wah-pay-toan bands of Dakota or Sioux Indians.

ARTICLE 1.

It is stipulated and solemnly agreed that the peace and friendship now so happily existing between the United States and the aforesaid bands of Indians, shall be perpetual.

ARTICLE 2.

The said See-see-toan and Wah-pay-toan bands of Dakota or Sioux Indians, agree to cede, and do hereby cede, sell, and relinquish to the United States, all their lands in the State of Iowa; and, also all their lands in the Territory of Minnesota, lying east of the following line, to wit: Beginning at the junction of the Buffalo River with the Red River of the North; thence along the western bank of said Red River of the North, to the mouth of the Sioux Wood River; thence along the western bank of said

Sioux Wood River to Lake Traverse; thence, along the western shore of said lake, to the southern extremity thereof; thence in a direct line, to the junction of Kampeska Lake with the Tchan-kas-an-data, or Sioux River; thence along the western bank of said river to its point of intersection with the northern line of the State of Iowa; including all the islands in said rivers and lake.

ARTICLE 3.
[Stricken out.]

ARTICLE 4.
In further and full consideration of said cession, the United States agree to pay to said Indians the sum of one million six hundred and sixty-five thousand dollars ($1,665,000,) at the several times, in the manner and for the purposes following, to wit:

1st. To the chiefs of the said bands, to enable them to settle their affairs and comply with their present just engagement; and in consideration of their removing themselves to the country set apart for them as above, which they agree to do within two years, or sooner, if required by the President, without further cost or expense to the United States, and in consideration of their subsisting themselves the first year after their removal, which they agree to do without further cost or expense on the part of the United States, the sum of two hundred and seventy-five thousand dollars, ($275,000):*Provided*, That said sum shall be paid to the chiefs in such manner as they, hereafter, in open council shall request, and as soon after the removal of said Indians to the home set apart for them, as the necessary appropriation therefor shall be made by Congress.

2d. To be laid out under the direction of the President for the establishment of manual-labor schools; the erection of mills and blacksmith shops, opening farms, fencing and breaking land, and for such other beneficial objects as may be deemed most conducive to the prosperity and happiness of said Indians, thirty thousand dollars, ($30,000.)

The balance of said sum of one million six hundred and sixty-five thousand dollars, ($1,665,000,) to wit: one million three hundred and sixty thousand dollars ($1,360,000) to remain in trust with the United States, and five per cent interest thereon to be paid, annually, to said

Indians for the period of fifty years, commencing the first day of July, eighteen hundred and fifty-two (1852,) which shall be in full payment of said balance, principal and interest, the said payment to be applied under the direction of the President, as follows, to wit:

3d. For a general agricultural improvement and civilization fund, the sum of twelve thousand dollars, ($12,000.)

4th. For educational purposes, the sum of six thousand dollars, ($6,000.)

5th. For the purchase of goods and provisions, the sum of ten thousand dollars, ($10,000.)

6th. For money annuity, the sum of forty thousand dollars,($40,000.)

ARTICLE 5.

The laws of the United States, prohibiting the introduction and sale of spirituous liquors in the Indian country shall be in full force and effect throughout the territory hereby ceded and lying in Minnesota until otherwise directed by Congress or the President of the United States.

ARTICLE 6.

Rules and regulations to protect the rights of persons and property among the Indians, parties to this treaty, and adapted to their condition and wants, may be prescribed and enforced in such manner as the President or the Congress of the United States, from time to time, shall direct.

In testimony whereof, the said Commissioners, Luke Lea and Alexander Ramsey, and the undersigned Chiefs and Headmen of the aforesaid See-see-toan and Wah-pay-toan bands of Dakota or Sioux Indians, have hereunto subscribed their names and affixed their seals, in duplicate, at Traverse des Sioux, Territory of Minnesota, this twenty-third day of July, one thousand eight hundred and fifty-one.

<u>Indian Affairs: Laws and Treaties</u>. Compiled and Edited by Joseph Kappler. Vol. 2. Washington: Government Printing Press, 1904, p. 588-590.

APPENDIX F

TREATY WITH THE SIOUX—MDEWAKANTON AND WAHPAKOOTA BANDS, 1851 – AUGUST 5, 1851

Articles of a treaty made and concluded at Mendota, in the Territory of Minnesota, on the fifth day of August, eighteen hundred and fifty-one, between the United States of America, by Luke Lea, Commissioner of Indian Affairs, and Alexander Ramsey, governor and ex-officio superintendent of Indian affairs in said Territory, commissioners duly appointed for that purpose, and the Med-ay-wa-kan-toan and Wah-pay-koo-tay bands of Dakota and Sioux Indians.

ARTICLE 1.

The peace and friendship existing between the United States and the Med-ay-wa-kan-toan and Wah-pay-koo-tay bands of Dakota or Sioux Indians shall be perpetual.

ARTICLE 2.

The said Med-ay-wa-kan-toan and Wah-pay-koo-tay bands of Indians do hereby cede and relinquish all their lands and all their right, title and claim to any lands whatever, in the Territory of Minnesota, or in the State of Iowa.

ARTICLE 3.

[Stricken out.]

ARTICLE 4.

In further and full consideration of said cession and relinquishment, the United States agree to pay to said Indians the sum of one million four hundred and ten thousand dollars, ($1,410,000,) at the several times, in the manner and for the purposes following, to wit:

1st. To the chiefs of the said bands, to enable them to settle their affairs and comply with their present just engagements; and in consideration of their removing themselves to the country set apart for them as above, (which they agree to do within one year after the ratification of this treaty, without further cost or expense to the United States,) and in consideration of their subsisting themselves the first year after their removal, (which they agree to do without further cost or expense on the part of the United States,) the sum of two hundred and twenty thousand dollars ($220,000.) *Provided*, That said sum shall be paid, one-half to the chiefs of the Med-ay-wa-kan-toan band, and one-half to the chief and headmen of the Wah-pay-koo-tay band, in such manner as they, hereafter, in open council, shall respectively request, and as soon after the removal of said Indians to the home set apart for them as the necessary appropriations therefor shall be made by Congress.

2d. To be laid out, under the direction of the President, for the establishment of manual-labor schools; the erection of mills and blacksmith shops, opening farms, fencing and breaking land, and for such other beneficial objects as may be deemed most conducive to the prosperity and happiness of said Indians, thirty thousand dollars ($30,000.)

The balance of said sum of one million four hundred and ten thousand dollars, ($1,410,000,) to wit: one million, one hundred and sixty thousand dollars ($1,160,000) to remain in trust with the United States, and five per cent. interest thereon to be paid annually to said Indians for the period of fifty years, commencing on the first day of July, eighteen hundred and fifty-two (1852,) which shall be in full payment of said balance, principal and interest: said payments to be made and applied, under the direction of the President as follows, to wit:

3d. For a general agricultural improvement and civilization fund, the sum of twelve thousand dollars, ($12,000.)

4th. For educational purposes, the sum of six thousand dollars, ($6,000.)

5th. For the purchase of goods and provisions, the sum of ten thousand dollars, ($10,000.)

6th. For money annuity, the sum of thirty thousand dollars, ($30,000.)

ARTICLE 5.

The entire annuity, provided for in the first section of the second article of the treaty of September twenty-ninth, eighteen hundred and thirty-seven, (1837,) including an unexpended balance that may be in the Treasury on the first of July, eighteen hundred and fifty-two, (1852,) shall thereafter be paid in money.

ARTICLE 6.

The laws of the United States prohibiting the introduction and sale of spirituous liquors in the Indian country shall be in full force and effect throughout the territory hereby ceded and lying in Minnesota until otherwise directed by Congress or the President of the United States.

ARTICLE 7.

Rules and regulations to protect the rights of persons and property among the Indian parties to this Treaty, and adapted to their condition and wants, may be prescribed and enforced in such manner as the President or the Congress of the United States, from time to time, shall direct.

In witness whereof, the said Luke Lea and Alexander Ramsey, Commissioners on the part of the United States and the undersigned Chiefs and Headmen of the Med-ay-wa-kan-toan and Wah-pay-koo-tay bands of Dakota or Sioux Indians, have hereunto set their hands, at Mendota, in the Territory of Minnesota, this fifth day of August, Anno Domini, one thousand eight hundred and fifty-one.

Indian Affairs: Laws and Treaties. Compiled and Edited by Joseph Kappler. Vol. 2. Washington: Government Printing Press, 1904, p. 591-593.

Bibliography

"Minnesota Treaties." *The U.S.-Dakota War of 1862.* Accessed on March 27, 2015. http://www.usdakotawar.org/history/treaties/minnesota-treaties.

"Reverend Stephen and Mary Riggs." *The U.S.-Dakota War of 1862.* http://www.usdakotawar.org/history/reverend-stephen-and-mary-riggs.

33 Congress, 1 Session, *Senate Executive Documents,* no. 61, p. 324, (serial 699).

Clemmons, Linda M. "We Will Talk of Nothing Else: Dakota Interpretations of the Treaty of 1837," in *Great Plains Quarterly.* Summer, 2005.

──────. *Conflicted Mission: Faith, Disputes, and Deception on the Dakota Frontier.* St. Paul: Minnesota Historical Society Press, 2014.

Clodfelter, Michael. *The United States Army Versus the Sioux, 1862-1865.* Jefferson, North Carolina: McFarland and Company, Inc., 1998.

Delo, David M. *Peddlers and Post Traders: The Army Sutler on the Frontier.* Helena, Montana: Kingfisher Books, 1998.

Folwell, William Watts. *A History of Minnesota.* Vol. 1. St. Paul: Minnesota Historical Society, 1922.

Frémont, John Charles. *The Exploring Expedition to the Rocky Mountains, Oregon and California.* New York and Auburn: Miller, Orton and Mulligan, 1856.

Glewwe, Lois A. *Dakota Soul Sisters: Stories of the Dakota Missionaries.* Accessed on March 15, 2015. http://dakotasoulsisters.com.

Heard, Isaac V.D. *History of the Sioux War and Massacres of 1862 and 1863.* New York: Harper and Brothers, 1865.

Heilbron, Bertha L., Editor. *With Pen and Pencil on the Frontier in 1851: The Diary and Sketches of Frank Blackwell Mayer.* St. Paul: Minnesota Historical Society, 1986.

Hughes, Thomas. *Old Traverse des Sioux.* St. Peter, Minnesota: Herald Publishing Company, 1929.

Hughes, Thomas. *The Treaty of Traverse des Sioux in 1851, Under Governor Alexander Ramsey, With Notes of the Former Treaty there in 1841, Under Governor James D. Doty of Wisconsin,* in *Collections of the Minnesota Historical Society.* Volume 10, Part 1. St. Paul: Minnesota Historical Society, 1905.

Kane, Lucille M. "The Sioux Treaties and the Traders." In *Minnesota History.* Vol. 32, No. 2. June, 1951.

Lass, William E. *Minnesota: A History.* 2nd Ed. New York: W.W. Norton and Company, 1998.

Long, Stephen H. *Voyage in a Six-Oared Skiff to the Falls of St. Anthony in 1817.* Carlisle, Massachusetts: Applewood Books, 1860.

Nute, Grace Lee. *The Voyageur.* St. Paul: Minnesota Historical Society, 1987.

Oneroad, Amos E. and Alanson B. Skinner. *Being Dakota: Tales and Traditions of the Sissetons and Wahpeton.* St. Paul: Minnesota Historical Society Press, 2003.

Prucha, Francis Paul, Ed. *Documents of the United States Indian Policy.* 3rd Edition. Lincoln, Nebraska: University of Nebraska Press, 2000.

Riggs, Stephen R. *Mary and I: Forty Years with the Sioux.* Boston: Congregational Sunday School and Publishing Society, 1888.

Robinson, Doane. *A History of the Dakota or Sioux Indians.* Vol. 2. Aberdeen, South Dakota: News Printing Co., 1904.

Snyder, Rebecca, Ed. *The 1851 Treaty of Mendota: A Collection of Primary Documents Pertaining to the Treaty.* South St. Paul, Minnesota: Dakota County Historical Society, 2002.

Timmerman, Janet. *Joseph LaFramboise: A Factor of Treaties, Trade, and Culture.* Master's Thesis. Kansas State University, 2009.

United States Office of Indian Affairs. *Annual Report of the Commissioner of Indian Affairs, for the Year 1851.* http://digital.library.wisc.edu/1711.dl/History.AnnRep51.

Williams, J. Fletcher. *A History of the City of St. Paul and the County of Ramsey, Minnesota.* St. Paul: Minnesota Historical Society, 1876.